381

D0519717

RETAILING
AN INTRODUCTION

We work with leading authors to develop the strongest
educational materials in business and finance, bringing
cutting-edge thinking and best learning practice to a
global market.

Under a range of well-known imprints including
Financial Times Prentice Hall, we craft high quality
print and electronic publications which help readers to
understand and apply their content whether studying or
at work.

To find out about the complete range of our
publishing please visit us on the World Wide Web at:
www.pearsoned.co.uk

Roger Cox and Paul Brittain

RETAILING
AN INTRODUCTION

Fifth Edition

FT Prentice Hall
FINANCIAL TIMES

An imprint of **Pearson Education**

Harlow, England • London • New York • Boston • San Francisco • Toronto • Sydney • Singapore • Hong Kong
Tokyo • Seoul • Taipei • New Delhi • Cape Town • Madrid • Mexico City • Amsterdam • Munich • Paris • Milan

Pearson Education Limited
Edinburgh Gate
Harlow
Essex CM20 2JE
England

and Associated Companies throughout the world

Visit us on the World Wide Web at:
www.pearsoned.co.uk

———————————

Fourth edition published 2000
Fifth edition published 2004

© Pearson Education Limited 1988, 2004

The rights of Roger Cox and Paul Brittain to be identified as
authors of this work have been asserted by them in accordance
with the Copyright, Designs, and Patents Act 1988.

ISBN-13: 978-0-273-67819-9

British Library Cataloguing-in-Publication Data
A catalogue record for this book can be obtained from the British Library.

10 9 8 7 6 5 4
09 08 07

Typeset by 35 in 9/12pt Stone Serif
Printed in Great Britain by Henry Ling Limited, at the Dorset Press, Dorchester, DT1 1HD

The publishers' policy is to use paper manufactured from sustainable forests

Contents

Preface

This book provides a comprehensive introduction to all aspects of retailing and the fundamental elements of retail management and a retail organization's activities, so that the reader will have a solid platform on which to build.

Intended not only for college and university students studying retailing, the book is also an invaluable tool for those already working in selling, marketing or retailing who require further knowledge of the way retailing works. It is also the perfect resource for aspiring retail managers who may have received little formal training on the subject.

Organization

The book is divided into three major parts. Part One is concerned with the structure of retailing, the relationship between the consumer and retailer, and the methods of researching that interaction. There are also chapters on international retailing and the retailing environments.

Part Two is devoted to the retail mix – that special blend of strategies that a retailer can use to appeal to target customers. Location, merchandise, pricing, advertising and atmosphere and layout are key elements in this section of the book.

Part Three deals with the administrative side of retailing. It demonstrates that planning, particularly financial planning, and the measurement of performance are just as vital in retailing as in any other business enterprise. The role of technology in retailing, retailing and the law and the future of retailing are also explored.

New to this edition

A major new feature of this fifth edition is its coverage of the internet and online retailing. This reflects the tremendous interest in this aspect of retailing and its potential to transform the way retailing is practised. A new chapter (Chapter 21) is devoted to general management, focusing particularly on the skills managers need in this very people-orientated industry. There is also a new section (in Chapter 26) on supply chain management, as well as a fully updated bibliography and list of retail trade associations.

Retailing in the twenty-first century

Today the revolution in the world of retailing is continuing. The pace of change is increasing and retailers, interacting as they do on a daily basis with consumers, are in a good position to capitalize on these changes and so increase market share. But the manufacturer who is two or three steps away in the distribution chain is fighting back by utilizing direct marketing techniques to communicate directly with customers.

Many traditional store-based retailers have also branched out by the rapid development of home shopping through the internet. It all adds up to a fascinating, fast-changing and dynamic environment.

Students of retail management today encounter an exciting subject dominated by innovative brands such as Virgin, Nike, FCUK and Microsoft. This is not the end of the story – the future beckons with even greater challenges to come!

Acknowledgements

We are grateful for the support and excellent suggestions we have received from many people in the course of writing this book. In particular we thank the following reviewers for their detailed comments:

Graham Beaver, Nottingham Trent University
Grete Birtwistle, Glasgow Caledonian University
Christopher Moore, Glasgow Caledonian University
Tony Robertson, The Co-operative Group
Leigh Sparks, University of Stirling
Paul Whysall, Nottingham Trent University

A big thank you to the entire Pearson Education team, including Thomas Sigel, Senior Acquisitions Editor; Peter Hooper, Editorial Assistant; Karen Mclaren, Senior Editor and Leigh-Anne Graham, Marketing Manager.

Roger Cox
Paul Brittain

Part one

Retailing and the consumer

1 The retail industry

Introduction

Retailing is one of the most important industries in the UK. Napoleon Bonaparte's jibe about 'a nation of shop-keepers' still has a ring of truth. This chapter considers the functions of retailing, together with some of the more recent trends in retailing and theories of retail change.

1. Definition

Historically retailing has been viewed as the sale of goods to the consumer through retail shops. However, retailing today should be viewed as being rather broader.

Retailing is the sale of goods and services to the ultimate consumer for personal, family or household use. Thus retailing involves more than selling tangible products. The purchase of a service such as a haircut or dry cleaning is also a retail transaction. Purchases for business or industrial use are not retail transactions.

2. Place of the retail stores sector in the economy

Despite the wider definition of retailing suggested above, the retail stores sector is particularly important because:

(a) It is the final link in the chain of production that begins at the extractive stages, moves through the manufacturing processes and ends by the distribution of goods (and services) to the final consumer.

(b) It is the second largest employer in the UK with over 3 million workers involved.

(c) It accounts for 23 per cent of the gross domestic product.

(d) It accounts for about 35 per cent of consumer expenditure.

(e) It is an important tax collection point, e.g. value added tax.

3. *Functions of retailing*

The retail outlet may provide some or all of the following services to its customers:

(a) Convenient location.

(b) An assortment of merchandise appropriate to the particular market (i.e. allows choice).

(c) Breaking of bulk so that small quantities can be sold.

(d) Processing of merchandise to more acceptable forms.

(e) Holding of stock for instant availability at relatively stable prices.

(f) Helping to effect change in ownership of goods.

(g) Causing goods to move through the distribution system, e.g. from manufacturer to retailer to consumer.

(h) Information not only to the consumer but to suppliers.

(i) Product guarantees, after-sales service and dealing with customer complaints.

(j) Credit and hire-purchase facilities.

(k) Some facility for social intercourse.

Trends in retailing

4. *Demand for retail products and services*

There is a trend showing consumer expenditure shifting from spending on goods to services. For example, catering (restaurants and cafés), holidays and home entertainment, and financial services have all performed well during the period from 2000. Food expenditure has remained relatively static after taking inflation into account, while expenditure on clothing and footwear has shown negative growth.

5. *Number of shops*

In 1971 the Census of Distribution showed that there were 504,781 retail outlets in the UK. This number has now declined to 310,000 outlets, although the rate of decline has dropped markedly in the period from 2000. The reasons for the decline in the number of retail outlets are as follows:

(a) Competition from multiples, who with their tremendous buying power and economies of scale make it increasingly difficult for many independent traders to stay in business.

(b) Multiples rationalizing their businesses, generally by closing down smaller units and opening fewer, larger ones.

(c) Large supermarkets and superstores with a wide range of goods on offer, which have led to increasingly large quantities of merchandise being handled by a comparatively small number of outlets.

A similar tendency towards reduction in the number of retail outlets may be observed both in Western Europe and the USA.

6. Retail polarization

This is the trend towards both larger and smaller retailers with medium-sized retailers encountering the greatest difficulty. The larger stores are offering the customer 'one-stop' shopping and the smaller retailer can be successful through specialization (e.g. Benetton).

7. Mergers and acquisitions

Many store groups have combined to form even larger groups. This trend has been particularly prevalent in food retailing but is by no means confined to it. Recent acquisitions in the electrical and catering sectors illustrate how successful retailers feel they can bring their formula for success to bear on less successful groups and achieve improved operating efficiencies.

8. E-tailing

There has been a rapid expansion of e-commerce (the sale of goods or services over the internet or other online system) since 1998 due primarily to the growth in availability and falling costs of technology. This has occurred both in the B2B (business-to-business) and B2C (business-to-consumer) sectors.

B2C, also known variously as e-retailing, online retailing, online shopping or e-tailing, really started to take off in 2002 when familiarity with the processes increased and security fears subsided. By the end of 2010 it is predicted that e-tailing will account for 15 per cent of all UK retail sales.

The growth of e-tailing initially seemed to pose a significant threat to traditional store-based (bricks-and-mortar) retailers; however experience is proving that, in fact, many of the more successful online retailers are traditional retailers who have embraced the internet and added an online facility to their traditional stores to become multiple-channel (bricks-and-clicks) retailers. This is discussed in more detail in Chapter 26.

Shopping via non-computer devices such as interactive digital television and mobile phones (m-commerce) is also predicted to make an increasing impact in the next few years.

Theories of retail change

Four theories of retail institutional change have originated in North America, but they are equally applicable in the UK.

9. Natural selection in retailing

Charles Darwin's biological theory of natural selection has been plagiarized and paraphrased to 'retail types (or units), which best adjust to their environment, are most likely to survive'. The department store is often cited as an example of a retail type failing to adapt quickly to changes in external conditions like sub-urban growth and congestion in town centres. These very factors have, of course, helped the out-of-town stores.

The major environmental factors affecting retailing are:

(a) Changes in the consumer character:

    (*i*)   demographic, e.g. population age changes
    (*ii*) social, e.g. product and service preferences
    (*iii*) economic, e.g. changes in real incomes.

(b) Changes in technology, e.g. greater ownership, use of motor cars, food freezers, microwave ovens, mobile phones and personal computers.

(c) Changes in competition, i.e. changes in the levels of competitive strength within the areas of influence.

It will be seen that these factors may react upon the environment in both a friendly and an unfriendly way depending on the type of retail organization.

10. The wheel of retailing

This theory, first championed by Professor McNair of Harvard, postulates that an efficient innovatory form of retailing (such as discounting) enters the market and attracts the public by its new appeal. Growth and maturation occur, during which market shares are increased, but trading-up occurs and finally the firms become high-cost, high-price retailers and once again vulnerable to the next innovator. Reasons for its occurrence include:

(a) **Organizational deterioration**. As young innovators age they become more conservative and may seek greater social acceptability. Again, they may be unable to recruit management capable of extending the life of the innovation.

(b) **Economic factors**. The popularity of non-price competition produces higher gross margin requirements as an institution matures. This suggests that non-price competition is less ruinous than price competition.

11. General–specific–general cycle or accordion theory

This describes the tendency for retail business to become dominated (alternatively) by generalists, then specialists and then generalists again. The switch to the specialist store from the old-time 'general' store occurred because:

(a) The greater variety of customer goods available could not be accommodated in the old general store.

(b) Growth of cities meant that consumer markets allowed profitable segmentation.

(c) The specialist store provided a social content to the shopping trip which was required as society became more complex and impersonal.

The tendencies helping to create the new 'general' store (superstore or hyper-market) include:

(a) Joining complementary lines, e.g. meat, groceries and produce.

(b) 'Creaming', i.e. taking the most popular lines from other retail outlets' ranges, e.g. paperbacks, confectionery, to create small but sure profits.

(c) 'Scrambling', i.e. the taking of risky merchandise from other outlets by buying high-margin, lower stockturn lines, e.g. unit audio, expensive toys.

(d) Adding complete ranges 'borrowed' from other institutions, e.g. Tesco selling non-food to increase the physical density of shoppers in its stores.

(e) The growth of shopping centres. Large modern air-conditioned centres, particularly those with a substantial food complement, are somewhat like huge general stores. Note also the return to small convenience stores that are now competing successfully primarily by staying open for long hours.

12. The retail life cycle

The retail life-cycle theory is based on the product life-cycle theory – details of which may be found in any standard marketing text. The retail life-cycle theory suggests that retail institutions also have a life cycle, which can be divided into four phases: innovation, growth, maturity and decline.

(a) **Innovation stage.** The new retailer will have few competitors, rapid growth in sales but low profitability due to start-up costs, etc.

(b) **Growth phase**. Sales growth is still rapid and profitability is high due to the economies of scale now possible. However, competitors will spot this and begin to encroach on this market.

(c) **Maturity stage.** There are many competitors, sales growth has declined and profitability moderates.

(d) **Final decline phase.** Sales and profits fall and new, more innovatory retailers are developing and growing.

It has also been suggested that the life cycle of retail institutions is getting shorter.

Progress test 1

1. Describe the position that retailing holds in the economy.

2. What functions does the retailer carry out?

3. What have been the main trends in retailing over the last ten years?

4. Summarize three theories of retail change.

5. Aldi, the German supermarket chain, has been expanding its retail concept in the UK. Its style of operation is 'no frills' – minimal decor, secondary locations, small to medium sized units of 10–15,000 square feet and restricted product ranges but very low prices.

   On the other hand, Sainsbury's, Tesco and Safeway have all been adding extra customer services to achieve competitive advantage. Making reference to retailing theory, examine the viability of Aldi's price-led approach.

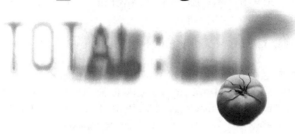

2 Retail organizations

Introduction

The retail industry is extremely diverse and, because there are so many different kinds of retail firms, classifying them all into one neat system has proved difficult. This chapter begins by considering the different forms of retail organization, then discusses non-store retailing and concludes with a consideration of wholesale organizations.

1. Classification of retail firms

Retail firms can be classified into a number of categories by:

(a) **Legal form.** The three basic legal forms of ownership are sole proprietorship, partnership and limited liability company (private or public).

(b) **Operational structure.** There are three operational structures: the independent trader (usually operating only one retail outlet); the multiple or chain store; and the consumer co-operative.

(c) **Range of merchandise.** Some retail businesses offer a wide range of goods. Examples of these include variety stores like Marks & Spencer or department stores like Harrods. Others concentrate on narrow ranges like health foods, leather goods or greetings cards, and these are called speciality stores or niche retailers.

(d) **Degree of service.** Although many retail outlets have been converted or built to self-service or self-selection standards, there are others that offer their consumers services such as delivery, credit, gift wrapping, repairs, etc. Many former self-service retailers are now looking at ways of gaining competitive advantage by adding new customer services.

(e) **Pricing policy.** Some retailers choose to emphasize low price rather than the service element of their retailing mix. Aldi, the German food retailer, expanded very rapidly by pricing below the competition. Others choose to price above the competition knowing that they will generate business on the basis of some other attribute such as convenient location or exclusive image.

(f) **Location**. With the increasing cost of town centre sites and traffic congestion, many retailers have sought edge-of-town locations, whilst others have preferred to stay in 'cluster' locations in town centres.

(g) **Size of outlet**. The average size of many multiples' branches has increased quite markedly over the past few years as more and more firms become large and medium-space users. The term 'superstore' has been used to define outlets between 25,000 and 50,000 square feet and hypermarkets are those stores over 50,000 square feet. Many outlets are now being built in the 50,000–100,000 square feet range. The number of superstores and hypermarkets in the UK increased from two in 1963 to 400 in 1986 and currently stands at 1,200.

(h) **Method of customer contact**. Most retail transactions are conducted by face-to-face contact in retail stores. However, a significant proportion of retail sales is generated by non-store retailing operations such as mail order catalogues, telephone selling, vending machines, door-to-door selling, mobile shops, and increasingly via the internet.

It will be seen that some of these categories overlap but they are all important in specific marketing situations. The conventional and most common classification of retail organizations is based primarily on operational structure and range of merchandise.

Having attempted a classification scheme for retail organizations and noted the degree of overlap between categories that continue to blur as firms diversify and respond to the changing environment, it is now appropriate to consider the main types of retail organization in more detail.

Independent traders

2. Definition

The great majority of shops in the UK are still owned by a single individual or sole trader. Independents are defined as retail organizations (other than co-operative societies) with less than ten branches. The usual number of branches controlled by the sole trader is one or at the most two. The market share of the independent, particularly in the food trades, has been falling for some years and the number of independently owned shops in most trades has diminished.

3. Disadvantages of the sole trader

These may be summarized as follows:

(a) Price competition from retail multiples who can reduce their costs through bulk buying and other economies of scale.

(b) Lack of specialist expertise in retail functions, e.g. buying, in-store merchandising, accounting, or possibly lack of time to carry them out adequately.

(c) Lack of capital to expand and improve the business.

(d) Inertia – the small trader may not wish to expand because of the extra problems expansion brings.

(e) Due to high accommodation costs the independent often lacks the advantage of being in a large shopping centre with heavy pedestrian traffic generation.

(f) Changing shopping habits brought about by increased car usage has concentrated purchases in large, well-located 'one-stop' stores.

4. Advantages of the sole trader

Although the multiple usually has the edge over the small trader in price competition, the latter often wins in terms of service competition. The small trader can offer the customer the following advantages:

(a) Personal relationship with customers.

(b) Convenient locations for 'walk-in' trade from customers' houses or places of work.

(c) More flexible merchandising policy, allowing for individual tastes.

(d) Longer and more convenient opening hours.

(e) Overheads can be kept low because of cheap sites, use of family assistance, etc.

(f) Some of the advantages of the multiple can be gained by membership of a voluntary group (*see* **33**), e.g. bulk-buying, national advertising, specialist services, etc.

5. Future prospects

The independent traders' share of the retail market has now fallen to about 23 per cent (down from 54 per cent in 1961). In the grocery sector the independent was fighting back by adopting a convenience store format with longer hours of trading and personalized services to a local community; however, the multiples have now spotted this opportunity and are moving in with their own offerings (e.g. Tesco Express, Sainsbury Local and Co-op Welcome).

Multiple or chain stores

6. Organization

The large multiple retail organization is usually a public limited liability company (plc) and therefore in common ownership with a degree of centralized control. A large multiple is defined as an organization (other than a co-operative) with ten or more branches. The chain is often made up of speciality shops, i.e. those selling a related range of merchandise (for example furniture, clothing or books and periodicals). Variety chains like Marks & Spencer, and some branches of the larger food multiples like Asda, are exceptions to the rule on related merchandise, however, and stock a very wide range of foods and non-foods. The multiple, by opening many branches, is able to attract a larger market. Multiples currently take over 70 per cent of all retail sales (up from 32.5 per cent in 1961).

7. Characteristics

The characteristics of many multiples are bound up with economies of scale and are:

(a) Centralized buying.

(b) Concentration on fast-moving lines – manufacturers' brand leaders or own-labels.

(c) Merchandise largely promoted through a mixture of national advertising and open in-store displays.

(d) Located in major shopping destinations alongside other multiples (giving them the advantage of associated sales).

(e) Relatively low prices.

(f) Strong corporate identity, most noticeable in shopfronts, fascias, in-store fittings and advertising.

(g) Centralization of many other functions such as advertising, personnel recruitment and training, operating policies, etc.

While the above is true for general-line multiples, many specialist multiple chains are now becoming prominent through targeting a well-defined consumer group and providing a range of merchandise to suit the needs of that target group. The Next chain is such an example, and although centralized buying is a characteristic of this chain, low pricing is not and the service element is stressed to a greater degree than other multiples. Similarly, many general-line multiples formerly very strong in the high street have moved out to larger, lower cost, edge-of-town locations.

Co-operative societies

8. Origins

The Co-operative Movement began in Rochdale in 1844. A co-operative society is defined as a co-operative retailing organization trading on co-operative principles, affiliated to the National Co-operative Movement (through the Co-operative Union) and registered under the Industrial and Provident Societies Acts. Because many retail co-operative societies operate branches, they are in this respect similar to multiple chains, but in the form of organization and control they are in many ways quite different. Today the Co-operative Movement as an entity is still one of the UK's biggest retailers.

9. The principles of the Movement

The principles of the Movement applicable to retailing are:

(a) Voluntary and open membership.

(b) Democratic control; one member, one vote.

(c) Payment of limited interest on capital.

(d) Surplus allocated for co-operative development, the common good or in proportion to the members' transactions.

One big problem has been the conflict between principle **(b)** and the need to fight the growing power of the multiple retailers. Co-operative market shares have declined substantially and, in an effort to counter this, attempts have been made to merge societies into larger, more powerful units.

10. Problems

The main problems facing the co-operatives have been as follows:

(a) **Poor management**. Although some successful societies have attracted high-calibre management, many of the smaller less successful societies have not. This largely stems from the inexperience and inefficiency of lay boards of directors and the lack of promotion opportunities and financial incentives for executives in some societies.

(b) **Unco-ordinated marketing**. Sometimes two or even three buying groups attempt to cover merchandise in some society areas.

(c) **Too much decentralization**. Local society boards of directors sometimes wish to remain in office and this reluctance to merge with other societies has reduced opportunities for scale economies.

(d) **Too many societies**. Strenuous efforts have been made to reduce the number of societies by merging them into regional societies. In 1960 there were 875 societies and this fell to just over 200 by 1977. Today there are just 33 societies.

(e) **Too many shops**. One aim of the Co-operative Movement has been to provide shopping in the most convenient places for 'walk-in' shoppers. Shop numbers fell by over half to 14,000 between 1961 and 1973. Today the total stands at fewer than 5,500 outlets but recently there has been a significant increase in the number of Co-op neighbourhood supermarkets and C. Stores.

(f) **Lack of an up-to-date image**. Co-operative stores are often regarded as old-fashioned, while the typical customer is slightly older and of a slightly lower socio-economic group than the typical multiple grocery customers.

(g) **Financing**. The main source of funds for development has been members' savings and profit retentions, but these are insufficient. The Movement has therefore often found it necessary to borrow money at commercial rates. However, it is itself involved in finance through both the Co-operative Bank and Co-operative Insurance Society.

11. Solutions

The Co-operative Movement has tackled these problems in the following ways:

(a) **Professional management**. Better managers are being recruited at all levels, but most particularly in the larger, more successful societies.

(b) **Marketing**. In theory, there is nothing to stop individual retail societies negotiating separate agreements with manufacturers, but in practice virtually 100 per cent of all packaged food and groceries are bought through the Co-operative Retail Trading Group (CRTG). The CRTG also carries out national negotiations for a much wider range of goods, especially for the national advertising programme of promoted lines.

(c) **Warehousing**. This has been streamlined to eight regional distribution centres in the UK.

(d) **New development**. Most societies are disposing of their superstores and, in line with the retail polarization trend, medium-sized units are being closed while the smaller units are being converted to the convenience store format with later opening hours.

12. Present trends

Although co-operative societies have declined seriously in trade share from the late 1950s, recent results show a slight reversal of the trend. Comparison with experience abroad is largely impossible because historical factors have caused shares to vary from country to country, e.g. in Sweden co-ops take about 20 per cent of retail trade compared with very little trade in the USA.

Department stores

13. Definition

A department store is defined as a large store selling, under one roof but in physically separate departments, four or more different classes of consumer goods, one of which is women's and girls' clothing. Some large departmental store groups like John Lewis, House of Fraser and Debenhams own up to 100 branches and these chains are called multiple department stores. There are also a number of much smaller chains of department stores, e.g. Beales, and also a few autonomous units. Within the larger groups central buying is the norm, but often the accent is on customer service with each department carrying out its own buying, merchandising and stock control. Scope for economies of scale in buying is therefore narrower. Department stores have seen a gradual erosion of market share as the large supermarket groups have added non-food merchandise to their retail offer. Refurbishment of city centre stores and the quality of management will be the key to the future success of department stores.

14. The general principles of operation

The general principles of operation of department stores are:

(a) Siting in major shopping centres or locations supported by potentially large catchments.

(b) Freedom for the customer to move around the store and view.

(c) Relatively high prices with margins large enough to cover heavy staffing, the range of services offered and high accommodation costs.

(d) Provision of a large number of specialized goods in one location, which allows some associated sales. (However, many of the larger groups have been carrying out range pruning.)

(e) Special staff expertise in particular products.

(f) Wide range of customer services such as delivery, credit, the making-up of soft furnishings and the provision of restaurants, cloakrooms, telephones, etc.

(g) Space concessions offered to 'shop-within-shop' operations (often manu-facturers) like Wedgwood or Berkertex.

15. Future trends

Department stores are expected to maintain their proportion of trade. This implies that their ability to withstand the dynamic trading of the leading multiple shops will continue. Movement towards new shopping centres, new centres of population and to the suburbs is expected to continue. In both Europe and the USA department stores have been one of the most successful types of retailing. (It has been suggested that variety stores such as Marks & Spencer in the UK have helped to hinder departmental growth here; this former type of retailing is not quite as popular abroad.)

Discount stores

16. Characteristics

Cut-price retailing has been common in the UK since the abolition of retail price maintenance in 1964. Every retail sector indulges in it, some firms to a greater extent than others. Discount stores tend to have characteristics such as:

(a) Very low prices.

(b) Low gross margins.

(c) High degree of self-service.

(d) Low-cost fittings.

(e) No free services, such as delivery.

(f) Reliance on heavy advertising in nearby large population centres.

(g) Relative isolation of locations from conventional shopping areas with consequently low rents predominantly in 'edge-of-town' sites. The dependence is therefore on shoppers requiring:

  (i)   good communications
  (ii) plenty of car parking
  (iii) visibility of the site from some distance.

Pure discount stores (such as the original Comet electrical operation) became very successful in the late 1960s and early 1970s on the basis of the discount concept. However, the 'wheel of retailing' has turned and distinctions between Comet and other electrical retailers are no longer marked. Similarly, Asda, which started as a food discount chain, now has a substantial number of own-label products and is similar in trading style to the other large supermarket groups.

Out of the various discount sectors, DIY retailers are the largest. These are closely followed by food discounters and carpets and furniture retailers. A new wave of limited-range food discount retailers such as Aldi, Netto and Lidl entered the market in the late 1980s when the UK recession began to bite and customers were again increasingly looking for the lowest possible prices; their success, however, has been limited and they are not now thought to pose a major threat to the major grocery retailers. More recently the UK has witnessed the growth of discounted 'designer' clothing stores (sometimes also referred to as factory outlets) which sell well-known brands at discounted prices.

Superstores and hypermarkets

17. Superstores and hypermarkets

The development of very large retail units grafting substantial non-food sales to a supermarket operation started in the early 1960s in the UK. Applying the basic principles of discount stores, low prices and minimum service, growth has been spectacular. From two stores in 1963 to 210 in 1978, the current total is over 1,200.

Superstores have a sales area of 25,000–50,000 square feet, while the term 'hypermarket' is reserved for units with over 50,000 square feet of selling area. Their characteristics are:

(a) Substantial surface car parking spaces under the control of the superstore retailer and serving the superstore largely or exclusively.

(b) A range of 25,000–50,000 individual items, covering most foods and many non-foods (the latter may take up 40 per cent of the total selling area).

(c) A broadly similar pricing, service and general marketing strategy to the discount store.

(d) The provision of often cut-price petrol retailing adjacent to the store and its car park.

(e) The comprehensive in-store use of information technology such as electronic point-of-sale (EPOS) equipment, and advanced food preparation equipment, e.g. for in-store bakeries.

Many planning problems have been encountered by retailers eager to open these very large stores. Now, many local authorities are reluctant to give permission to units that they believe might help to blight town centres and put many small independent retailers out of business.

The proportion of retail sales captured by this sector has increased from 2.7 per cent in 1980 to over 7 per cent in 1986, and today well over 50 per cent of grocery sales are transacted by superstores.

Franchising

18. Franchising

Franchising is the granting of sole selling rights within a given geographical area. The franchising company (the franchisor) supplies equipment and/or raw materials for a licensee who either pays a franchise fee or a percentage of turnover, or contracts to buy supplies from the franchisor (or a mixture of these methods of payment). The licensee is also helped in finding a location and is trained in all aspects of the business. Franchising is most frequently found in retail catering (Wimpy, McDonald's, Kentucky Fried Chicken), car maintenance and launderettes, but also in many other trades such as electrical retailing and bridal wear.

Franchising really took off in the USA in the 1960s and now accounts for well over a third of all retail sales there – it is not difficult therefore to see why many retailers feel there is a lot more potential in the franchise business format in the UK. (Franchising now accounts for about 30 per cent of retail sales in the UK.)

Mail order

Mail order retailing – using the mail to get orders and/or facilitate delivery – takes several forms as follows:

19. Mail order catalogues

This category involves two types – the general merchandise catalogue and the specialist catalogue. Examples of the latter are the specialist seed, bulb and plant catalogues. But the general merchandise catalogue is by far the more important in this sector, incorporating familiar names such as Kays, Littlewoods, Freemans, Grattan and Empire Stores.

Mail order catalogue retailing currently accounts for 3.7 per cent of all retail sales as compared to 4.7 per cent in 1976. However, the last few years have seen a slowing of the downward trend with the introduction of several new specialist catalogues.

From the mail order operators' point of view, the advantages of the system are:

(a) No conventional retail overheads.

(b) Lower buying costs possible.

(c) Less under-employment of staff than in conventional retail outlets (i.e. no peaks and troughs in the daily sales volume).

(d) Relatively high margins for the retail sector.

The disadvantages are:

(a) High working capital ratio (which means that a higher proportion than normal of net assets are earning less than average returns).

(b) Fixed prices (the catalogue is prepared many months beforehand).

(c) High commission, credit and carriage costs (particularly for returned goods).

(d) Inflexibility (e.g. lines cannot be altered quickly to take account of new situations).

The advantages of the general merchandise mail order catalogue to the customer are:

(a) 'Free' credit.

(b) Price stability over the lifetime of the catalogue.

(c) Savings in transport fares and petrol.

(d) Wide selection of merchandise.

(e) Approval facility.

(f) 'Armchair shopping' for groups such as the elderly, people with mobility problems and families living some way from shopping centres (i.e. convenience).

Free credit, it is said, far outweighs the advantages to customers of lower prices obtainable elsewhere, but in any case the structure of mail order trading is not conducive to competition in terms of price.

Mail order catalogue retailing has been stimulated by the launch of mail order catalogues by mainstream retailers such as Marks & Spencer with its home furnishings catalogue and the Next chain's launch of the Next Directory.

20. Direct response advertising

This is the use of advertising in newspapers or magazines to describe a product and stimulate the customer to write or telephone for it. Firms such as Coopers of Stortford have used this method successfully to sell anything from men's handkerchiefs to mini torches. Most national newspapers have a Saturday bargain-squares section advertising all manner of postal bargains.

21. Direct mail

This is the use of advertising literature sent directly to the potential customer for the purpose of selling goods or services. The Reader's Digest has been particularly successful in selling books in this manner and CDs, DVDs and collectors' pieces are also sold via direct mail.

Service retailing

22. Service retailing

As disposable incomes rise, so consumer spending has shifted from purchasing essential items to goods and services that increase the consumer's quality of life. There has been a marked increase in the provision of primary services as the focal point for retail transactions. In the same way as a product satisfies the needs and wants of consumers, so can a service. The prime difference between products and services is the intangible nature of the service (i.e. you cannot touch it).

Service retailers have existed for many years – shoe repairers, travel agents and dry cleaners being some examples. However, many new service retailers are now being established and are thriving. Examples are the amusement or 'theme' parks, health clubs and gyms.

As well as increasing disposable incomes, the growth of service retailing has been fuelled by:

(a) An increasing number of working women.

(b) Changing lifestyles with increasing emphasis on leisure activity, health and personal care.

(c) New service offerings – for example, private health screening.

Other forms of retail selling

23. Markets

Although traditional markets account for less than 1 per cent of total retail turnover, they affect general retail sales wherever they are held because of their attraction. Many of the older provincial markets like Nottingham and the Bull Ring in Birmingham have been successfully accommodated in new shopping centre schemes.

24. Mobile shops

These are travelling shops and are distinct from vehicles from which milk, bread and certain other goods are delivered regularly to an established list of customers.

25. Automatic vending

Selling out of machines has been part of the retail scene for many years (particularly for cigarettes and confectionery) and there has been something of a recent boom in auto-vending, notably in closed, relatively vandal-proof areas such as sports centres and airports. The possible limitation of the closed area reduces the main advantage of the machine in that they can be in operation for 24 hours a day, 7 days a week.

26. Door-to-door trading

Selling by travelling salespeople has declined since the days before the Second World War, but household goods (Betterware) and cosmetics (Avon) are still sold in this way. A variety of foodstuffs is also regularly delivered in the UK to the doorstep, e.g. milk and soft drinks.

27. Party selling

This idea, which originated in the USA, has been quite successful in the selling of the Tupperware brand of plastic containers and in children's clothing. It involves a local person organizing a party demonstration in his or her own home. Although homeware parties have declined, lifestyle parties (e.g. Ann Summers) have increased.

28. Club trading

Some retailers encourage people to join a club, paying a weekly sum for the article they wish to buy. This is still a popular method for the purchase of large items especially for Christmas.

29. E-tailing

E-tailing (the supply of goods and services for personal or household use by consumers via the internet or other electronic channels) is now a well-established form of retailing. The advantages to the consumer of convenience, ease and the saving of time and money, coupled with a growing familiarity with the technology and reduction in fears over security has ensured its success.

Equally there are several advantages for the retailer. There are savings to be made on wages and premises, orders can be accepted 24 hours a day and there is the ability to reach a much larger audience than with a traditional store.

Interestingly, however, many of the more successful online retailers are traditional retailers who have added an online facility to their traditional stores to become multiple channel retailers (*see* Chapter 26).

Shopping via interactive digital television is predicted to make an increasing impact in the next few years. The system allows retailers to send detailed product information to the consumer's set-top box, which can then be accessed by the consumer and an order for the product placed.

Mobile commerce (m-commerce) is still very much in its infancy but there are some clear theoretical advantages to the system. For example, shoppers heading to their nearest shopping centre could receive messages alerting them to the special deals on that day or to interact with a store's computer network to ease the chore of buying groceries.

Wholesale organizations

30. Definition of the wholesaler

The wholesaler is an organization, independent of producer and retailer, which undertakes the classic functions of distribution. These functions are:

(a) Merchandise selection.

(b) Forward buying.

(c) Warehousing.

(d) Breaking bulk.

(e) Financing, i.e. credit.

(f) Presentation, e.g. preparation, packaging.

(g) Levelling out of price variations.

31. Basic types of traditional wholesaler

(a) **General.** This involves the stocking of a wide range of merchandise.

(b) **Specialist.** This type keeps stocks of particular categories of goods, e.g. toys, electrical goods, etc.

Both these types of wholesaler may operate nationally and may employ staff to call on retailers, either to sell or to deliver goods or to do both.

32. Changes in wholesale patterns

The wholesaler in the traditional mould has been declining due to changes in the structure of retail distribution, e.g. fewer, larger multiple-owned shops with direct deliveries from manufacturers. New types of wholesaler have arisen, namely voluntary groups, cash-and-carry warehouses and warehouse clubs.

33. Wholesale-sponsored voluntary groups

These are often large organizations like Spar, Mace and Costcutter, which sell to the group's retail members.

The advantages to the member of the 'symbol' group are:

(a) Bulk-buying by the group means bigger discounts and thus the possibility of lower prices to compete with the multiple.

(b) The problems of administration of buying and so on are largely taken from the group member.

(c) Group 'own-brand' products help to give a corporate multiple-type image; this is boosted by national group advertising, sales promotion and display cards.

(d) In larger group wholesale chains, financial assistance and advice on development are available to the member.

The disadvantages of being a member are:

(a) A minimum weekly order must be placed with the local warehouse.

(b) A member may be asked to keep special accounts.

(c) For the larger member with very big stores, membership is less advantageous because the local warehouses often do not stock the very broad ranges needed for modern superstore operation.

34. Cash-and-carry wholesalers

The basic elements of cash-and-carry are:

(a) A wholesale warehouse.

(b) Customers are traders.

(c) Complete or partial self-service.

(d) Payment always in cash.

(e) Customers carry their own goods away.

The advantages to the retailers are:

(a) Lower buying prices.

(b) The ability to purchase as necessary, i.e. the retailer can use the cash-and-carry as a stockroom.

(c) Time saved in dealing with representatives, receiving and checking goods, invoices, etc.

(d) A better knowledge of what is available.

(e) Greater contact with the wholesaler in connection with exchange of views, etc.

The advantages to the wholesaler are:

(a) Better net margins.

(b) Greater contact with retailers.

35. Significance of cash-and-carry

Although there was a great upsurge in cash-and-carry development up until the early 1990s this seems to have stabilized at near saturation point in some areas. Many of the large groups have rationalized their chains by closing down badly sited branches and extending those outlets that have proved to be profitable. Others such as Makro have followed the US warehouse club format, which targets the small business customer, but also serves an increasing number of non-business customers.

Progress test 2

1. What are the main bases for classifying retail firms?

2. What problems face independent traders and how have they tried to overcome them?

3. What are the characteristics of a multiple?

4. How has the Co-operative Movement attempted to regain its position in UK retailing?

5. Describe the characteristics of a department store and compare them with discount stores.

6. What are the three forms of mail order retailing?

7. What functions does the wholesaler carry out?

8. How do voluntary groups operate? Do they have any disadvantages?

9. Multiple retailing has assumed a dominance over consumer channels of distribution that is becoming increasingly difficult to break. How do you account for this dominance and what are the implications of this situation for other distributive organizations?

10. Recent advances in IT have resulted in significant increases in e-tailing – home shopping and the delivery of products and services direct to the consumer via the internet. Discuss the implications for the traditional store-based retailer.

3 Economics of retailing

Introduction

Like all businesses, retail firms seek to expand their top-line revenues as well as attending to bottom-line costs and enhancing their pre-tax profitability.

There are a number of theoretical models that can be used to illustrate how firms can improve their performance. This chapter explores how retail firms can become more efficient, how they can analyse their industry sector and how they can expand successfully.

Economies of scale

1. Economies of scale

It is well known that the larger a company is, the more savings or economies it can make. This could be because fixed costs are spread over a greater volume of output, thus helping to reduce average costs, or the sheer size of variable inputs like raw materials makes it cheaper to buy in bulk. The prospect of scale economies drives firms to grow in size and this phenomenon is common in retailing.

Economies of scale are divided into external economies, which are enjoyed by a whole industry sector, and those that accrue to the individual firm (internal economies).

2. External economies

(a) **Economies of concentration**. The term 'concentration' has several meanings in industrial economics. Here it refers to the trend for firms to congregate or 'cluster' in specific geographical areas. In distribution, retail parks are a good example, where DIY sheds, electrical retailers and supermarkets locate together to share advantages such as common road and parking facilities, specially designed buildings and access to car-borne customers, staff and suppliers.

(b) **Economies of information**. It is expensive to develop and maintain databases containing the myriad information required by management today. This is particularly so in financial services and commodity trading where prices change continuously. Companies like Reuters and Bloombergs supply up-to-date financial information online to subscribers. In the food manufacturing and distribution sectors the Institute of Grocery Distribution, for example, carries out research on behalf of its retail, wholesale and manufacturer members.

(c) **Economies of distintegration**. Whereas the term 'integration' means bringing together blocks of resources such as firms under a single ownership and control, distintegration in this case means contracting out the supply of goods and services to what are called outsourcers. It addresses the question of whether a company should make or buy in its supplies. Although quality, availability and service are important it may be that it is cheaper to source inputs from a specialist producer which may itself enjoy internal economies of scale. Typically retail firms buy their merchandise and services (like transport) from contractors (as does Marks & Spencer) rather than producing it themselves. Outsourcing has grown immeasurably in all sectors in recent years, underlining the belief that individual firms should focus on what they do best.

3. Internal economies

(a) **Technical economies**

    (i)   *Superior technique*. Large firms can make better use of larger pieces of equipment than small firms. A 100,000-square-metre warehouse used by a large superstore group could not be operated effectively for its own use by a village shop.

    (ii) *Increased dimensions*. The fact that a superstore is a hundred times larger than the village shop does not mean that it costs a hundred times more to build, operate and maintain.

    (iii) *Linked processes*. Today retail firms can use electronic data interchange (EDI) to link the outputs of their EPOS systems with warehouses and even suppliers. Thus data that has been collected by bar code scans can be transmitted down the telephone line to a manufacturer, which can produce replenishment stock immediately the data is received, if needs be. This reduces time and documentation as well as improving the quality of communication.

(b) **Marketing economies**. These accrue in the areas of both selling and buying.

    (i)   *Product*. Large firms buy in bulk and can earn substantial discounts from suppliers, thus reducing the unit costs of the merchandise or service bought in.

    (ii) *Price*. Companies can pass the savings made in buying on to customers. This works particularly well in product categories where there are many competing brands. Here demand is relatively price elastic and firms can leverage their revenues over and above the level of their price cuts. On the other hand if a retailer possesses a strong brand itself, like Tesco, it can use the price inelasticity here to raise prices.

(*iii*) *Promotion.* The cost of advertising and promotion can be spread over many units, reducing the promotional costs per customer to a minimum.

(*iv*) *Place.* Distribution costs can be reduced per unit by the larger size of 'drops' to each store.

(c) **Financial economies.** Larger firms can borrow substantial sums of money at preferential rates because of their size and their lower perceived risk. Equity funding can be created by share issues whose charges fall proportionately to the size of the offering. Larger firms can also generate increased amounts of pre-tax profit, which can be retained and used as internally sourced funding.

(d) **Managerial economies**

(*i*) Large firms set up functional groups to deal with marketing and human resources and these specialist departments are designed to provide added-value solutions (in recent years cross-functional teams and matrix organizations have been developed to avoid the bureaucratic effect and conflict created by the old-style departmentalization).

(*ii*) Delegation or empowerment is more possible in a large firm. This enables managers to concentrate on more important issues while allowing subordinates to take decisions without reference to them.

(e) **Risk-bearing economies.** The larger a company the more resources it can allocate to diversification if this is required. Some retailers have become mini-conglomerates and have ventured into other shopping formats, for example Kingfisher into electrical products.

Other retailers have crossed borders (*see* Chapter 5) like Tesco into Eastern Europe and Marks & Spencer into the Pacific Rim.

The idea of diversification or risk-bearing is to avoid the 'all-eggs-in-one-basket' syndrome. If a giant comes along and sits on the basket the result will be little more than the ingredients for an omelette. Having eggs in many baskets avoids the cyclical nature of economic activity. For example, the early 1990s economic downturn began in the USA in 1989 and ended three years later, having travelled round the world. Thus the advantage of market diversification. In terms of products, food is considered to be contracyclical in that households have to eat. Other products like furniture, although of a 'big ticket' kind, tend not to be purchased by households on a regular basis. Retailers need to study each product market to gauge the best economic mix to adopt. But if a business diversifies too far away from its core competences – what it understands and can do well – it may face other risks when things go wrong.

4. Existence of small retailers

One reason why small firms still exist in retailing is that there has been a polarization between large and small firms. This is not confined to retailing and is found in many service industries like accountancy and the legal services. Not every firm can obtain economies of scale, because of reasons such as lack of capital, unwillingness of owners to take on the extra responsibilities of growth or because there are opportunities in niche markets. In retailing the niche positions are often found in more isolated communities or in housing estates that are not well supplied by the bigger retail chains. If personal services are supplied such as dentistry, economies of scale are somewhat irrelevant. Imagine a dental surgery with 100 chairs in an open-plan environment. Even if the dental charges were low, how many patients would it attract?

Economies of experience and scope

5. Economies of experience

The longer a firm has been operating in a particular sector the greater the amount of learning it should have made about the market and its products. This should enable it to keep ahead of its competitors in terms of the four main factors that buyers look for in a purchase – quality, value, availability and service.

This is not to say that the first mover or earlier entrant to a sector will continue to lead. Newer entrants may learn faster or more efficiently than the original firm. A good example is how Tesco was able to replace Sainsbury's as leader in the grocery sector.

Economies of experience may make up for lack of scale economies. McDonald's, for instance, lacks some technical economies as a fast-food company. Its largest units, in Moscow, have 25 server positions and it is difficult to see how a larger unit than this could be effectively operated, constricted as it is by its service-market offering. Learning is carried out in the company's Hamburger University chain (local unit in London's Edgware Road) where managers and franchisees are trained to train their store crews. Experience learned and transmitted through the chain enables crews to work as teams to attain better quality (clean restaurants) and faster response to order times (a key success factor in fast-food operations). This is a good example of the learning organization (*see* Chapter 4).

Economies of experience may well have limitations and McDonald's is experimenting with more sophisticated cooking facilities in its restaurants. The company has also closed some of its units, e.g. in both north and south London.

6. Economies of scope

This means the ability of a firm to produce several different outputs from a common set of resources. These savings are obvious in a manufacturing system where standard parts (e.g. automotive platforms) can be made up into a variety of different products (e.g. saloon cars and pickup trucks). But by assembling diverse products in a store retailers are also providing economies of scope in the service sector. Again, a pizza restaurant buys in standard pizza bases upon which a wide variety of toppings are placed and cooked. As micromarketing develops and each customer is treated as an individual there may be more possibilities for economies of scope.

Structural analysis

Michael Porter's Five Forces Model (*see* Figure 3.1) enables planners to analyse the structure and relationship in an industry sector to determine its attractiveness.

7. Threat of new entrants

If a retail mode is relatively young or still in its growth stage it is possible that new firms may set up in competition to the existing players. There are very few barriers to entry in retailing. For example, both Tesco and Iceland set up in the food retailing sector from very small and humble beginnings but are now the top performers in their respective areas. But to grow, large amounts of capital and economies of scale may be required. William Low, the Scottish supermarket company, saw that it could not obtain 'critical mass' (a size large enough to enjoy scale economies) so it auctioned itself off to the highest bidder. Exit barriers are also low in food retailing. These refer to the ease with which a player in a sector can sell up. Exit barriers are high in the steel industry, for example.

8. Threat of substitutes

These can be defined as products or services that perform the same tasks as an existing offering but more cheaply or effectively. In retailing, different forms of retail channel compete for custom and a new and growing threat is from the internet (discussed in more detail in Chapter 26). The internet will become truly threatening when it drives down the price that shoppers pay to below that of conventional retail shops. Again, there is a gain in convenience as in mail order

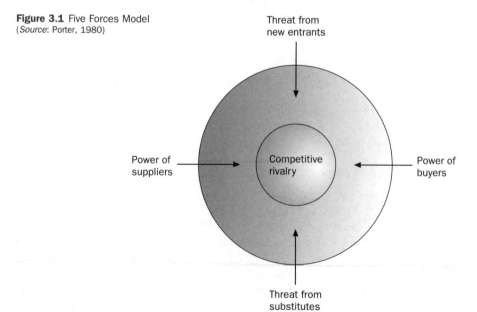

Figure 3.1 Five Forces Model
(*Source*: Porter, 1980)

shopping. E-commerce is continually improving its accessibility and performance and this will attract more personal computer users to link up to it.

9. Powerful suppliers

Vendors are more powerful than customers and thus able to raise their prices if they:

(a) Are relatively more concentrated (here concentration means market dominance expressed perhaps by share of market value).

(b) Offer unique or differentiated products such as branded goods (Coca-Cola, Nestlé or BMW are companies with substantial brand equity).

(c) Can threaten to integrate forward (i.e. buy up their customer, acquire one of its competitors or set up organically as a new competitor).

(d) Are a larger supplier to other firms or industries.

Another problem for the customer may be that switching costs (the cost of searching for and appointing a new supplier) may be more than the extra charges it pays the existing supplier.

10. Powerful buyers

Customers are in a stronger position to force down supplier prices if:

(a) They are relatively concentrated (e.g. the UK retail grocery industry).

(b) They make bulk purchases (e.g. Tesco as the biggest UK food retailer).

(c) The product they are buying is undifferentiated or of a commodity type (this will make the price on offer more elastic because there are many substitutes).

(d) The customer can integrate backwards and acquire the supplier's business.

11. Competitive rivalry

This involves the extent of competition between firms within an industry. This will depend on:

(a) **The stage of sector life cycle**. Most of the retail industry as presently constituted on a location basis is mature and therefore less competitive than a few years ago. Oligopolies have crept into areas such as food retailing.

(b) **The importance of fixed costs**. In womenswear retailing, for example, the high fixed costs of town centre locations mean that when demand weakens, these stores have to cut prices and increase volumes in order to pay their rents, thus increasing competition and the possibility of category killers entering the market.

(c) **Size of new units**. Hypermarkets have wiped out many small shops due to their huge size and the ranges offered, economies of scale and so on.

(d) **Exit barriers**. It may be difficult for retail companies to leave the industry because there exists no demand for their type of merchandise or their premises. The need for planning permission to change use may also slow up the recycling process. Family firms may face emotional exit barriers (the Letts brothers of the diary firm lost it because they were only interested in passing it on to their sons).

Business integration

Business integration means the bringing together of blocks of resources, like firms, under common ownership and control. It is often carried out in order to support growth strategies and to obtain economies of scale. There are four main types of business integration.

12. Horizontal integration

This occurs where similar firms at the same stage of the process of production and distribution come together in a merger or takeover situation (mergers are usually seen as friendly acquisitions while takeovers are often hostile). Clear-cut examples of horizontal integration in retailing would be Tesco's acquisition of Hillards and William Low, two small regional supermarket companies.

13. Vertical integration

Here, firms at different stages of the production/distribution chain join together to gain control of manufacturing or of distribution. Retailers do not normally indulge in this kind of integration because of difficulties in maintaining profitable links between production and distribution. When Body Shop announced a restructuring in January 1999 only 25 per cent of its manufacturing operation at Littlehampton was being used. Laura Ashley also rid itself of its clothing factories during its many restructurings. It makes more sense today to disintegrate operations by outsourcing product manufacture to specialist suppliers. Marks & Spencer has done this successfully for decades. Again, Benetton, the Italian knitwear manufacturer, outsources its distribution through an international franchise system.

14. Lateral integration

This type of integration falls between the former two. There is a connection but not a direct one between the two (or more) firms involved. A good example was the penchant for airlines to buy hotel chains during the 1980s. On the face of it there were synergies in this link up, but this kind of integration often falls apart when a serious economic recession sets in. One retail example is the Co-op Group which carries out manufacturing of food and other goods and is also the largest provider of funeral services in the UK. The outputs of the production side are sold through Co-op superstores (an example of scope economies).

15. Conglomeration

Retail conglomerates became popular during the 1980s retail boom. Conglomeration involves bringing together several types ('trades') of retailer. Next built up a chain of shops that extended from clothing to jewellery to florists but has now cut back to a core clothing offer. Boots the Chemists took over a group that included Halfords (motor accessories) and Do It All (DIY products). The idea behind conglomeration is to spread risk but today the general view in many industries is that 'sticking to the knitting' (focusing on core strengths) is the best policy. This does not preclude supermarkets 'creaming' and 'scrambling' (*see* Chapter 1).

16. Demerger

Recently there has been a trend towards breaking up all sorts of company. The idea here is to improve shareholder value by focusing a group away from its former parent. Examples involve Argos (ex-BAT) and Selfridges (ex-Sears).

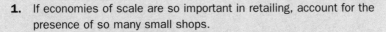

Progress test 3

1. If economies of scale are so important in retailing, account for the presence of so many small shops.

2. What is meant by economies of experience? Do they always accrue to the firm that has been longest in the market? If not, why not?

3. Carry out a structural analysis for a retailer with which you are familiar. What conclusions do you come to?

4. What is the point in integrating organizations?

5. Why are demergers popular today?

4 Grand strategies

Introduction

The term 'grand strategy' refers to the overarching plan that may have a time horizon of up to five years ahead and that motivates the whole of a business, as explained in the introduction to Chapter 6. This chapter considers what kinds of strategy are available, the relationships of organization and culture to strategy, and how an organization is designed to enhance its value.

1. Grand strategies

Figure 4.1 shows that the overall strategies of a business ('grand strategies') take up the peak of the organization's pyramid, while operating strategies, discussed in Chapter 6, flow from these.

Figure 4.1 Grand strategies as a proportion of the organizational pyramid

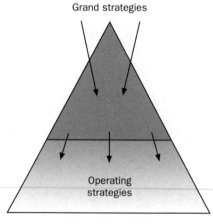

Grand strategies

Operating
strategies

Organizational pyramid

The operating strategies 'put flesh on the strategic skeleton' and are activated by the functional departments or multidisciplinary networks or whatever organizational form is adopted to implement strategy.

Main types of grand strategy

For the purposes of this text, which is operationally orientated, we have simplified grand strategy types into three.

(a) **Growth strategies**. The adoption of an expansion plan that is aimed at increasing market share and profitability is partly determined by the economic cycle and by competitors. It is clearly a popular approach with shareholders, management groups, suppliers and other stakeholders.

(b) **Recovery strategies**. Because the economic cycle goes down as well as up there is sometimes a need to turn a loss-making business round or to retrench, which involves divesting non-performing parts of a business.

(c) **Sell-off or liquidation**. Occasionally businesses are so badly affected by competition and economic recessions that they are sold off completely (a so-called 'exit' strategy). Again, some profitable businesses may not be able to grow enough shareholder value in the present form and rather than adopting a growth strategy they put themselves up for auction, such as William Low, the Dundee-based supermarket group that sold itself to Tesco.

2. *Bases of strategy*

Before a business can attempt to define an effective grand strategy it needs to identify its present situation and to decide the best direction in which to move, along with a plan to support its aspirations. This process is discussed in Chapter 6, together with a description of SWOT (strengths, weaknesses, opportunities, threats), an essential part of any planning system. SWOT analysis reminds us that we need to assess the resource capability of the organization along with the opportunities and the threats in the organization's environment.

Strategic planning is about identifying the distinctive competence of an organization (what it does best that is relevant for at least the duration of the plan) and matching it with the opportunities identified within the environment. This process should show capabilities in the organization that give it an advantage over other, competing organizations. If no capability is identified managers need to buy in appropriate skills and assets, acquire them or pursue a joint venture (*see* Chapter 5).

3. *Strategic connections*

Before we discuss how strategy is formulated it is important to explain further how strategy connects with the rest of the organization.

(a) **The vision**. This involves a view of what the organization and its core competences should be in the future. For example, how will home shopping affect the physical locations of shops? People who get the vision right before others have a head start in building a new and perhaps sustainable competitive advantage.

(b) **The mission**. This is a statement of the overriding purpose of the organization, which often encapsulates the expectations of the key stakeholder groups (these are groups of people who have interests in the company and perhaps some power to influence its policies), e.g. customers (who want quality, value, availability and service), shareholders (who want income and capital growth) and single issue groups (who want retailers to do many things such as to avoid buying merchandise from overseas factories that use child labour). This is a process of inclusion that reduces the possibility of threats from stakeholders.

(c) **Objectives**. These are decision rules that enable management to guide and measure the firm's performance towards its mission or purpose, e.g. to achieve net profits of £x million by the year 2010.

(d) **Grand strategy**. This is the long-range plan that supports the objectives of the business, as discussed earlier in this chapter.

(e) **Goals**. These are specific milestones such as annual profit performance standards. These are associated more with operational systems in the organization.

(f) **Standards**. These are very specific performance indicators that refer to individual store sales and profitability. Indeed, they can include departmental performance within the store.

It can be seen that the hierarchy or pyramid of activity can be broken down into a series of quantitatively assessed performance indicators. These set standards for monitoring and evaluating performance within the total strategic plan. Unless detailed monitoring is done at 'grass roots' level on a continuous basis the strategic objectives of the business may not be met. Clearly, this achievement not only requires the provision of appropriate resources at each level but the motivation of staff in all functions. All this folds back into the vision, mission and strategy of the organization and, critically, to the quality and consistency of top management, whose role is crucial to the ultimate success of the organization.

Culture and organization

Top management is responsible not only for the direction the business is moving in but also for its culture and organization.

4. Culture

The culture of an organization can be defined as the impact of influences on it over time in forming its value and belief systems. The history of an organization is crucial in its culture, along with the present-day influence of stakeholder groups that may challenge the organization's current policies (Shell's petrol retailing in Germany was affected by environmental groups in 1995). Culture influences the assumptions that company managers and staff have in the organization itself, and their attitudes to external groups, e.g. stakeholders. This forms a paradigm or mindset – 'the way we do things here'. The paradigm may have to change with the strategy.

5. Organization

This is the way in which management relates resources within the overall system in pursuit of objectives. Organization is now regarded as an important factor in success. The wrong organization can produce poor results. For example, some retail organizations have formed into tall, bureaucratic pyramids which make it more difficult for communication to flow upwards or even downwards.

Currently, Marks & Spencer has been cited as an example of an organization that has too many managerial layers. The term 'learning organization' has been recently coined. In order to survive along with it, the people in an organization must use experience to adapt to the ever-changing environment. As indicated above, the paradigm may have to change to reflect a new reality. To enable change to occur in an orderly manner, managers have to learn to deal with change, i.e. change management. Good examples of change management occur in the IT sector with firms such as Dell and Sun.

Management quality

6. Management quality

The ability of managers to cope effectively in very dynamic conditions such as we are experiencing today is a crucial factor in success.

It is sometimes suggested that different types of managers are required for each stage in the cycle that retail companies may experience. For example, in a start-up situation an entrepreneurial business person is required who can assess and cope with risk. Such a person may be incapable of managing growth (the famous inventor Edison had to be removed from the boards of several companies he had founded). A growth manager is able to control a situation where costs may be overtaking revenues and where competition is stealing ahead. Inevitably the company life cycle moves from growth to maturity to decline (the retail life-cycle theory is discussed in Chapter 1). A recovery specialist may then have to be brought in to turn the company round. In retailing, this is often not the end of the story. Cases like Laura Ashley and Marks & Spencer are all too frequent, underlining the fact that some retail organizations can often misread or fail to notice the enormous shifts in shopping patterns that have occurred during the past 25 years. Recovery specialists ('company doctors') have to have the required skills, knowledge and attitude to turn round businesses that have lost their way. These specialists require interpersonal and analytical skills, along with vision and the experience of previous successful turnaround situations.

Managers must assess strategies from the point of view of their suitability (do they add value to the existing business?), feasibility (can resources be made available to implement them?) and acceptability (will all key stakeholders accept them?). Above all, managers must be leaders and motivators who seek to include all employees as part of the mission and the team.

The value chain

7. Introduction

'The value chain' is a term coined by Michael Porter to describe areas in which a company's critical success factors lie. These synthesize into the distinctive competence of a firm which, if relevant to the target consumer, could provide the competitive advantage that the firm can use to move ahead of competition and thus become more profitable. Porter developed the idea of the value chain to help companies in this particular part of their strategy planning. The value chain breaks up a firm into its strategically relevant activities in order to understand the behaviour of costs and the existing and potential sources of differentiation. This approach is very relevant to retailing as the four diagrams in this section show (*see* Figures 4.2 to 4.5). It involves an analysis of activities in the firm that together produce synergies and add value to the eventual outcomes (synergy is the concept that in certain circumstances the whole is greater than the sum of its parts).

8. Value activities

The value chain is made up of two sets of activities that should create value (and subsequent profitability). These are primary activities and support activities.

Figure 4.2 Porter's value chain
(*Source*: Porter, 1985)

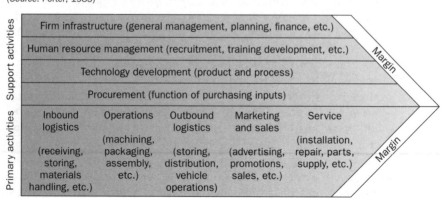

(a) **Primary activities**. There are five generic categories of primary activities:

(i) *Inbound logistics*. In retail terms this would include costs of unloading vehicles, storing merchandise and so on.

(ii) *Operations*. The merchandising of products received within specific locations and layouts and using particular space allocation.

(iii) *Outbound logistics*. This, in retailing, involves systems such as self-checkout operations by customers and delivery systems.

(iv) *Marketing and sales*. Advertising the store's offer and inducing visits by use of sales promotion.

(v) *Service*. This might involve installation and after-sales service.

(b) **Support activities**

(i) *Procurement*. This refers to the purchasing methods and not to actual merchandise. Improved purchasing can make big differences in retail profits because so much of the revenues of a retailer are reimbursed to suppliers.

(ii) *Technology development*. The introduction and development of systems such as EPOS (electronic point of sale), EFTPOS (electronic funds transfer at point of sale) and EDI (electronic data interchange) are examples of how retailers can improve profits by reducing costs.

(iii) *Human resource management*. As service providers, retailers are highly dependent on the skills, knowledge and attitudes of their staff so that recruitment, selection, training, development and payment of all types of personnel are critical to success.

(iv) *Firm infrastructure*. This involves general management, planning, finance, accounting, legal and other aspects of company operation. The quality of management (as discussed in Chapter 6) is of vital importance.

9. Cost behaviour

According to Porter, there are ten elements, called cost drivers, that affect the performance of the activities discussed above. In today's deflationary environment, it is essential that retailers take cost out of the value chain and the entire supply chain.

(a) **Economies or diseconomies of scale** (discussed in Chapter 3).

(b) **Learning**. This has been referred to in terms of experience and the 'learning organization'.

(c) **Pattern of capacity utilization**. Many supermarkets have attempted to increase numbers of customers at off-peak times by offering them inducements such as sales promotions. Such shifts in volume may improve scale economies.

(d) **Linkages**. These are complicated connections within the company's value chain but also outside it. Suppliers can be encouraged to improve their value and quality while intermediaries and customers can be helpful by buying bigger and by spreading the word. IT systems can help immeasurably here (*see* Figure 4.5).

(e) **Interrelationships**. This involves sharing activities such as joint venturing or use of concessions (e.g. designer clothing manufacturers in Harrods).

(f) **Integration**. Here a firm has an in-house capacity rather than one that is shared. This may involve computer operations that may be cheaper to run in-house than using an outsourcer.

(g) **Timing**. An obvious advantage here would be first-mover advantage, e.g. a category killer's entry into a mature market. But late movers can also gain advantage such as purchasing the latest equipment.

(h) **Discretionary policies independent of other drivers**. This involves what Porter classes as generic strategies, where firms can opt for a low-cost positioning or can provide a differentiation offer. For example Aldi and Lidl are positioned in the UK grocery market as limited range discounters whereas Waitrose is a higher cost differentiated offer.

(i) **Location**. This is discussed in Chapter 11; it offers value, for example, to convenience store users as it does to superstore shoppers (a good example of different bases for synergy).

(j) **Institutional factors**. These are external factors that are driven by government regulations, trade unions and so on. The impact of the Competition Commission on supermarket policies is a case in point.

Clearly the analysis of the organization's value chain is a complicated and time-consuming activity. Company management should attempt this task in order to

Figure 4.3 A value chain for Marks & Spencer
(*Source*: Porter, 1985)

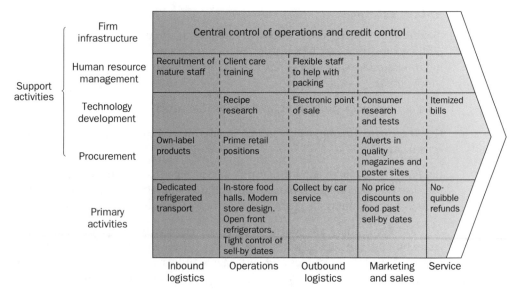

Support activities	Firm infrastructure	Central control of operations and credit control				
	Human resource management	Recruitment of mature staff	Client care training	Flexible staff to help with packing		
	Technology development		Recipe research	Electronic point of sale	Consumer research and tests	Itemized bills
	Procurement	Own-label products	Prime retail positions		Adverts in quality magazines and poster sites	
Primary activities		Dedicated refrigerated transport	In-store food halls. Modern store design. Open front refrigerators. Tight control of sell-by dates	Collect by car service	No price discounts on food past sell-by dates	No-quibble refunds
		Inbound logistics	Operations	Outbound logistics	Marketing and sales	Service

Figure 4.4 A value chain for a limited range discount food retailer (based on KwikSave)
(*Source*: Porter, 1985)

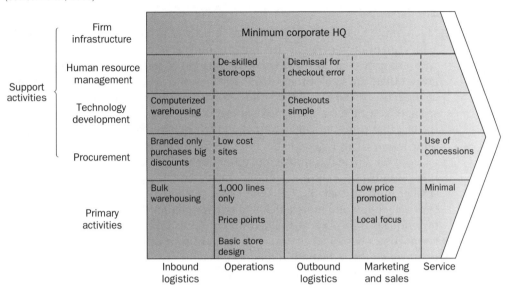

	Inbound logistics	Operations	Outbound logistics	Marketing and sales	Service
Support activities — Firm infrastructure	Minimum corporate HQ				
Human resource management		De-skilled store-ops	Dismissal for checkout error		
Technology development	Computerized warehousing		Checkouts simple		
Procurement	Branded only purchases big discounts	Low cost sites			Use of concessions
Primary activities	Bulk warehousing	1,000 lines only Price points Basic store design		Low price promotion Local focus	Minimal

identify competitive advantages, as shown in the two contrasting retail value chains illustrated in Figures 4.3 and 4.4.

The value chain does not finish at the boundaries of the individual organization, however. Figure 4.5 illustrates how it extends back to suppliers and forward to customers. Through systems such as efficient consumer response (*see* Chapter 26), other members of the supply chain add their own values.

Figure 4.5 The extended value chain based on a manufacturer
(*Source*: Porter, 1985)

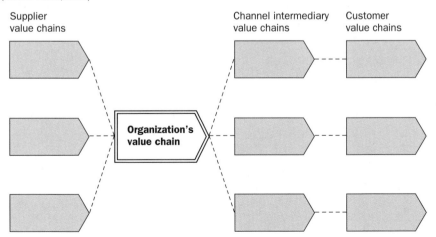

Synergy

10. Synergy

Much of the methodology and activity described in this chapter is aimed at the achievement of 'synergy' in the organization. The idea of synergy is associated with economies or cost savings of various kinds and means that the whole is greater than the sum of the parts. A key task of management is to use resources in the most productive way possible. Today, a common phrase in management speak is 'getting more out of less'. Students and others are sometime puzzled by the fact that concepts can be turned on their heads to demonstrate precisely the same lessons. This reflects major changes in conditions – new scenarios – which require very different contingent plans. A case in point is that of demergers. While there are advantages of scale, it often makes sense to break up organizations into smaller units so that they become closer to their customers and staff and are thus able to respond more quickly to environmental change. Thus the demerger of Selfridges from Sears or the flotation of Argos from its parent group. Synergy is sometimes described as $1 + 1 = 3$, but, again, it could be $2 - 1 = 3$. The basis upon which this 'equation' is produced may be very different in order to mirror the external realities surrounding the business in question.

Progress test 4

1. What is meant by the term 'grand strategy'?

2. Explain the difference between vision, mission, and objective.

3. How do the culture and organization of a company affect its strategy?

4. Why is the quality of management crucial to business success?

5. What relevance does the value chain have for retail managers?

6. How can a retailer develop synergies in its value chain? Give examples.

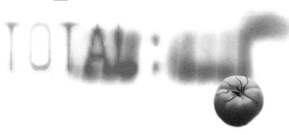

5 International retailing

Introduction

Retailing, which is one of the world's biggest but most localized industries, is undergoing a change that many observers would have dismissed 20 years ago. This chapter considers the factors that influence cross-border retailer moves, the methods used by firms to cross borders, and guidelines for cross-border moves.

1. International retailing

The recent explosion in international or cross-border retailing belies the bad experiences of retail companies like the Burton Group in France or Carrefour in the UK during the 1970s. Of course there have been well-established international retailers such as Woolworths for many years but they were the exception rather than the rule. Political, legal, economic and sociocultural factors militated together against any mass migration of retail brands over international boundaries. This was largely true of most products and services, which had to be extensively modified or rebranded for export. The costs of such effort were often seen as largely non-productive and the failure rates were seen as too high. In any case there was no need to attempt to operate in cross-border fashion except for large consumer packaged goods manufacturers like Heinz, Unilever, Coca-Cola and Nestlé. But as early as 1985 in the UK the retail sector was showing signs of maturity in falling returns on capital investment, increased price competition and greater advertising expenditure; many observers commented that there were too many stores in the wrong place and/or in the wrong hands – reflected by the epidemic of takeovers. This maturation of the market is one of the so-called 'push' or threat factors causing retailers to look overseas. These push factors as well as 'pull' factors are discussed in the next two sections.

2. Push factors

(a) **Saturation**. The biggest 'push' factor is saturation of domestic markets. While there is room for expansion at home, retailers have no need to look abroad, but that option is fast disappearing.

In the UK for example retail chains' share of the grocery retailing market increased from under half in 1973 to over 80 per cent by 2000. A similar pattern can be seen in such countries as France, Germany, Belgium and the Netherlands.

With such levels of concentration at home, companies are moving into countries with less developed retail markets like Spain or buying existing chains in developed markets. In the UK this latter option is no longer possible for grocery supermarket chains. After the acquisition of Hillards (Yorkshire) and William Low (Scotland) by Tesco there is only one regional grocery chain left in the UK.

(b) **Recession**. Another threat or push factor has been the severity of recent recessions. Clearly, retailers like other sectors see the need for a portfolio of assets covering economies that offer contracyclical advantages, i.e. when your own economy is down, other nations' economies could be booming.

The strategic need to maintain and enhance growth in a fast-changing set of environments is a paramount objective for retail managers in all sectors. If one door closes then another has to be found. In this case the door is abroad.

(c) **Planning restrictions**. Growing aversion to the spread of hypermarkets and retail parks has taken hold in several European countries. In the UK the Department of Environment published new planning guidelines in 1993 called PPG6, calling for town centre development to be favoured over out-of-town localities. After two years it became apparent that the guidelines had produced a decisive shift away from out-of-town shopping. As a result Sainsbury's, the grocery supermarket chain, was building only 12 new stores in 1995 out of an original 20 planned. Sainsbury's says it is now winning only one in ten planning appeals against seven in ten previously.

In France, inventor of the hypermarket, restrictions were introduced in 1973 when the number of hypermarkets soared to more than 200. Paris alone was surrounded by eight giant regional centres. Controls were toughened in 1993 and now every centre needs permission from a government body composed of local mayors, trade and consumer groups. France's Promodès says that because of planning restrictions it can only open one hypermarket a year at home and that is why it has become a major player in Spain. As a result some Spanish local authorities are becoming worried and Catalonia for example has banned developments of more than 2,500 square metres.

Controls of some sort are also applied in Germany, Denmark, Finland, Belgium and Holland.

In the USA, with the greatest number of shopping malls in the world, growth has slowed since 1989 not so much because of planning problems but the increasing competition in a saturating market.

3. Pull factors

There are several factors that can be seen as opportunities rather than threats.

(a) **Falling barriers to market entry**. The European Union (EU) now offers a more standardized environment for retailers in terms of the movement of goods and, more importantly, because of the introduction of the euro, a common currency. From 1 January 1999 11 countries in the EU started to use the euro. This may help to harmonize prices throughout Europe but whatever happens European retailers need to change their operating systems to accommodate the new currency. The creation of a single European market of 320 million consumers has also made Europe a much more attractive market for US retailers. The crumbling of the Berlin Wall and the collapse of communism has opened up not only Eastern Europe but the countries of the CIS (the old USSR). The EU expanded to 25 members in 2004.

Trade blocs elsewhere such as NAFTA (the North American Free Trade Area) have encouraged American retailers to look next door at Mexico and Canada. Japanese department stores spread across Asia in the 1980s and in the 1990s began gaining a foothold in London.

(b) **Supplier strategies**. Manufacturers of goods for retail distribution are becoming more international themselves. Groups such as Unilever are restructuring manufacturing operations on a pan-European basis and are adopting international marketing campaigns. A sign of this is the growing importance of internationally recognized brand names ('global brands') in consumer goods. Nestlé for example has rebranded all the Rowntree products since that confectionery company was taken over, using the Nestlé logo.

(c) **Strategic retail alliances**. Since 1988 some European food retailers have formed joint ventures, forming eight loose alliances. This could lead to joint buying and greater pressure on food manufacturers to sell at common prices. The internet has spawned GNX and WWRE: retailer supply chain networks that include many big international retailers.

(d) **Identification of less developed markets**. From the 1970s the Southern European markets of Spain, Italy and Portugal were invaded from the north. Four of Spain's top five food retailers are now French-owned, for example.

(e) **Converging consumer tastes**. Increasing foreign travel by consumers and the spread of cross-border mass media such as satellite television are creating 'common denominations in consumer tastes'.

(f) **Possible economies of scale**. *See* Chapter 3.

4. Cross-border trends in Europe

As can be seen from Table 5.1, of the retailers with international operations in Europe, only a handful had an international presence in the 1950s. By the 1960s most European markets had foreign entrants, although even France had only half a dozen non-domestic operators. The 1970s witnessed something of a polarization

Table 5.1 Internationally active retailers in Western Europe by destination country and decade of entry

Destination country	1950s and earlier	1960s	1970s	1980s	1990s
Austria	1	1	16	23	92
Belgium	–	4	19	61	166
Denmark	–	3	7	10	51
Finland	–	1	–	7	27
France	1	6	10	34	101
Germany	–	2	8	27	134
Greece	–	–	1	8	47
Ireland	–	4	2	13	79
Italy	–	2	–	15	76
The Netherlands	1	3	12	21	80
Norway	–	5	1	15	38
Portugal	–	–	–	15	104
Spain	–	3	8	31	113
Sweden	–	3	5	6	52
Switzerland	–	2	12	26	65
UK	1	1	5	26	130
Total of above	4	40	106	338	1,355

Note: Data relates to those operations where date/decade of entry is known, and is based entirely on published and primary information gathered for this report.
Source: Retail Intelligence

in terms of the direction of international expansion within Europe; some core markets such as Belgium and Austria hosted a relatively substantial number of non-domestic operators (19 and 16 respectively), while other markets, particularly those on the periphery such as Finland and Greece (0 and 1 respectively), had little or no overseas interest shown in them. Given the size of the UK market, it is probable that the limited interest shown in it (5 foreign operations compared with 10 in France and 8 in Germany) was partly due to its island status.

As noted above, the 1980s witnessed a boom in international retail activity, with foreign operations being identified for this decade in all of the 16 markets covered in the table. While the peripheral markets, such as Sweden, still only played host to a limited number of non-domestic retailers (6 operations), other centrally located countries such as Belgium, France and Germany were attractive to numerous foreign players (61, 34 and 27). The acceleration of retail internationalization within Europe continued into the 1990s; all markets now have a significant number of foreign operators and most markets have many more times the number of non-domestic operators than in the 1980s.

Growth in European retail internationalization during the 1990s was not just a reaction to mature, saturated and highly regulatory home markets. Developments in IT and other technology made operational issues, such as international logistics, simpler. Similarly the extension of the EU and establishment of the euro could be argued to have facilitated cross-border expansion, and certainly placed emphasis on opportunities for pan-European growth. In terms of consumer market homogenization, the extent to which a 'Euro-consumer' exists (or ever will) continues to be discussed. Perhaps more importantly than total consumer convergence many retailers identify similar consumer groups and demands in a number of European countries. In addition, internationalization levels have increased as less developed European markets such as Italy and Greece have been considered ripe for exploitation, while the emergence of new international markets, such as in Latin America and Asia have highlighted opportunities for overseas growth.

While it is possible to trace an acceleration of international retail activity in European markets, this trend should be placed in context. Certainly, the economic climate of growth in the late 1980s saw many smaller retailers announcing overseas expansion plans, but the economic downturn of the early 1990s and the 1998 recession ensured that many of these did not take place, as companies instead sought to consolidate their position at home. It also meant that some international retailers withdrew from non-domestic interests, examples include C & A's shutdown in UK, Marks & Spencer's closure of its continental European branches and Tesco's disposal of its Catteau chain in France. Thus the increasing rate of international activity has occurred in a period of restructuring and retreat, as well as continued moves into the international arena.

Table 5.1 illustrates the number of retail operations that have entered individual Western European markets prior to and during the 1950s, and in subsequent decades. The figures are not cumulative: they show the number of new entrants that decade, not the total amount of international activity in each market. The data includes all retailers identified as still having operations in 1998. Retailers that made international moves and have subsequently withdrawn are not included here, so the figures quoted will actually underestimate the real level of international activity. Retail Intelligence has identified over 500 retail companies that have crossed borders. We have not discussed wider international moves here in detail, the foregoing section being indicative only.

Cross-border strategy

5. Strategic methods

The word 'strategy' is from the Greek for 'general' and this suggests a plan that will support a major directional move by a corporation. We see in Chapter 6 that a retail company like Marks & Spencer can adopt a market development strategy and move into overseas markets for the reasons discussed earlier in this chapter.

Having decided, after due research and analysis, to carry out a cross-border move the retail company has three broad methods by which such a strategy can be implemented. These are organic growth, acquisition or joint venturing. We examine each option along with its benefits and problems and give examples of success and failure in each category.

(a) **Organic growth**. This involves a company starting from scratch in a new market. Also termed internal development, a firm buys in the basic resources needed to set up its own operations, in this case, abroad. Given the perceived differences in tastes and cultures in each country it may seem strange that organic growth has been a popular method of implementing cross-border strategies. Even stranger, much organic growth has been seen in the retail food sector. One has only to look at the entry of German food retailers Aldi and Lidl into the UK. Differences in food tastes between the UK and elsewhere were underlined by the failure of Campbells Foods when it first entered the UK market with its own US range of soups which proved a failure in the UK. Things are clearly changing when Toys 'Я' Us (USA) and IKEA (Sweden), retailing toys and furniture respectively, can develop organically not only in the UK but across the world.

(b) **Acquisition growth**. Here companies buy up local firms. Whereas organic growth can be time-consuming, growth by takeover can be fast, with the added advantage of buying local knowledge (the problems of 'cultural shock' have to be managed in advance for success).

Examples of successful acquisition include Sainsbury's and its purchase of two New England (USA) supermarket chains, and Kingfisher also buying a French electrical retailer, Darty.

Some retailers have had well-publicized problems with their international ventures. They include Dixons, the electrical stores group with its acquisition of the US Silo chain, Marks & Spencer, which made a costly entry into the Canadian market, and Britain's Signet (formally Ratners), which bought into the US retail jewellery market.

(c) **Joint ventures**. These are also called strategic alliances and include franchising as well as other looser affiliations. The two leading retail franchise groups are McDonald's (USA) and Benetton (Italy). The advantage of this type of joint venture is that the entrepreneurial skills of local business people can be harnessed to the pull of a proven international brand so that a 'symbiotic' relationship can be developed. Joint venturing reduces the risks of investment in overseas markets.

6. International retailers

The following are brief summaries of six companies' strategic methods.

(a) **IKEA**. This Swedish company is the world's largest furniture retailer with over 140 stores in 29 countries. IKEA breaks the rule that product should be tailored to local taste when it opens a store in a new country. The secret is to offer a range of quality furniture at prices customers can afford. This approach is followed rigidly in each country – unless there is a major customer revolt. Sales of beds in the USA were very slow until the company realized that Americans liked bigger beds than Swedes and ordered larger sheets and beds from its suppliers. Kitchen units also had to be enlarged to accommodate plates large enough for pizza, and, in Belgium, IKEA stores are allowed to stock leather-covered sofas. IKEA's secret is said to be its rigorous cost control systems and its decision to take a stake in some of its 2,000 suppliers in 70 counties. IKEA's prices are 20 per cent below the average in furniture retailing.

(b) **Toys 'Я' Us**. Like IKEA this US company is a 'category killer' as the world's largest toy retailer. It operates 400 stores internationally on the same basis as its US chain of cut-price toy warehouses. Unfortunately, the company has been struggling for years against stiff competition in the USA from discount stores and membership warehouses that sell best-selling toys at even lower prices than Toys 'Я' Us. In late 1998 the company announced the closure of 50 of its European stores, where it has also been suffering from poor returns; European wages, property and distribution cost much more than in the USA (a factor that has proved the undoing of many other US retailers attempting to penetrate the European market). Toys 'Я' Us also announced that it was to start remodelling its stores with a new format that would present goods in a completely different way. By 2004 these moves had not been particularly successful.

(c) **Metro**. This German-based group is the world's second largest retailer after Wal-Mart. Unlike IKEA and Toys 'Я' Us, it is a conglomerate retailer with interests in cash-and-carry, hypermarkets, DIY and electronic media shops. Formed in 1996, the original Metro merged with the Kaufhof and Asko retailing groups. It has since bought the Makro European cash-and-carry business and is now represented in most major European countries from the UK to Poland and Greece. It is therefore a pan-European retail business that can take full advantage of changes such as the introduction of the euro in 1999. This so far successful format could be the future of European retailing – further concentration of power within a relatively small group of large conglomerates. Kingfisher of the UK appears to be pursuing a similar policy with its purchase of Darty (electricals) and merger with Castorama (DIY) in France to add to its Comet and B&Q formats in UK.

(d) **Wal-Mart**. Wal-Mart is the largest retailer in the world and its success is partly attributed to its small-town roots. Founded by Sam Walton in a hamlet near Bentonville, Arkansas in 1962, Wal-Mart lacked customers, staff and supplies. Walton thus had to do things differently by offering incentives: profit-sharing for the staff, partnerships for suppliers and for customers friendly service and 'everyday low prices'. As a result costs had to be kept low. When moving cross-border, however, the company failed to adapt its culture in some markets. For example in Germany it did not anticipate the inflexibility of employees and the strength of trade unions. German staff were embarrassed by the Wal-Mart 'cheer' and hid in the toilets. German shoppers care more about price than friendly staff and packing of purchases. Incompetent management was blamed for the blunders.

(e) **Ahold**. At its core, this Dutch group owns Albert Heijn, the supermarket chain that has 28 per cent of the Dutch market, three times more than its nearest competitor. But, unlike Metro or Kingfisher, Ahold has ignored the huge markets on its doorstep like the UK, France and Germany. Instead it has opted for expansion in the USA where the availability of new premises makes organic growth easier. The American market is also geographically fragmented and is also said to lag behind European best practice in food retailing techniques. Over 20 years Ahold has built up a presence on the American east coast through six supermarket chains. It is now one of the top food retailers in a rapidly con-solidating market. In 1997 it bought the 18 per cent of Giant supermarkets owned by Sainsbury's, whose experience in the USA has been poor. The com-pany will continue to operate behind multiple storefronts because of US regional loyalties but is developing central buying and distribution by collecting data on purchasing from its scanning tills. Ahold even believes it could be in line to build a national supermarket chain in the USA but financial problems emerged in 2003, casting a shadow over this aim. Meanwhile, the company is developing interests in the Iberian Peninsula, Eastern Europe, Latin America and Asia.

(f) **Muji**. This Japanese retailer has bucked the recent trends in Japan by declar-ing record profits. The name Muji means 'no brand' in Japanese and with its 248 stores it is tackling the Japanese recession with excellent marketing and efficient distribution. It is a general retailer selling everything from parkas and bicycles to ramen noodles. It offers a no-frills approach based on Chinese suppliers who manufacture 80 per cent of its apparel, its largest product category, and 50 per cent of its household goods. Currently its affordable prices spell enormous success for the company.

The quick snapshot of six international retailers above is not meant to be even vaguely comprehensive. But it does point up some common attributes – and failings. Size is crucial for scale economies (*see* Chapter 3), which reflect on relative costs and prices. Links with suppliers are also crucial, as is distribution. Product styles and store formats need to be attractive. Retailers must be very aware of the various business cycles and how they will affect performance.

7. Impact of international retailers

Apart from the advantages that retailers gain from cross-border moves as pre-viously discussed, retailers also bring changes to the markets they enter:

(a) They may alter the competitiveness of the national markets. Wal-Mart is clearly seen as a significant force in UK food and non-food retailing.

(b) They bring innovation. Zara, a Spanish-based clothing retailer, has revolu-tionized merchandising practice by quickly scrapping ranges that do not sell, and replacing them.

(c) They may influence management practices. In Chapter 21 some doubt is expressed about the historical competence of UK retail management. Certainly in other industry sectors the introduction of quality circles, empowerment and other techniques have helped to upgrade industry practices.

On the question of globalization some writers suggest that this has not properly occurred because important markets like the UK lack some of the key world players in the sector.

8. Cross-border strategy guidelines

Frank Woolworth opened his first store outside the USA in 1909. The Brenninkmeyers, who founded the C & A empire in The Netherlands, opened their first foreign outlet in Germany in 1911 and in the UK in the 1920s. A lull then occurred which was only broken decisively during the 1980s. The world has now become borderless for many more retail companies.

Despite all the difficulties, more and more retailers will enter foreign markets over the next decade. Some guidelines on how to do it have begun to emerge.

(a) **Study the market**. Toys 'Я' Us says that it looks at new markets for several years before taking the plunge. It has considered Mexico for five years, and 'three times we decided not to go in', says Larry Bouts, the firm's international director.

(b) **Decide on your pace**. After observing Australia for four years, Toys 'Я' Us opened 17 stores in its first 18 months. A slow build-up 'gives less leverage with suppliers and real-estate developers, and means less customer awareness', Bouts says. But others, including Wal-Mart and Marks & Spencer, start with small pilot investments in new markets, allowing fine-tuning before any full-scale commitment.

(c) **Think about local partners**. Many international retailers use joint ventures to help them deal with local politics, regulations and suppliers. Picking the right partner can be crucial: Wal-Mart's success in Mexico owes much to its alliance with Cifra, the country's top retailer. Conversely, Carrefour blames the failure of its hypermarkets in the UK on the shortcomings of its local partner, an investment company.

(d) **Adapt to local conditions**. This may mean local sourcing, or adjusting ranges to fit local tastes and constraints. For example in Marks & Spencer's shops in Hong Kong food accounts for only 10 per cent of sales compared with 40 per cent in the UK, because the company found it could not get local supplies of acceptable quality.

(e) **Stick to core skills**. Newcomers must ensure that their logistics and computer systems can be made to work in new markets, and that they can maintain their reputation for quality, low prices or service. This means that exporting single-format businesses has proved easier than, for example, department stores.

(f) **Develop local management**. This is the key to understanding new markets, and the biggest constraint on international expansion. Transferring a retailer's corporate culture across borders is perhaps the trickiest part of internationalization.

Ignore some or all of these rules if they clash with your corporate culture or business methods. IKEA jumps into new markets without local partners and with only cursory research. The firm says it needs to be in a market to understand it, and needs to have achieved a high volume of sales before it can profitably adapt its products to local tastes.

Despite the complexities, venturing abroad will be a main source of growth for both European and American retailers in the next few years. But even as they stride out, American retailers in particular are looking anxiously over their shoulders at a new threat in their own backyard. What if new technology allows their customers to dispense with stores altogether? What if consumers find they can do their shopping from home? (The potential threats from e-commerce are discussed in Chapter 26.)

Progress test 5

1. The phrase 'push and pull' is commonly used in marketing. Explain, with examples, what it means in the context of cross-border retailing.

2. Describe the various entry methods used by retailers when moving into overseas countries. Discuss their relative advantages and disadvantages.

3. Outline the broad reasons for retail companies choosing one country or countries rather than others.

4. Discuss the risks inherent in cross-border retailing and offer some prescriptions for success.

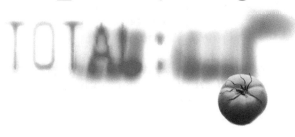

6 Retail planning and strategy

Introduction

Until fairly recently many retail companies have grown in a largely unplanned way, but before a company can begin to suggest to itself the sort of policies it should be pursuing to reach its corporate goals, it must decide what sort of company it is today and where it wants to get to within a finite time-scale. This chapter considers the planning process, and the general and specific retail strategies that retailers can pursue.

1. Planning

Many retail companies now use corporate planning techniques or variants thereof. Corporate planning has been described as the total planning of a company's entire resources for the achievement of both long- and short-term objectives. Although the term 'corporate planning' may sound rather grand, the techniques of corporate planning are just as applicable to the corner shop as they are to the multiple.

2. The process

The retail planning process can be divided into three discrete yet interlinked steps. The first step is a statement of the retail mission which answers the fundamental question, 'What business am I in?' From this, objectives are established to answer the question, 'Where do I want to go?'

The statement of objectives will naturally lead to a series of strategies for achieving those objectives – thus answering the third question, 'How do I get there?' These strategies will relate firstly to target markets (for example to serve the total market or only a specialized part of it). Once it has been decided who the target customer is, retail mix strategies are developed to meet the needs of those customers in terms of merchandise, price, location, promotion, level of service, etc.

What business am I in?

The answer to this question is often far less obvious than would at first appear. For example, what business is a florist in – the flower business or the gift business? The definition chosen will materially affect how that retailer interprets such aspects as customer requirements and competitors.

3. The retail mission

The retail mission is a statement of the overall purpose of the organization and will evolve from a close study of the environment in which the retailer sees itself operating. For example Burton's retail mission is 'To serve the clothing needs of UK males aged 25–34 who are looking for great value clothing with a fashionable edge'.

4. Situation analysis

The situation analysis (sometimes also known as the marketing or retail audit) will involve investigation of the defined market in terms of market size and market trends as well as looking closely at the competition – its strengths and weaknesses and market shares. The potential customers should be studied to determine their motivations, how, why, what and where they buy, and if there are needs that are not being totally satisfied. The larger forces in society should also be studied to detect social and economic trends and the effects of technology and government. Finally, in the situation analysis the retail organization must look at itself, determine its strengths and weaknesses and build on those strengths to exploit gaps unfilled due to the weakness of competition or simply not identified as yet (*see* Figure 6.1).

5. SWOT

A SWOT analysis should then be produced defining S (strengths), W (weaknesses), O (opportunities), and T (threats) for both the retailer's own organization and also that of the competition in relation to those factors already identified through the situation analysis.

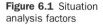

Figure 6.1 Situation analysis factors

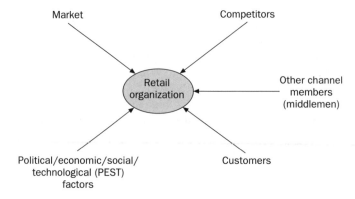

For example, factors to be considered in determining strengths and weaknesses will include location, merchandise, personnel, store layout, management capability, financial aspects and market share position.

6. Level of generalization

The question to be addressed now is, 'At what level of generalization should this situation analysis be carried out?', and the apparently rather unhelpful answer is at a level that is meaningful to the individual retail organization. Thus the multiple retail organization may well be concerned at a national or even international level, whereas the corner shop may only be interested in an area of a few hundred households. It is helpful, however, that the analysis, even for the smallest operator, starts off with an investigation of the national picture through which identifiable trends can be detailed, which can then be revisited within the contexts of the local catchment area.

For example, it is unlikely that the size of the market in cash and unit terms for pizzas in the Nottingham area is immediately accessible. However, national data is available which can then be extrapolated to the local level on a consumption per capita basis.

Where do I want to go?

7. Objectives

After completing the situation analysis, objectives (goals or targets) need to be set so it is clear what job has to be done and whether the goals have been reached at a specified point in time; and to ensure the organization is moving in a direction consistent with the corporate mission.

The variety of objectives the retailer seeks to achieve varies widely but generally falls within four broad areas: corporate, financial, marketing and organizational.

(a) **Corporate objectives**. These are an extention of the personal beliefs of the most senior executives. Thus, for example, corporate objectives are often stated in terms of growth, profitability and prestige as: 'To increase our net sales area by one million square feet and investment in new stores of over £1 billion over the next five years'.

(b) **Marketing objectives**. These should be defined in terms of sales, market share, communications, customer service, etc.

(c) **Financial objectives**. These would include targets for profit and return on investment.

(d) **Organizational objectives**. These might specify employee turnover and quality of labour force.

How do I get there?

8. Strategy

Having identified a direction through the objectives, it is now time to consider alternative ways (strategies) of achieving those objectives.

Once again, the appropriate level of generalization is necessary. It is therefore useful to develop strategy at the general level and the specific level.

General retail strategies

These will focus upon growth, selectivity and productivity.

9. Growth strategies

No business can stand still, because it needs to adapt to change. Growth can be achieved by pursuing a number of different routes. These may be described in terms of the merchandise offered and customers chosen as the target market (*see* Figure 6.2).

(a) **Penetration**. This relies on the retailer aggressively seeking to increase its market share. This strategy has been pursued very successfully by Tesco in the grocery retailing field where increase in market share has been won at the expense of direct competitors such as the small grocer and the Co-ops.

(b) **Merchandise development**. There is a limit to the growth that can be achieved by penetration strategies and most retailers pursuing growth will look to add new merchandise to appeal to their customers and thus generate extra sales. This merchandise development strategy has been successfully pursued by Marks & Spencer, moving into food retailing, then into furniture and subsequently financial services. Next has also been successful in offering its prime target customer – the 25–40-year-old fashion-conscious female – a greater range of merchandise, which now also includes accessories and gifts.

(c) **Market development**. This strategy can be pursued in two ways:

(*i*) *New areas*. New customers can be sought in geographic areas not presently served, for example Asda's move south, or Tesco's move into overseas markets.

Figure 6.2 Growth strategies

		CUSTOMERS	
		Existing	*New*
MERCHANDISE	*Existing*	Penetration	Market development
	New	Merchandise development	Diversification

(*ii*) *Existing areas*. Alternatively, market development may involve attracting new customers in the same geographical area. This approach has been used by a number of retailers with varying degrees of success, for example Currys' attempt to appeal to the discount-orientated customer with its out-of-town electrical discount stores. The difficulty is that if the merchandise remains the same but a new group of customers is being sought, some other element of the retail mix has to change to appeal to them. As in the example above, price can be the variable that is changed. Location may also be changed and the image of the store could be modified, as for example with MFI's attempts to move up-market.

(d) **Diversification**. New merchandise for new target customer groups is the most expensive of the growth strategies. It is possibly the riskiest of the growth strategies but can bring the highest rewards. Dixons' purchase of PC World and The Link was an example of a diversification strategy.

10. Integration

An alternative strategy for retailers is to seek to minimize conflict in the channel of distribution by ownership of channel members, acquisition or merger. Thus, Thorntons, for example, manufactures quality chocolate and confectionery products and also sells them through its own retail outlets. MFI, the flatpack furniture retailers, acquired the Hygena furniture manufacturing business in order to cut out the intermediary's profits and derive the benefits of assured continuity of supply and economies of scale.

11. Selectivity strategies

Next is a good example of a retail organization that had lost its direction – trying to meet the needs of too many markets. A new approach was devised, which laid down a strategy for reducing the range of merchandise in order to appeal to a more well-defined target group of customers. This strategy resulted not only in a reduction of merchandise lines, but in some cases also, in order to be consistent with this policy, a reduced geographical scope – pulling out of certain geographical areas.

12. Productivity strategies

Productivity strategies concentrate on producing better results with the same mixture of resources or the same (or better) results with fewer resources. Thus, as in many areas of business, the 80/20 rule applies – 80 per cent of profit is generated from 20 per cent of the merchandise offered, and if those high turnover lines are identified then increasing inventory turnover can be achieved. Productivity strategies also involve closely monitoring costs and identifying ways of reducing costs, for example in staff, energy usage, etc.

While much of the emphasis in productivity strategies is directed towards improving operating efficiency, managerial efficiency is also an important element. Training of managers is an expensive business and thus it is essential that an organization reduces its managerial turnover and drop-out rate to maximize its managerial training resources.

Specific retail strategies

The retailing concept proposes that the most critical factor in determining the success of a store is the identification and satisfaction of customer needs. Thus specific retail strategies should address this objective requiring the retailer, first, to identify the target customers and then to satisfy their needs through an appropriate retail mix strategy – considering location, merchandise, price, communication, store atmosphere and layout, and customer service.

13. Segmentation strategy

Segmentation is concerned with identifying subsets within a market – groups that have something in common that will differentiate their needs and wants from other groups. Following the identification of these subsets, three strategic alternatives are available.

(a) **An undifferentiated strategy**. Here group differences are ignored and a standardized retail mix is developed to suffice for the whole market.

(b) **The differentiated approach**. This entails developing different retail mixes for different segments.

(c) **The concentrated strategy**. This focuses on one segment as the target market and develops a distinct retail mix to satisfy that discrete segment.

Segmentation strategy is examined more fully in Chapter 10.

14. Location strategy

Where the retail organization chooses to locate can make the difference between success and failure. Additionally a location that is right for one type of retailer (e.g. a discount furniture warehouse) could be totally wrong for another (e.g. an exclusive high-class fashion retailer). Location strategy is examined more fully in Chapter 11.

15. Merchandise strategy

Arguably the most important strategic choice is what product to offer. However, a product is much more than a tangible good. The consumer's perception of a product is anything that satisfies a particular need or want and as such the retailer must consider much more than a physical offering or technical specification. (More depth on merchandise strategy will be found in Chapter 12.)

16. Pricing strategy

Price is often considered a surrogate indicator of quality and consumers often make a judgement on products or indeed on the store as a result of their response to the price of merchandise. Thus for example a retailer could adopt a strategy of offering goods at relatively high prices in order to be consistent with a general strategy of appealing to consumers who are wanting exclusivity. Pricing strategies are considered in more detail in Chapter 15.

17. Communication strategy

The retailer has to communicate with customers, initially to make them aware of its offerings and then to stimulate interest and desire. The techniques available to the retailer include advertising, personal selling, sales promotions and public relations. Through the use of these communication tools the retailer establishes a position in the consumer's mind that hopefully will move the consumer to choose that store in preference to competitors. (*See* Chapters 16–18.)

18. Store image and customer service strategy

In addition to the four communication tools listed above, it can be seen that everything the retailer does communicates something to the consumer. Thus the exterior of the store, window displays, the interior design and layout all combine to communicate a store's personality and to add to the image that the consumer has of that store. This image is further modified by the number and quality of services that are available to the customer and the basis on which they are offered.

Chapter 19 explains store image further and Chapter 20 deals with customer services.

It is important that the strategies adopted are consistent with the defined objectives, and as such each strategy is integrated within the framework of the others. Thus for example a discount pricing strategy would not be consistent with an objective of establishing an up-market image for the store. Similarly, the location of the store should be chosen to reflect the needs of the defined customer group, and although there are always exceptions to every rule the consumer has come to expect lower prices out of town.

19. Control and continuity

Success cannot be achieved without a reliable feedback mechanism. This will allow modifications to the plan on a rolling basis to fit in with changes in the external environment. It will also show how actual progress matches the plan so that extra throttle or a touch on the brakes can be administered. The plan should be thoroughly reviewed:

(a) Annually to take account of the company's progress.

(b) Whenever there is a distinct change in the company's market, e.g. the merger of two large competitors.

(c) Every five years to modify basic objectives and to make out a new checklist of strengths and weaknesses.

Progress test 6

1. What are the three interlinked steps in the retail planning process?

2. What is a SWOT analysis?

3. Describe the three general retail strategies of growth, selectivity and productivity.

4. What is the function of the feedback mechanism in retail planning?

5. What is meant by the retail mix? Describe the retail mix of a retailer of your own choice and analyse whether it is appropriate or not.

7 Retailing research

Introduction

Management is essentially concerned with planning, decision-making and control. To manage an enterprise successfully, information is required. This chapter considers the role of retailing research in the provision of information, the sources and collection of information and the various types of retailing research.

1. Information

As has been seen, the planning process has been described as an attempt to answer three fundamental questions:

(a) What business am I in?

(b) Where do I want to go?

(c) How do I get there?

To answer questions, information is required, and the way this information is provided is through the use of research.

2. Retailing research defined

To focus our attention on the retail situation the term 'retailing research' will be used to mean marketing research within the retailing context. Retailing research involves the systematic design, collection, analysis and reporting of data and findings relevant to a specific retailing situation.

3. Importance of information

Information and information management is important to the retailer because of the increasing pace of environmental change to which the retailer must adapt. Changes in the age profile of the population, more single-parent households and increasing disposable income are among a myriad of changes that all have implications for retailers. Additionally, new technology in retailing, new products and new types of store all go to produce an extremely complex environment that the retailer must monitor and react to.

4. The retail information system

The retailer should set up a system to organize and retrieve information. This should set out well-defined procedures and practices by which people and equipment generate information in a form that, and at a time when, retail decision makers require it.

The retailing research process

Effective retailing research involves six steps:

(a) Define the problem.

(b) Define the research objectives.

(c) Determine the sources of information.

(d) Collect the information.

(e) Analyse the information.

(f) Present the findings.

5. Define the problem

For example, a large furniture retailer wishes to find out whether providing a play area for children within the store will be worthwhile. A definition of this problem could be, 'Will offering a play area create enough incremental business to justify the initial cost and loss of selling space?'

6. Research objectives

The research objectives could then be to determine:

(a) The type of customer who would make use of the service.

(b) How valuable this type of customer sees the service.

(c) Whether this customer would spend more time in-store if the children could be left.

(d) Whether spending more time in-store would lead to increased expenditure.

Sources of information

The next stage of retailing research is to develop a procedure for gathering the required information in the most efficient manner.

7. Four sources

There are four sources of information acquisition:

(a) Internal sources – within the company.

(b) External sources – outside the company.

(c) Secondary data – gathered originally for another purpose.

(d) Primary data – gathered to solve the specific problems at hand.

8. Order

Remembering that the information must be obtained in the most cost-effective manner, the order in which attempts are made to access information from the four sources is important. This would therefore normally be:

(a) First, internal secondary sources.

(b) Second, internal primary sources.

(c) Third, external secondary sources.

(d) Fourth, external primary sources.

The task is of course completed when we have the information required, which would ideally be as early in the above sequence as possible in order to minimize cost.

9. Internal secondary sources

Retailers gather large quantities of data internally, which may be invaluable for research purposes.

EPOS systems can provide information on sales of products by units and value and much more besides. Customer order forms contain information about the location of customers. Credit records too may have location details and frequency of purchase. Accounting records will be useful for sales history and forecasting trends, while previous research (primary) may now be used as internal secondary data for the purposes of the new search.

The use of store cards or 'loyalty' cards such as the Tesco Clubcard or Boots Advantage card can provide detailed information on items sold, price, when sold, inventory and also promotion evaluation; in fact the challenge now is not just to provide information but to present it in the most useful manner.

10. Internal primary sources

Employees of the retail organization can also be a useful source of information. Sales assistants, checkout operators and delivery people all come into contact with customers and receive comments about the store, price, service, etc.

11. External secondary sources

There is a tremendous range of external secondary data available. This can be divided into three main types:

(a) Government statistics, for example Monthly Retail Sales, Annual Business Inquiry, Census of Population, Consumer Trends, Family Expenditure Surveys, General Household Surveys, Economic Trends, Regional Trends and Social Trends.

(b) Periodicals and books, for example, *Retail Directory, Retail Intelligence, Market Research Great Britain, Kompass, International Journal of Retail & Distribution Management*. Also specialist publications such as *The Grocer, Electrical Retailing*, etc.

(c) Reports from specialist retail research organizations such as Experian, Verdict Research, Mintel, AC Nielsen and Taylor Nelson Sofres.

12. External primary sources

Suppliers and competitors may be sources of information but consumers are the most common source of external primary data.

13. Advantages and disadvantages

The advantages of secondary data are essentially low cost and speed of access. The disadvantages can be numerous, including data being out of date, different units of measurement, different definitions, etc.

Primary data offers the retailer the advantage of timeliness but the disadvantage is the cost and the time involved in collecting the data.

Collecting the information

Internal data is obviously available in-house and external secondary data should be relatively easy to access through public libraries or, in the case of commercial data, through the company concerned. However, gathering external primary data will require more time and effort. External primary data can be gathered in three main ways: observation, experiments and surveys.

14. Observation

The observation technique simply involves the observation and recording of behaviour. The advantage of this method is that respondent co-operation is not required and therefore the results obtained are more likely to be a true reflection of the facts than if a questioning technique is used. Observation of the consumer can be carried out either by an individual or through the use of devices such as video cameras.

Personal observation is often employed in-store to determine customer flow patterns and general shopping behaviour. Customer traffic counts may also be done this way. Mechanical observation can also be used for traffic counts, as well as more sophisticated observation such as customer/sales assistant interaction.

15. Experiments

Experimental research uses the scientific methodology of selecting a matched group of subjects, subjecting them to different treatments, controlling extraneous variables and then measuring the observed differences. An example of experimental research would be to reduce the price of a merchandise item and to monitor the effect on sales. All other factors such as promotion, shelf location, etc., should be kept constant and sales in one week could be compared with sales in the experimental week at a reduced price. The difficulty with this type of research is ensuring that the only factor that changed is the price or the variable that is to be changed. Similar experiments can be carried out with different promotions, shelf locations, displays, etc.

16. Surveys

The survey method is perhaps the most common way of generating external primary data. It essentially uses some type of questionnaire as the mechanism for gathering information, and this questionnaire can be administered personally, over the telephone, via the mail or internet.

(a) **The personal interview or face-to-face method**. This allows a lot of detailed data to be gathered because people quite often like to be asked their opinion and to offer it to another person who is interested. High response rates are therefore achieved by this method but there is a danger of the results being inaccurate due to interviewer bias – that is the interviewer may in some way (perhaps unconsciously) influence the answers given.

(b) **The telephone survey**. This offers a quick and relatively inexpensive method of administering a questionnaire. It allows person-to-person contact, which facilitates probing and explanation, but respondents soon tire of a telephone administered questionnaire and therefore it is only suitable for short, simple information gathering. There is also the problem that information can only be gathered from respondents who have a phone.

(c) **The postal survey**. A questionnaire is mailed to respondents, thus offering the retailer the opportunity of reaching many potential respondents over a wide geographical area. The greatest difficulty with mailed questionnaires is the low response rates, which are often well below 25 per cent. This leads on to the problem of non-response bias, that is bias against those not answering the questionnaire. It is highly probable that those answering a mailed questionnaire do so because they are interested in the subject, or are perhaps more educated or articulate. Thus they may not be wholly representative of the total number of people who received the questionnaire. None the less, mailed questionnaires are popular with retailers because they are seen to be economical and versatile.

The survey technique is most useful for obtaining information about customers' knowledge, beliefs, attitudes, preferences and so on, but because the methodology deals with these qualitative or subjective areas, it is vitally important that the questionnaire is designed properly.

(d) **Online surveys**. An increasingly popular way to undertake surveys is via the internet as it offers a fast and cost-effective method for researchers to reach their target audiences. Online research is still in its infancy – internet surveys represent less than 5 per cent of the value of research conducted in the UK. However, it is a technique that is steadily growing and has already proved highly effective in certain instances, for example when conducting research into retailers' websites.

There are a number of advantages to conducting retailing research online, including:

(*i*) large numbers of respondents can be surveyed at one time

(*ii*) international boundaries no longer need to be an obstacle to research – worldwide surveys can be conducted at the click of a button

(*iii*) it can be an inexpensive way to conduct large surveys

(*iv*) it allows for a very rapid turnaround – research can be undertaken and results received within a few days.

For a business that needs to gain a general view from a large cross-section of the population, and in as short a time as possible, there is no doubt that online research offers certain benefits.

However, despite its convenience, online research has limitations, which need to be considered from the outset. These include:

(*i*) DIY surveys (where the clients put the questions directly to the respondent without a professional researcher as an intermediary) may compromise objectivity of questioning and impartial interpretation

(*ii*) research conducted via internet surveys can only target internet users and, more specifically, it can only target internet users who are prepared to answer online questionnaires – currently still a small percentage of the population; there is therefore a danger that a truly representative sample will not be drawn

(*iii*) while suitable for quantitative surveys, electronic surveys are not so suitable for gathering qualitative information, because online focus groups are difficult to run and it is difficult to obtain in-depth information.

Potentially, the most valuable use of online research is in conjunction with more traditional forms of market research, whether it be quantitative or qualitative. Completing a questionnaire on the internet could be offered as an alternative to a telephone or postal questionnaire. Alternatively, a business could conduct a broad-brush electronic survey, and follow up the outcome with more targeted, personal interviews.

Questionnaire design

17. Structured or unstructured

The design of the questionnaire must be such as to provide the appropriate information in a form most suitable for interpretation. Thus the major design issue is to choose between a structured or an unstructured questionnaire.

The highly structured questionnaire consists of a series of questions and a predetermined set of answers set by the researcher (closed questions). The other extreme is the highly unstructured questionnaire where the general area for scrutiny is predetermined but the questions are allowed to develop during the information-gathering process and the respondents are allowed to answer in their own words (open-ended questions).

Each type is appropriate to a particular situation: structured when the expected answers are known; unstructured when the researcher cannot predetermine answers or wants to research the widest possible interpretation of issues.

18. Wording and sequence

In preparing the questionnaire the researcher must also carefully choose the questions asked and the wording and sequence in which questions are asked.

Thus each question must provide data that contributes to the research objectives. The wording of questions should be simple, direct and unbiased. The questionnaire should start with a question that will create interest, while difficult, personal or classificatory questions should be reserved for the end.

Sampling

The retailer must select respondents to answer the questionnaire. It will usually choose a sampling procedure, since administering the questionnaire to the total population (a census) would be far too expensive and time-consuming.

19. Random sampling

The technique of random (or probability) sampling gives each member of the population a chance of being selected, but in practice is difficult to conduct.

20. Non-probability samples

As a matter of course many retailers resort to talking to customers at a store or shopping centre. This is a form of non-probability sampling known as a convenience sample (i.e. convenient to the retailer). Other forms of non-probability sample that aim to be somewhat more scientific in approach are the judgement sample and the quota sample.

(a) **The judgement sample**. This is based on the judgement (expertise) of the retailer. For example, it may describe a typical customer as a 25–45-year-old female. Thus respondents who answer this description may be selected.

(b) **The quota sample**. The sample is selected in proportion to characteristics in the population considered to be important discriminants (e.g. by income, age and sex).

Analysing the information and presenting the findings

21. Analysis

The next step is to analyse the data and extract pertinent information. Data is tabulated and averages and measures of dispersion calculated.

22. Presentation

Since the purpose of acquiring information is to enable the retail decision maker to choose the best alternative solution to a retailing problem, it is incumbent upon the researcher to present the research findings in a form suitable for that purpose. Thus the presentation of findings should concentrate on the major issues that are relevant to the retailing decisions facing management. Too many numbers, charts and sophisticated statistical techniques will only lose sight of the issues and lessen the import of good research.

Types of retailing research

Many research techniques have now been developed to meet the specific needs of retailers, for example store audits, pricing checks, exit surveys, diaries, mystery shopping, accompanied shopping, discussion groups and observation.

23. Store audits

Conducted in the store, store audits involve checking stock on the shelves – usually with the retailer's permission, but sometimes 'incognito'. Store audits provide information on:

(a) Stock movement.

(b) Market share.

(c) Shelf facings.

(d) Prices.

(e) Promotions.

24. Pricing checks

In addition to store audits, prices can also be checked with consumers. The process involves structured interviews and provides information on:

(a) What consumers are prepared to pay.

(b) Opinions of prices charged.

(c) Thresholds at which consumers would switch to an alternative product or brand.

(d) Perceptions of value for money.

25. Exit surveys

These involve stopping shoppers as they leave a store and conducting a short structured interview. Exit surveys provide information on:

(a) Profiles of shoppers.

(b) Where they live.

(c) Where else they shop.

(d) What they intended to buy and what they actually bought on this trip.

(e) Their opinions of the store.

26. Diaries

These are usually self-completion and involve consumers recording their shopping activities for a week or a month. They provide information on:

(a) Where they have shopped.

(b) When they shopped.

(c) What they bought.

(d) How much they spent.

(e) How quickly the product was used.

27. Mystery shopping

This technique involves mystery shoppers visiting outlets pretending to be genuine consumers. Visits involve observation, interaction with staff and going through the purchase process. Immediately after the visit, a questionnaire is completed as a record of the trip. It provides information on:

(a) Staff and the service they offer.

(b) General appearance of the store.

(c) Quality of displays.

(d) Customer care.

28. Accompanied shopping

Shoppers are accompanied by an interviewer while on a shopping trip. The technique involves the interviewer observing, talking to the consumer and possibly taping the discussion. After the shopping trip is completed a written report is prepared, which provides information on:

(a) Shopping behaviour.

(b) Store layout.

(c) Product displays.

(d) In-store promotions.

(e) Staff and service.

(f) Factors influencing consumer choice.

29. Discussion groups

These may be conducted in-store or away from the store, and involve a skilled moderator talking with consumers for anything between one and three hours. The group size can range from three to nine respondents and the discussion provides an opportunity to go into more depth when gathering information. Discussion groups are more flexible than using a questionnaire format and allow consumers to express their views in their own words. The discussions are taped, transcribed and a content analysis is carried out; then the findings are reported, often supported by verbatim quotations from the consumers in the discussion groups.

30. Observation

Consumer behaviour is 'observed' usually without their knowledge and often with the use of film or video equipment. Records are made of:

(a) The direction in which shoppers moved.

(b) Products browsed.

(c) Products purchased.

(d) The order in which products are browsed/purchased.

(e) Time spent at displays.

The observation method can be combined with other research techniques to provide more information about the shopper.

31. Website research

The philosophy of website design is simple. Web pages should load quickly, navigate easily and deliver efficiently. It is important to measure the performance of a website or internet strategy. In most cases this research is aimed at measuring return on investment (ROI).

(a) **Competitor research.** The websites of all major competitors should be checked for site structure and keyword usage. Knowing the weaknesses and strengths of these companies' websites could save a lot of time when it comes to deciding what emphasis should be applied to various search terms. No search engine or directory ranks a web page in exactly the same way. They each have their own specific criteria for this. Research in this area is designed to help keyword selection in order to achieve a high ranking position with search engines, and to deliver high-volume traffic. This research includes:

    (*i*)   analysis of keywords and key phrases for site and product relevance

    (*ii*) analysis of how many competing web pages use the same phrases or words (*iii*) analysis of how well competing sites are ranked for important keywords

(*iv*) selection of those keywords that can improve web page optimization

(*v*) choice of additional search terms

(*vi*) selection of a definitive list of most effective search terms to be used in the website.

(b) **Criteria for successful websites**. Most websites measure their effectiveness by looking at the web visitor statistics and trying to calculate a cost per visitor and a return per visitor. The situation, however, is a lot more complicated than this. As an example, a recent study showed that for every purchase made on a popular retail website, another three visitors then visited the bricks-and-mortar store to make the final purchase. This meant the actual ROI of the website was four times that given by the website statistics.

Web metrics is about measuring the effectiveness of a site. But much more important than that, it is about feeding back these measurements and making the website more successful. Research on the performance of a website should address the following issues:

(*i*) *Effectiveness*. Can a given task be performed without any significant difficulty? Any website that makes such tasks difficult to achieve for some or all users is, in a sense, 'failing'.

(*ii*) *Efficiency*. Are tasks completed quickly and easily? A website that makes the most routine tasks take multiple actions to complete is inefficient and will waste users' time.

(*iii*) *Satisfaction*. Is the website enjoyable to use? Does the user intuitively know where to go and what to do? Users who become frustrated with a website, or who blame themselves for failure, are likely to avoid using that website in the future.

(c) **Measuring website visitor behaviour**. Specialized software is available to help the research of the behaviour of visitors to a website. The questions to be answered are: where they come from, what they do and where they go. These include such issues as:

(*i*) how many and which visitors see each page

(*ii*) how long they stay on average

(*iii*) how many entered on a particular page

(*iv*) how many leave from this page

(*v*) which page visitors to this page came from, and which pages they see next.

Websites receive visitors from search engines, pay-per-click programmes and other partnerships. Most researchers count the number of visitors who enter the site, and may even track how many visitors are brought by using each different keywords with the search engines. But what happens after a visitor arrives at the site? With a first-time visitor, there is a critical short time of seconds while the visitor decides whether your site is relevant, whether to stay at your site or go on to another. What links do users choose? Just how do they navigate through the site? What paths do they follow? Which users are more or less likely to buy?

Progress test 7

1. What is retailing research?

2. Describe the retailing research process.

3. What are the four general sources of information acquisition?

4. Describe the three ways of gathering external primary data.

5. Under what circumstances would you consider using an unstructured questionnaire?

6. What is random sampling? How useful is it in retailing research?

7. What are the main sources of information available to a small business wishing to start a first specialized lighting shop? What information is it essential to have before investing any money and how would this information be accessed?

8. What particular problems are faced when doing marketing research within the retail sector? What techniques are available to overcome them?

9. As deputy manager of a large department store you have been asked to assist in the training of Eddie, an 18-year-old trainee. As part of his training programme, briefly explain the value of marketing research to the retailer.

10. Eddie and Rita Robertson have decided to open a new menswear shop in Chester. They believe there is potential for a retail outlet serving the busy businessman who wants a little more than a 'Marks and Sparks pinstripe suit' but is not sufficiently fashion orientated ('poserish' as Eddie describes it) to find 'Next for Men' attractive. They wish to be businesslike in their approach and they have decided to check out their hunch by carrying out marketing research.

    Identify the sources of information that are available to them and how they might go about gathering information.

11. A leading chain of confectioners/tobacconists/newsagents (CTNs) with over 750 shops located primarily in tertiary trading locations is coming under heavy pressure from supermarkets, petrol forecourt shops and others taking increasing shares in its main merchandise areas. A consultant to the company has suggested abandoning the strategy of remaining a CTN and has suggested the company should focus on its prime benefit to the customer – convenience. Make recommendations for suitable forms of retailing research to evaluate the viability of this suggestion.

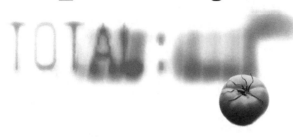

8 The retailing environments

Introduction

> The retailer is part of the larger environment. This chapter considers the two levels
> of the retailing environment – the micro-environment and the macro-environment.

1. Environmental change

The retailer must monitor changes and adapt in such a manner as to thrive in the
new environment. Additionally, forecasting changes in the environment will then
allow the retailer to plan the adaptation process. The process of monitoring and
gathering information on the retail environments can be seen as part of the
retailing research function and many of the sources of information on environmental change are those described in the previous chapter.

The retailing environment can be thought of as having two levels – the micro-
environment and the macro-environment (*see* Figure 8.1).

2. The retailing micro-environment

This consists of those elements within the environment that immediately impinge
upon the retailer on a day-to-day basis and that require immediate responses.
Customers, competition and other distribution channel members can be defined
as the members of the micro-environment.

3. The retailing macro-environment

This is made up of those elements within the environment that are not controllable by the retail organization and that consist of the larger societal forces such
as demographic, economic, cultural and social, political, legal, technological and
natural factors.

Figure 8.1 Retailing environments

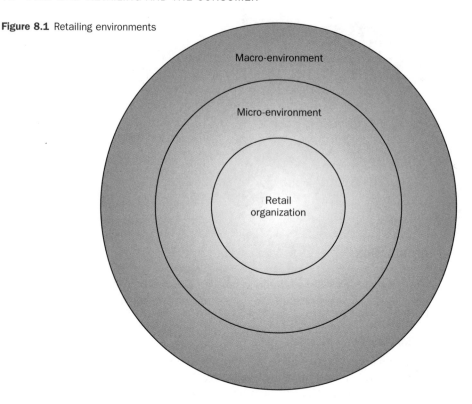

The retailing macro-environment

4. Demographic factors

The retailer must scrutinize demographic data to determine what is happening to its customers and the implications for the business. At present in the UK there is a slowly rising population but in terms of age distribution there is a very marked increase in the older age groups (people are living longer). Women are delaying having their first child and are having fewer children. There is an increasing number of households, but this increase is primarily of the one person or one parent type.

There is an increasing number of working women (up from 8.4 million in 1971 to 12.2 million in 2003) and their profile is changing. They are now likely to be married and have children, often working for personal satisfaction rather than simply for the money. Therefore, with less time for shopping and the preparation of meals, there has been an increase in one-stop shopping and the purchase of convenience foods.

There has also been a geographical shift away from inner cities to the suburbs and also to some extent from the North to the South.

5. Economic factors

The standard of living of the population is increasing and can be measured by a number of criteria. Real personal disposable income per head is increasing and is reflected in the increasing penetration of consumer durables in UK homes. Most householders now have a television and refrigerator, but sales of dishwashing machines are now increasing as other needs are satisfied. The percentage of owner-occupied dwellings has also increased significantly over the past 20 years.

Other economic factors that the retailer must monitor are the rate of inflation and the cost of credit.

6. Cultural and social factors

Individuals are becoming more self-centred and show a greater need for self-expression. This is reflected in the growth of 'designer' labels and specialist clothing shops. People are paying more attention to their quality of life, and healthy living and concern for the environment are current issues. There is a growing 'consumer movement' which requires business to operate in the best interests of the consumer. Lifestyles are changing, which can, in part, be explained by the increasing number of people travelling abroad and introducing foreign ways of life, food and goods into their own lifestyles. There is a greater amount of design and in some markets a greater emphasis on quality rather than price. These changes in society will be reflected in the wants and needs of customers and the retailer must be aware of these changes in order to fulfil the primary role (to anticipate and satisfy these wants and needs).

7. Political factors

Differing political philosophies can have a major effect on retail organizations. The problems of inflation, foreign competition and unemployment will be tackled in different ways according to which political party is in power. For example, a Conservative government is more likely to lean towards a *laissez-faire* attitude with market forces determining the course of events and a minimum of political intervention.

A government's economic policy can also have a major effect on interest rates, taxation – either direct or indirect – credit, and a host of other factors that will affect the retailer, the volume of business and profitability.

8. Legal factors

Closely associated with political philosophy is the role of the law and regulating authorities set up to administer and enforce the law.

The Office of Fair Trading, the Equal Opportunities Commission, the Health and Safety Executive, among others, are bodies that have been set up by the government which can and do bring retailers to task when appropriate. In addition many laws relating to the management of a retail establishment exist and are constantly being modified. For example, the law as it relates to labelling requirements, pricing, credit and hours of trading is constantly being updated and therefore changing the way in which the retailer operates.

9. Technological factors

Changes in technology not only affect the products that retailers sell but also the way they sell them. Most particularly the influence of information technology (IT) and the development of sophisticated data capture facilities has led to the revolutionizing of certain sectors of the retail industry.

For example, the introduction of electronic point-of-sale (EPOS) equipment provides retailers with detailed information which allows for extremely efficient stock control systems, price change procedures and up-to-the-minute sales reports.

The introduction of electronic funds transfer at point-of-sale (EFTPOS) systems, allows the transfer of funds from a customer's account to the retailer's account without the need for paperwork.

E-commerce is now well established in the UK; the facilities exist and will be increasingly used, with significant consequences for all retailers – large or small.

10. Natural factors

Environmental groups have brought to the public's attention the problems of pollution, energy shortage and the diminution of limited natural resources. This public awareness of environmental issues has resulted not only in the creation of a Green political party but has also led to shifts in consumer buying, for example the growth of the Body Shop chain on the basis of providing cosmetics made entirely of natural ingredients – no money wasted on fancy packaging, no animal testing of products, and refillable bottles.

The retailing micro-environment

The elements of the micro-environment – competitors, distribution channel members and customers – influence retail decisions on a daily basis, so it is important to monitor changes in the micro-environment and also observe how it interacts with the larger societal forces of the macro-environment.

11. Competitors

Within any market there will be competition to satisfy the needs and wants of the participating customer. Wherever there is an opportunity, someone will spot it and attempt to capitalize on it. No retailer can afford to rest, even if it has a commanding market share, because its very success will signal to the others that there are opportunities within that market place that are just too tempting to resist. The retail market place has been likened to a battleground with retailers competing with each other to win the favours of the customer.

12. Who are the competitors?

The first step in formulating a competitive strategy is to define the competition. This can be accomplished by looking at the two variables of the store and the product. Competition can be between two retail stores of the same type, e.g. Tesco and Sainsbury's, or between different types of retail store selling the same product, e.g. Tesco competes with Boots in the toiletries market.

Retailers often define their competition as similar retail stores but this is not necessarily the most appropriate approach. For the consumer the starting point in the purchase process is an awareness of a need or a want. This leads in a series of steps to the final purchase of a product or service to satisfy the need/want. Along this route the consumer will ask the question, 'Where can I go to purchase this product or service?' and at this point will have a set of possibilities. This set of stores ('the evoked set') will then be considered and a choice made on which to go to.

This concept is important to the retailer because it implies that the retailer cannot simply rely on a consumer instinctively knowing that particular goods are available from a particular store, but that the objective of the retailer must be to figure in the consumer's awareness – and this is achieved by communication.

13. The perceptual map

Within the set of possible stores the consumer will have an image of each and will be comparing attributes of one against the other within the framework of a 'perceptual map'. That is, consumers can be asked to rate attributes of different stores along a number of dimensions, e.g. quality and value for money, and different stores are then plotted on this graph to determine their position on the perceptual map, i.e. how close they are together. By adopting this approach the retailer can not only determine the competition but also the closest competitors (*see* Chapter 10: **13**).

14. Market shares

Another way of measuring the strength of the competition is to determine their share of the market. It is a reasonable assumption that the market leaders are doing something right or they would not be in the leading position. However, this analysis can be taken a stage further by looking into the market shares not only by the type of retail store but also by the product type, and in this way identification of weaknesses can come to light.

15. Competitors' retail mix

Other elements of competitors' retail mixes should also be monitored to detect strengths and weaknesses. Location, price and communications, as well as product, may prove to be a retailer's Achilles heel and provide an opportunity for exploitation.

16. Competitive strategy

Through this competitor analysis will come an understanding of the competition that will allow forecasting of their behaviour and anticipation of how competitors will react to the retailer's own strategy. This leads to evolving the most appropriate strategy to counter the competition. There have been many interesting competitive battles on the British retailing scene and none more so than in the field of grocery retailing. It is fascinating to observe the strategies being adopted by Tesco and Sainsbury's in their battle for market share. In the late 1970s the battleground shifted from an emphasis on price to quality. Since 2000 choice and additional customer services have been highlighted. Safeway's growth through acquisition put it in the big league and Wal-Mart's takeover of Asda has put the focus back on price with its 'Everyday low price' (EDLP) policy.

17. Other channel members

The retailer, by definition, is the final link in the distribution chain. Products may well pass from the original manufacturers through several intermediaries (agents, wholesalers, etc.) before reaching the retailer. If anything goes wrong with a single link in the chain the retailer, being the last link, suffers. For this reason it is imperative that the retail organization approaches channel decisions in an informed and systematic way. The basis on which each link in the chain operates is that it receives some benefit (usually financial) for some service performed (e.g. breaking bulk, transport, storage, etc.).

18. Co-operation and conflict

The ideal situation is established where there is complete co-operation between channel members and they all work together for mutual benefit. However, conflict may arise when one channel member feels that another is gaining at their expense or is getting an unfairly large cut of the rewards.

19. Power

At this stage the concept of power within the channel is raised because the exertion of power can reduce conflict and/or raise co-operation. Within a number of retail sectors, for example grocery retailing, the balance of power has shifted from the manufacturer to the large multiple who can now dictate terms. This has implications both for manufacturers who plead that they are not making sufficient profit to invest in research for new products, and for consumers who may, as a result, get a reduced choice. The small retailer also complains that it is not able to compete with the very low prices offered by the large supermarkets.

20. Vertical marketing systems

What then are the responses of retailers to this channel evolution? One has been the growth of vertical marketing systems (VMS) whereby channel members forge formal links, for example by contract, to enable maximum co-operation between channel members, thus acting as a unified system. There are three types:

(a) **A corporate VMS.** All stages from manufacturing to retailing are under one ownership, e.g. Thorntons, the Co-op Group.

(b) **An administered VMS.** Each channel member is independent but responds to a dominant member's efforts to effect co-ordination, e.g. Marks & Spencer.

(c) **A contractual VMS.** This has shown the greatest growth through the legal or contractual basis for co-operation. There are three types of contractual VMS:

  (i) *The retailer-sponsored VMS.* For example the Londis group of grocery retailers: it consists of a group of independent retailers who join together to gain buying economies. Participating members are required to purchase a proportion of their stock (usually 30–50 per cent) through the group.

(*ii*) *The wholesale-sponsored VMS.* For example Spar: it is similar to the retailer-sponsored VMS but is initiated and sponsored by a wholesaler. In addition to the economies of bulk buying, participating members receive assistance with merchandising, layout, pricing, etc. and are perceived by the customer to be part of a larger group which carries out national advertising.

(*iii*) *The manufacturer-sponsored VMS.* Also known as franchising, this involves two parties – the franchisor and the franchisee. The franchisor has developed a successful business format that is made available to the franchisee for a financial consideration (usually an initial lump sum plus a continuing percentage commission on turnover). Explosive growth has been experienced by some franchise operations, while others have been less successful. Benetton, Burger King and Domino's Pizza among many others are household names in the field of franchise.

The final element of the micro-environment is the customer and forms the basis of the following chapter.

Progress test 8

1. What are the two levels of the retailing environment?

2. Describe the main demographic trends of interest to retailers.

3. What are the major technological factors affecting retailing?

4. What are the elements of the micro-environment?

5. What is the significance of the concept of power within the channels of distribution?

6. How does the formation of a vertical marketing system (VMS) help the retailer?

7. Analyse the changes occurring in the retail environment and discuss the possible implications of such changes for retailers in the next decade.

8. Mike Johnson is a successful retailer of mid- to high-priced furniture in Grantham. He realizes, however, that the retail environment has changed a great deal since he began in the furniture trade in 1965. He thinks he needs to conduct an analysis of the retail environment but does not know where or how to begin.

   (a) What factors in the external environment should Mike monitor?
   (b) How can he get information on these factors?
   (c) If Mike finds that most of his customers are two-income families, how might he wish to react to this information?

9. A VMS operates when manufacturer, wholesaler and retailer act as a unified system to achieve operating economies and maximum market impact. Illustrate by reference to two examples how operating within a VMS may give competitive advantage.

9 Consumer buying behaviour

Introduction

The consumer is the focus of all retail decisions. It is therefore important to appreciate how consumers go about making their buying decisions. This chapter considers how consumers decide upon what product to buy, the brand, and the store to buy them from, as well as the factors influencing these choices.

The buying process

1. The decision process

The buying process is essentially a decision process designed to provide solutions to problems. The first stage in the process is the awareness of a need or a want; this is followed by an information-processing stage prior to the purchase decision. But the buying process should not be considered complete until the product/service has been used and resulted in satisfaction or dissatisfaction in the original need or want (*see* Figure 9.1).

Figure 9.1 The stages of the buying process

Felt need/want
↓
Pre-purchase activity
↓
Purchase decision
↓
Use behaviour
↓
Post-purchase feelings

2. The felt need/want

Human beings have certain fundamental needs for survival: food, water, shelter (warmth) and security. These may be satisfied in quite simple ways or through the expression of more complex requirements – wants. For example, the need for water is as a result of a basic biological requirement. However, this water may be delivered as water, or the human being (consumer) may express a preference for Coca-Cola or lemonade or a myriad of other products designed to satisfy the want for more than just plain water. This felt need or want can be considered as a problem. The natural response of the human being to this problem state is to seek a solution, and the process of seeking a solution leads naturally to the search for information and the exploration of alternative ways of resolving the problems.

This problem state may be expressed in a vague way, for example, 'I am bored', or in a specific way, 'I want to go to Alton Towers'.

3. Pre-purchase activity

This stage is concerned with gathering information and processing it to allow the consumer to move towards a purchase decision. The mnemonic AIDA simply describes the stages of pre-purchase activity. First, consumers become *A*ware of products or services that may satisfy their requirements. *I*nterest is generated which becomes more intense as more information is gathered, resulting in a *D*esire to obtain the item, and finally *A*ction – the decision to purchase. This same process has been described as Awareness → Knowledge → Liking → Preference → Conviction → Purchase. It is clear that there are two key elements to this – first, the information search and, second, the evaluation of alternatives.

The extent of the information search is dependent upon the perceived difficulty in resolving the problem. For routine grocery purchases, the consumer evolves an automatic pattern of behaviour that requires minimal information search and alternative evaluation. However, for a high involvement purchase (i.e. where the risk of making the wrong decision is great, e.g. financial outlay for a new car), the information search will be extensive.

The generation and evaluation of alternatives centre around the product, the specific brand and the store, and which of these three takes precedence will again depend on the nature and extent of the perceived problem.

Therefore, the sequence for the weekly grocery trip will probably be store–product–brand. However, for purchase of a new motor vehicle it will probably be product–brand–store.

The implications for the retailer are clear. It must attempt to make the problem-solving process easier by ensuring that the customer includes its store in the list of alternatives and has a positive image of the store as being the place that will stock the customer's preferred product/brand. Successful retailers have realized that the key lies in targeting a well-defined group of customers and then offering them the type of product or service they require. In turn this customer will come to regard the store in precisely that light – i.e. 'My kind of store'.

Repeated satisfaction will generate loyalty to the store, so that in any decision relating to 'Where can I obtain that product?', the same store will be at the top of the list. The authors of this book even have experience of people who would not move to a new area unless there was a particular grocery store there – so loyal were they in the belief that only that store (Sainsbury's) could satisfy their particular grocery requirements.

4. The purchase decision

The purchase decision is not a single decision but a bundle of decisions, any one of which can result in a change of mind and an alternative route being followed. Thus, for example, a consumer may have decided on a product, brand and store but is finally persuaded that this is in fact the wrong choice because the price in that store is not competitive or because the sales staff have not been helpful.

So the actual time of purchase is important since it can either help or hinder the decision process. Helpful, courteous and attentive sales assistants are essential. Information provided in-store can lead to additional purchases or trading up. In-store promotions and store design and layout will provide the right incentives and atmosphere for purchasing.

Finally, the purchase transaction is important as it is the last impression the customer has of that purchase situation. Ease of purchase, lack of queues, credit facilities, treatment by sales personnel and efficient handling of problems, comments or complaints, can make a lasting impression. Difficulty in these areas can lose a sale or even lose a customer permanently.

5. Use behaviour

As was stated previously, the product is not purchased for its own sake but for its ability to satisfy a need. For example, the PC is not purchased because it is a computer but because with it the customer can manipulate information and play games. Much is to be learnt by understanding why consumers buy products. For example, a customer buys a printer and brings it back two weeks later demanding a refund because 'it is not up to the job'. A little questioning reveals that they really need a printer and a copier. Knowing this the retailer is able to save the day by offering the customer, for very little extra outlay an all-in-one printer that not only prints and copies but scans as well.

Other questions the retailer can ask about the product in use are: Who uses the product? When and where is it used? What other products is it used with? The answers can provide opportunities for ensuring customer satisfaction, and additional sales.

Once again the satisfaction of customer needs is paramount. There is little point in making a sale but losing a customer. That customer talks to other people and bad news spreads very quickly. The sales assistant should determine the use the product is going to be put to, and then guide the customer to the right product. Often it is not possible to question customers in this informal way; therefore surveys should be carried out periodically to monitor customer satisfaction with the store and products purchased from the store.

6. Post-purchase feelings

Dissatisfaction with a product can be as a result of a genuinely disappointing performance of the product due to faulty manufacture, inappropriate use, etc. Sometimes, however, dissatisfaction is due more to psychological factors such as the tension created by wondering if the right choice has been made – particularly if the alternatives were also attractive. Also, even if the product appears to be performing well, adverse information provided by friends or neighbours may reduce satisfaction or cause consumers to fear failure of the product so causing them to return it and demand a refund.

Recognition of this phenomenon, known as post-cognitive dissonance, will lead the retailer to provide mechanisms for reducing this tension either at the time of purchase or shortly afterwards. A liberal returns policy will allow the customer to feel that even if the product is not quite right when they get it home, they are still able to get a refund without a problem. This reassurance actually makes it easier for the consumer to make the purchase decision. Also, the fear of product failure can be lessened by the retailer providing extended guarantees or making available products that offer a manufacturer's extended guarantee. Reassurance can also be offered that the customer has made the right choice by offering information on the number of other satisfied customers or the popularity of that particular product, e.g. 'The best selling car in Europe', 'The No.1 best seller', 'Brand leader', etc.

To reiterate, the importance of post-purchase feelings is not only their relevance to post-purchase satisfaction but also because they affect the consumer at the point of purchase and fear of making a wrong decision can result in a lost sale – or a lost customer. Consider your feelings if you had been persuaded by a retailer to purchase a product that proved to be unsatisfactory. What would your attitude be towards that store? Many customers do not like the hassle of returning goods but would simply choose not to shop in that store again.

The buying participants

The buying process has been described as a problem-solving exercise, designed to result in the satisfaction of a need or want. However, it should not be forgotten that the consumer does not live in a vacuum and there are many factors that will influence consumer behaviour in a particular buying situation. The four possible roles of the actors in the buying process – the buying participants – are considered below.

7. Influencers

These are the people who encourage, inform or persuade at any stage in the buying process. For example, a TV personality used in a commercial may influence choice, or a prominent member of society, e.g. doctor, or simply a neighbour or friend, will influence the buyer's thought processes. Retailers can use this concept most effectively in their promotion efforts, either using TV personalities to open new stores or through advertising. Also, the targeting of local opinion leaders as recipients of promotion messages or to generate publicity is an efficient way of influencing a larger audience.

8. Deciders

The actual purchase decision maker is clearly the prime target for promotional messages but quite often the purchase decision is not made by an individual but by a group of individuals. For example, the family may be considered the decision-making unit (DMU) for a new family car, while the husband and wife team may be the DMU for domestic durables such as lounge and dining room furniture. It is therefore important for the retailer to reach the DMU with promotional messages, particularly where more than one individual is involved in the buying process.

9. The buyer

The significance of the DMU is highlighted when the buyer is considered as the individual who makes the actual purchase. Consider the case of the husband with the wife's shopping list. Has he really had a significant say in which products/brands are on the list and which store is chosen? Perhaps this is an extreme but there will be many occasions where the buyer will merely be acting as a purchasing agent on behalf of another individual. The retailer should take care not to be misled into believing that the target market consists solely of those people who are seen in the store. Many retailers carry out in-store market research surveys asking detailed questions on standards of customer service, quality of merchandise, etc. Many of the responses will be irrelevant to the objective of determining factors for store choice if that shopper is merely acting on behalf of someone else who may hold totally different views.

10. Users

The final buying participant is the end user. The user of a product may have had no role in the initial product/store/brand choice but being the user of the product will either be satisfied or dissatisfied with it. This will usually be communicated to the purchaser who will react appropriately. How will user dissatisfaction influence future store choice? It may be a dissatisfaction with a product that results in a dissatisfaction with the store for selling such an inferior product. Or it may be dissatisfaction with the way the store handled the sale, e.g. by not providing users with sufficient information to enable them to make the best use of the product, or by offering inadequate post-purchase support, such as delivery, installation or after-sales service. Once again the implications for the retailer are clear. The user of the product must also be satisfied and this can best be achieved by determining who the user will be and providing services appropriate to the user's need.

A situation has now been described where the satisfaction of customer needs can be seen as rather more complex than the simple phrase suggests. Who is the customer? Is it the decider, the buyer or user? The answer will vary according to the specific buying situation but the retailer should know in order to maximize the chances of future sales.

Factors influencing choice

In the previous section (*see* 7) the role of the influencer was briefly described. However, the consumer is influenced by many factors in choosing the product/ store/brand complex. These factors may be perceived as internal variables – needs, motivation, personality, perception, learning and attitudes; or external – family, reference groups, social class and culture.

Internal variables

11. Needs

A need can be defined as an inner force that prompts or moves the individual to behaviour. A hierachy of needs has been described whereby there are different degrees of need, the most fundamtal being food, water and shelter which have to be met before other needs are felt. Second-order needs are for safety and security, which in turn, when fully satisfied, will lead to the need to belong and love. Finally, satisfaction of esteem (prestige, success, etc.) and self-fulfilment needs are sought.

Thus a retail organization may adopt a strategy of appealing to the need to belong, e.g. 'Your caring, sharing Co-op', or to esteem needs, e.g. prestigious stores such as Harrods.

12. Motivation

A motive is an internal energizing force that gives rise to behaviour. The retailer motivates customers through stimulation of a need or want that will be sufficiently strong to give rise to purchasing behaviour. There are two stages to the process. First, the retailer must generate awareness of the product or service as a satisfier of the need. Second, consumer motivation is enhanced by making the product more desirable. Both these objectives can be achieved through communication devices: providing information, demonstrating the satisfaction of need or providing incentives to action. Advertising and personal selling are useful as methods of increasing motivation; in-store the provision of discounts, special offers, competitions, etc. can raise customer desire to the point where action (purchase) is inevitable.

13. Personality

The way in which an individual interacts with the environment is termed personality. It is a complex concept and has given rise to many theories. One element of personality that has proved to be of particular value to retailers is the study of lifestyles. Lifestyles – how people lead their lives – can be measured by looking at three variables: activities, interests and opinions. Through measuring these dimensions it is possible to differentiate groups of consumers who lead their lives in a particular way.

Lifestyle retailing really started in the UK with the Next retailing group which originally defined its target customer as the fashion-conscious female, to whom price was a secondary consideration. Once this definition was available, other merchandise and indeed other stores were added to appeal to that same target customer.

14. Perception

Perception is the way in which an individual interprets the stimuli received from the environment. For retailers it is imperative that they realize that 'customer perception is reality'. In other words it is not what they are that is important but what they think they are. Thus some customers' perception of a store may be 'traditional, reliable, stable', i.e. a favourable impression. Others may interpret the same stimuli in a negative way as 'old-fashioned, dowdy, unexciting', i.e. an unfavourable response.

15. Learning

Learning can be thought of as modification of behaviour as a result of experience. Two important aspects of learning for the retailer are the concepts of reward and punishment, and the enhancement of learning by repetition. Thus a customer who constantly finds satisfaction of need through visits to a particular store will build up a loyalty to that store.

Stimulus generalization occurs when a customer responds in a particular way to one stimulus but then generalizes the response to other stimuli. For example, one rude assistant in one branch of Marks & Spencer may result in a response whereby the customer vows never to shop in any branch of M & S again. Or the purchase of a single item that proves unsatisfactory may result in a response that all merchandise from that store is considered unsatisfactory. The lessons for the retailer willing to apply learning theory are devastatingly clear.

16. Attitudes

An attitude is a learned predisposition to respond in a consistently favourable or unfavourable way with regard to a particular object or idea.

The measurement of attitudes through retailing research and the ways in which attitudes are formed and changed are important to the retailer. An attitude, once formed, is particularly resistant to change because it is an efficient way of operating. A predisposition to respond in a particular manner reduces the need for exhaustive evaluation of alternatives every time the consumer comes to make a decision. The retailer should therefore aim to generate a positive attitude towards the store and maintain it. It is far easier for a customer to move from a positive to a negative attitude than it is for a retailer to move the customer from a negative attitude to a positive one.

External variables

The degree of influence of external variables is illustrated in Figure 9.2, the family being the strongest.

17. The family

The influence of the family has been touched upon already when considering the buying participants. The degree of influence of the family will vary according to the situation and the product. The degree of influence of the partner, children or extended family in a purchase decision has implications for developing the retail strategy, perhaps most particularly with regard to advertising and sales promotion.

18. Reference groups

A reference group is a group with which an individual wants to be associated and whose beliefs, attitudes, values and behaviour he or she will seek to emulate. Reference groups influence decisions on store choice because members of the group are expected to adhere to group norms and act in particular ways acceptable to other members of the group. Teenagers are particularly prone to being

Figure 9.2 External factors influencing store choice

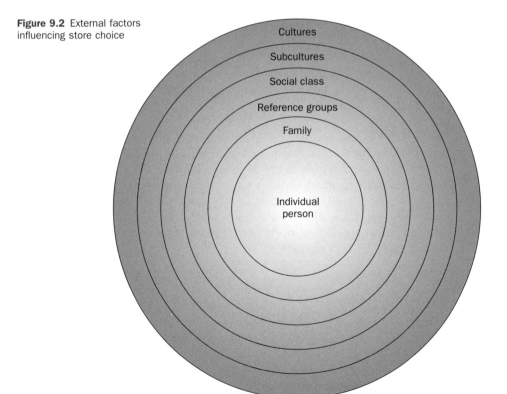

Cultures

Subcultures

Social class

Reference groups

Family

Individual person

highly influenced by reference groups, for example in their music and clothing tastes, but reference groups occur in all walks of life. Professional organizations, colleagues, neighbours and friends may all be regarded as reference groups. The retailer can use this concept by constructing advertising to appeal to the group, for example a fashion show for the local Women's Institute, or a display of new books at the local university.

19. Social class

The system of social stratification according to socio-economic groupings provides us with definitions of social class which, although everyone agrees are not as well defined as in the past, still provide a useful classification scheme for retailers. Certain retailers will design their retail mixes to appeal to certain social classes, but perhaps the greatest value of the classification system is in the determination of appropriate media to reach target audiences. Most newspapers and magazines have information on their readers which they make available to advertisers in order to persuade them to place ads in that particular publication. Frequently this will include data on readership by social class. The retailer can then match the cost of reaching its target audience in terms of social class against other competing publications, and thereby choose the most cost-effective.

20. Culture

The unique pattern of behaviour and social relations that characterize a society and distinguish it from others gives rise to the concept of culture. A society's values, ideas, attitudes, traditions, symbols or technology can all form the basis of culture. Thus it is possible to describe North American cultural values as achievement, success, progress, material comfort and freedom; and this may be compared with the Chinese culture.

21. Subculture

Perhaps the greatest value of the concept of culture to the retailer is at the level of subcultures. A subculture can be defined as a distinct cultural group that exists as an identifiable segment within a larger, more complex society. For example, we can describe a primary concern of the youth subculture as entertainment, music, cinema, etc., while the elderly subculture is more concerned with health care and gardening. Other subcultures could be defined according to religion, racial groups, political groups, etc.

Progress test 9

1. Describe the stages of the buying process.

2. What are the four types of buying participants?

3. How has the study of personality helped retailers?

4. How can retailers use the concept of reference groups in promoting their business?

5. Is the stratification of the population into social classes still relevant?

6. Define subculture and give an example.

7. What factors are likely to be most important to customers when selecting a store? (Illustrate your answer with reference to the purchase of furniture.)

8. Briefly describe the stages of the consumer purchasing decision process. Explain and evaluate the methods used by retailers to influence consumer choice and actions, in this process of decision-making.

10 Segmentation

Introduction

There is an old truism that 'you can't please all of the people all of the time!' In other words, with respect to retailing it is not possible to serve all types of customer. If this is attempted none will be served adequately. This chapter considers ways of splitting customer groups into different segments and the advantages and disadvantages of doing so.

Differing customer needs

Differing groups of customers have always had differing needs but this is particularly true today when consumers require a greater choice and are looking for satisfaction of their particular needs and have the spending power to demand it.

The retailer must instead look to satisfying certain groups of customers – this process is known as segmentation.

1. Definition

Segmentation is the dividing of a market into subsets of customers, any one or more of which can be selected as a target market to be satisfied with a distinct retailing mix.

2. Examples

Perhaps the best example of segmentation in action can be found in the retailing of clothing and fashion wear. Certain retailers have identified younger age groups as their target segment, e.g. Miss Selfridge. Next originally chose to serve the 25–40-year-old fashion-conscious female, whereas Marks & Spencer traditionally offered more conservative wear to slightly older age groups. An example of a retail organization that has learnt to its cost the lesson of segmentation is Arcadia.

This company was brought to its knees in the late 1990s because it was trying to be all things to everybody, offering a vast range of merchandise and serving a wide range of customers. The company was turned around by adopting the principles of segmentation and concentrating efforts on key target markets. Operation BrandMAX, as this segmentation process was named, resulted in Arcadia pulling out of certain segments altogether, e.g. Principles for Men. The main purpose of the BrandMAX strategy was to refocus on the best brands, which meant a greater emphasis on womenswear and the Dorothy Perkins, Evans and Top Shop chains. The results were dramatic – sales of ongoing brands increased by 40 per cent.

Having illustrated the results of adopting the segmentation strategy, it is appropriate to ask, 'How can we subdivide a market?'

Bases for segmentation

The objective of segmenting a market is to identify segments that offer the retailer an opportunity to serve that segment and thus truly and precisely satisfy customer needs. There are five bases for segmentation: geographic, geodemographic, demographic, psychographic and behavioural.

3. Geographic segmentation

Segmenting a market by geographic factors is a common retail practice. At the most general level many retailers restrict operation to the UK. It is only relatively recently that retailers have looked to overseas territories for growth with the same vigour as the manufacturing industry does. There are also groups of stores that restrict operation to a geographic region where they have a strong presence, e.g. Booths supermarkets in the North-West of England. There are, however, many retailers who have segmented their market geographically at the level of a town or as the corner shop in the local community.

4. Geodemographic segmentation

A particularly useful scheme for classifying residential neighbourhoods has been developed by the market analyst CACI which classifies every parish with a population of 50 or more into 11 groups. This scheme, known as ACORN (A Classification Of Residential Neighbourhoods), has been based on the principle that people living in similar residential areas will show certain similarities in their buying patterns. For example, people living in 'better-off retirement areas' will have very different buying requirements to those in the 'poorest council estates'. A similar system marketed by Experian is known as MOSAIC.

5. Demographic segmentation

Segmenting a market by demographic variables is probably the most widely used method.

(a) **Age and life-cycle stage**. Examples have already been given of retailers who target certain age groups and it is clear that consumers' requirements change with age. The teenager's requirement for cosmetics, records and cinema-going are replaced in young adulthood by home-furnishing and convenience food requirements, and so it goes on through the life cycle with older age groups pre-occupied with health and filling their leisure time.

(b) **Sex**. In the area of clothing retailers, there has long been a division between menswear and ladieswear. However, many other retailers also target predomin-antly male or female customers. Consider the target markets for a fishing tackle retailer and a specialist sewing machine retailer. The composition of the target groups has a major impact on the retail mix and particularly on the ways in which the retailer communicates with the different groups.

(c) **Family**. Two variables are important in segmenting by family factors – the family size and the stage in the family life cycle. Larger families may be more economy minded and purchase larger pack sizes, economy brands or own-labels. At the same time, the family with a youngest child under 3 years of age will differ in its requirements from a family with no children under 11. We recall here that the family may act as a decision-making unit in the purchasing process.

(d) **Income**. Segmentation by income is another long-standing retail practice. Retailers like House of Fraser aim to appeal to higher income groups by offering 'exclusive' products, higher-than-average prices and a greater range of customer services. Rising disposable income in the UK and the trend towards double-income families has offered greater opportunities for retailers targeting these higher income groups. With higher incomes comes a customer orientation towards quality of merchandise and service and a lesser emphasis on price.

(e) **Occupation**. At one time occupation was intimately linked with income. But this relationship is breaking down with many blue-collar workers earning more than others in professional and technical occupations. However, occupa-tion can provide a useful basis for segmenting markets due to the lifestyles that individuals in that occupation will lead. For example, one might expect a book retailer to target lecturers, school teachers and other professionals in preference to blue-collar workers. It is common to feel uneasy about these distinctions and to feel an element of snobbery and undesirable class distinction or discrimina-tion. However, it is as well to remember that the purpose of this discrimination is to serve the customer better. Thus McDonald's has targeted its segment and in this way serves its particular customers the way it wants; so equally Starbucks caters for another segment of the market and aims to please it with an alternative offering.

Similarly, other demographic variables that can be used as the basis for segmenta-tion are education, religion, race and nationality.

Table 10.1 Social class groupings

Social grade	Per cent of population	Social status	Occupation
A	2.7	Upper middle class	Higher managerial, administrative or professional
B	15.1	Middle class	Intermediate managerial, administrative or professional
C1	23.9	Lower middle class	Supervisory or clerical, and junior managerial, administrative or professional
C2	27.8	Skilled working class	Skilled manual workers
D	17.8	Working class	Semi and unskilled manual workers
E	12.7	Those at lowest level of subsistence	State pensioners or widows (no other earner), casual or lowest-grade workers

Source: Joint Industry Committee for National Readership Surveys

6. Psychographic segmentation

It has been said that the retail revolution that started in the 1980s was sparked by the application of psychographics, i.e. segmenting a market according to lifestyles. Lifestyle – the way groups of people lead their lives – is determined by attitudes, opinions and interests. For example, some individuals are particularly concerned with environmental issues – they will look for economy, safety and a consideration for ecology. The Body Shop is a retail organization that had this lifestyle group particularly in mind when formulating its retail strategy.

Social class is also an important element of psychographics ranging from the A group or upper middle classes through to pensioners who make up the bulk of the E group (*see* Table 10.1).

Personality is the third element of psychographics, with retailers looking for personality traits that they may use to segment the market. Individuals may be described as gregarious, ambitious, independent, self-confident, etc. and retailers may wish to appeal to individuals with one or more of these personality traits. Laura Ashley would seem to be appealing to the ambitious and/or self-confident, Benetton similarly has an appeal to certain personality types. Perhaps the aim of the retailer should be to project an image with which these personality types identify and feel most at ease. The family man may feel uncomfortable shopping in Top Man and the 'fast trackers' may feel equally uncomfortable in searching for clothes in Littlewoods.

7. Behavioural segmentation

In behavioural segmentation customers are grouped according to certain aspects of their behaviour in relation to the store, rather than as previously by inferring behaviour from other factors, e.g. demographic. A market can be segmented according to occasions, benefits and loyalty status.

(a) **Occasions**. Customers can be segmented according to when they develop a need. For example, a convenience store can specialize in serving people who normally do their main shopping at the supermarket but find they have forgotten certain items, run out of them or need them at a time when the supermarket is closed. In this way the convenience store is able to compete with the supermarket, not on price but on convenience and providing satisfaction to 'distress purchase' buying.

(b) **Benefits sought**. Considered by some as the most useful method of segmentation, benefit segmentation seeks to determine the prime benefit sought by shoppers. For example, certain shoppers may patronize a department store because the prime benefits they seek are quality merchandise and the facility for charging their account at the store. Others may seek the best possible price and want a discount for cash – the discount out-of-town factory outlets may well attract this type of customer.

(c) **Loyalty status**. Many retailers find that a high proportion of their turnover is generated by a small proportion of their customers. These individuals have developed a high degree of loyalty to that store and use it frequently. There are degrees of loyalty and retailers may attempt to identify those who are loyal to two or three stores and attempt to turn them away from competitors by provision of extra incentives (e.g. store loyalty cards) and thus convert them to loyalty to the individual store.

It should be stressed that segmentation is often achieved by combining two or more of the above variables. For example, a furniture retailer may combine income, age and sex as the variables that will define its target market. Similarly the '25–40-year-old fashion conscious female' defines a target market in terms of demographic and psychographic variables.

Advantages and disadvantages of segmentation

8. Advantages of segmentation

The purpose of segmentation is to define a group of customers that we wish to serve. By adopting this focused approach the retailer should be better able to:

(a) Spot and compare opportunities.

(b) Spot different responses to different stimuli; for example, a new advertising campaign or a change in price.

(c) Make fine adjustments to the retail mix.

In short the advantage of segmentation is to enable the retailer to identify more accurately customer needs and wants and satisfy them. The approach has been likened to the rifle bullet rather than the shotgun approach.

9. Disadvantages of segmentation

Targeting a well-defined segment has provided a new lease of life to many retailers who seemed to have lost their way (e.g. Woolworths, Arcadia), but there is the danger of:

(a) Becoming cost inefficient – i.e. by targeting a small group the retailer will lose economies of scale.

(b) Becoming too myopic in serving only one segment and missing opportunities that may arise in others.

(c) Trying to compete in too many different segments. The process of identifying segments naturally leads to the decision of which to serve. Many retailers find it difficult to jettison some segments, hoping that they will be able to attract some business from it. This leads to the 'Jack of all trades, master of none' syndrome which has been the downfall of many retail operations, particularly of the department store type.

(d) Becoming locked into a segment that is declining. Many small retail outlets have been lost because they served a segment that was in decline. For example, the changing retail environment has meant that for food purchases most people prefer to buy most items once a week at one outlet. Therefore, many fishmongers, butchers and bakers have lost out to the superstore where the convenience of one-stop shopping was the benefit sought by the customer.

Segmentation strategy

Having identified different segments through gathering information, the stage now reached is to determine which segments to serve.

10. Deciding factors

There are many factors that will impinge upon this decision, including:

(a) The size and profit potential of the alternative segments.

(b) The objectives of the retail organization.

(c) The strengths and weaknesses of the retail organization. For example, a small company with limited resources may find it impossible to compete in many different segments.

(d) The strengths and weaknesses of the competition. It is often preferable to attract a small segment where competition is weak than a large segment that is adequately served by strong competitors.

(e) Channel relations – it may be very difficult to break into a market segment, not because of direct retail competition, but because the intermediaries provide a significant barrier to entry, e.g. newspapers and magazines.

(f) Company image – a segment may be seen to offer significant potential but does not provide consistency with the company image.

11. Alternative strategies

There are three alternative segmentation strategies that may be adopted.

(a) **Undifferentiated**. The retailer recognizes that there are different segments but focuses on the common needs of consumers rather than their differences. Thus the retailer hopes to attract a sufficient number of consumers from all segments with one retail mix. Perhaps one of the most successful adopters of this strategy is the McDonald's fast-food chain which offers a highly standardized mix on a global basis.

(b) **Differentiated**. Here the response to the different segments is to design different retail mixes to satisfy the differing needs. For example, the Arcadia group operates a number of successful retail operations targeted at several different segments. The Evans chain is targeted at the larger woman, Top Shop and Top Man at the younger market, while Principles for Women aims at an older, more style-conscious group of customers.

(c) **Concentrated**. The concentrated strategy is aimed at gaining a larger share of one segment and is perhaps the most appropriate segmentation strategy for the new smaller operator. Many examples of successful operation of a concentrated strategy can be cited. For example, Mothercare became hugely successful serving the needs of the mother and baby. Tie Rack and Knickerbox have concentrated on providing a very wide choice of a specialist clothing item, but have run into difficulties with this strategy (*see* **9d** above).

12. Criteria for successful segmentation

It has been suggested that in order for segmentation to be most effective, the identified segments must be:

(a) **Measurable**. It is difficult to measure personality variables such as ambition or rebelliousness. Therefore demographic variables are often preferred as the basis of segmenting markets because, for example, it is easy to determine the population within a certain age band.

(b) **Substantial**. Having measured different segments it is then possible to determine which are sufficiently substantial to afford an opportunity for targeting and thence generating a profit.

(c) **Accessible**. There is little point in identifying a segment if it is not accessible – if it cannot be reached by communications such as advertising, personal selling, sales promotion or publicity. In order to serve a segment the retailer has to be able to communicate with it.

In addition, the retailer's segmentation strategy must be capable of being put into action. The question of action is directly linked to company objectives and of course resources.

13. Segmentation and positioning

As we have seen, the process of segmentation involves identifying different bases for segmentation and determining important characteristics of each segment. It is then necessary to evaluate the potential or commercial attractiveness of each segment and then to select one or more segments as the target markets.

Closely linked to the whole process of segmentation is 'positioning'. This is where the store is positioned in a given market in the minds of the targeted consumers. A 'perceptual map' can be drawn to show the position of the store and its competitors using important choice attributes. Thus price and range can be used to produce a perceptual map for grocery retailers (Figure 10.1).

It can be seen that on this map Asda would seem to have a satisfactory position, being perceived as providing a wide choice and lower-than-average prices. On the other hand, Safeway may be considered vulnerable since it is perceived as having higher prices and less choice. Equally there is a cluster of discounters operating within a very similar position in the market.

It is important to remember that positioning is not what you do to the store. Positioning is what you do to the mind of the customer. So you position the store in the mind of the customer.

Asda recently completed a successful repositioning exercise – in fact to get it back to the position it used to hold as being perceived as a provider of a good choice of quality merchandise at the best possible price, 'Asda-price.'

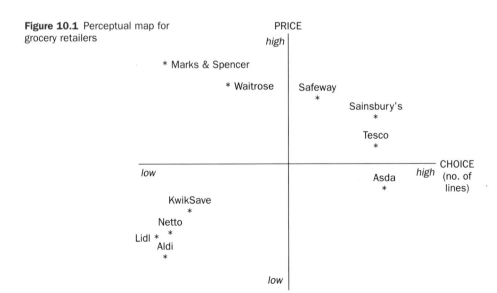

Figure 10.1 Perceptual map for grocery retailers

Progress test 10

1. What is meant by segmentation?

2. What are the bases for segmentation?

3. How has the ACORN classification scheme proved to be of use to retailers?

4. What are the advantages and disadvantages of segmentation?

5. Describe the criteria for successful segmentation.

6. A retailer, having conducted an extensive survey, finds that the customers most likely to patronize its store are in the 45-plus age group. It decides to mount a major effort to attract the 20–35 age group to try to convince them to use the store. It believes there will be a higher pay-off in attempting to recruit new customers than in reinforcing attitudes of current customers. What are the arguments for and against this strategy?

7. What advantages can you suggest for a retailer who decides to segment its market using geodemographics? What are the disadvantages of this methodology and how can they be minimized?

Part two

The retail mix

11 Store location

Introduction

It has been said that there are three criteria for success in retailing. They are location, location and location. This rather flippant remark serves to underline the importance of the location decision. This chapter considers the general area in which to locate a store and also how to choose a specific site.

1. The importance of location

Having the right location is important in terms of convenience to the customer but it is most important to the retailer because a mistake in the location decision is almost impossible to correct. If a pricing decision is wrong it can be changed, if the merchandise variety is wrong it too can be changed, but once the location is chosen the retailer is stuck with it. The store location decision should be approached bearing in mind three factors – the customer, the general area and the specific site.

2. Customers

The target market is the major determinant of the ideal store location. Thus, for example, if the target market is composed of individuals whose primary objective in selecting a store is convenience, then the store must be located conveniently for these customers. The definition of what is convenient may, however, differ according to customer type and merchandise required. In this way, a corner shop may be considered convenient for the purchase of a packet of sugar but may be inconvenient for the purchase of a full week's shopping if no car parking facility is available.

Similarly, an exclusive jewellery store will probably locate some considerable distance from its target market on the basis that convenience is not the major determinant of store choice for this type of merchandise; instead quality and service may be of greater import, and the ambience only available in a high class shopping area.

Determining the general area in which to locate

The decision on the general area is arrived at through a stepwise process:

(a) Catchment area analysis.

(b) Determining the sales potential of different areas.

(c) Choosing the area that would fit best (retailer objectives related to needs of target market).

Catchment area analysis

3. The catchment area

This is a term borrowed from geography which accurately describes the watershed effect that entices shoppers living within a shopping centre's sphere of influence into the centre and away from other shopping influences (*see* Figure 11.1). It

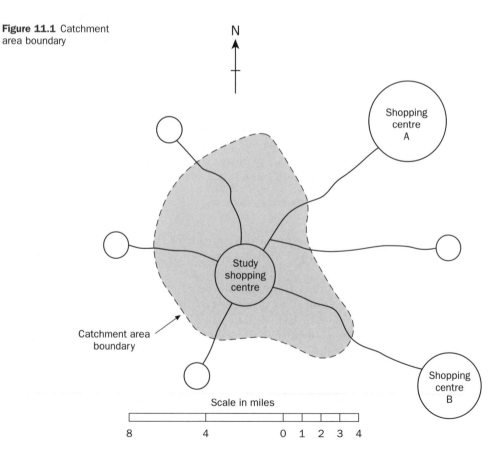

Figure 11.1 Catchment area boundary

may be defined as the geographical area from which a shopping centre (or large individual store) draws its custom. The main influences on catchment area size and shape are:

(a) Business attractions of the shopping centre. These consist of:

- (*i*) types of major store
- (*ii*) kinds and selection of merchandise offered
- (*iii*) delivery, credit and other retail services
- (*iv*) reputation of major retailers
- (*v*) banking facilities
- (*vi*) car parking facilities and restrictions.

(b) Social and leisure attractions.

(c) Population of area.

(d) Density of population.

(e) Type of consumer.

(f) Distance to travel and local 'psychology of distance'.

(g) Lines of transportation (including road and rail systems, bus routes).

(h) Lines of communication. These consist of daily newspaper circulation areas, sales and readership, and other local media such as radio, TV and magazines.

(i) Car ownership in the market.

(j) Nature and competition offered by other shopping centres within or near the market.

(k) Topographical nature of market area.

4. Quantifying the catchment area

The two main approaches to determining the local catchment area are:

(a) **Empirical theory.** This is made up of the following methods:

- (*i*) *Observational methods.* For example, by finding natural catchment boundaries like rivers and motorways on maps or by driving round the area.
- (*ii*) *Customer spotting.* This is based either on a shopper questionnaire or on an analysis of customer use of credit facilities and so on. A customer 'spot map' can be constructed from the questionnaires, etc., showing where customers live (*see* Figure 11.2).

(b) **Gravitational theory.** The best known of these so-called spatial interaction models, which is based on Reilly's Law, states that the frequency with which the residents of an intermediate settlement trade with two towns is directly proportional to the populations of the two towns and inversely proportional to the square of the distances of the two towns to the intermediate settlement. Reilly's Law can be modified to derive the 'breaking point' between two towns, which is

Figure 11.2 Customer spot map

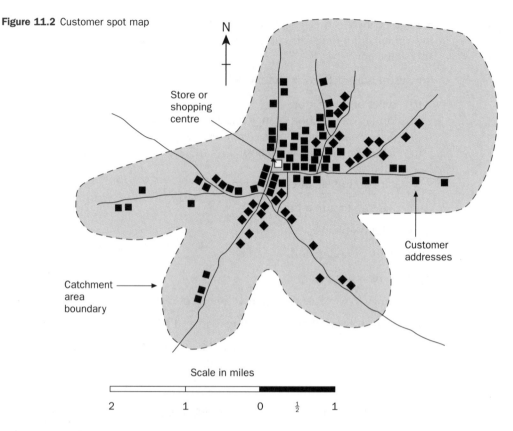

defined as the point up to which one town dominates and beyond which the other town is dominant. This is given as:

$$\text{Breaking point (in miles from town A)} = \frac{\text{Distance A to B}}{1 + \sqrt{\dfrac{\text{Population B}}{\text{Population A}}}}$$

The following example shows how a catchment area boundary is drawn using Reilly's method.

Example

Town A has a population of 40,000 and town B of 10,000. Town A is 6 miles from town B. Break-points for all surrounding towns can be calculated and a line drawn to connect these points, thus producing a catchment area boundary:

$$\text{Breaking point (in miles from town A)} = \frac{6}{1 + \sqrt{\dfrac{10,000}{40,000}}} = 4 \text{ miles}$$

Figure 11.3 Drawing a catchment
area boundary

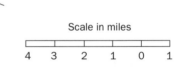

N

Catchment area
boundary

Road

Town B

Town A

Scale in miles

4   3   2   1   0   1

From either of these two basic types of catchment area appraisal, an idea of the
sphere of influence of a shopping centre can be gained. This sphere of influence
can be quantified by drawing a series of the break-points or a continuous line to
form the catchment area boundary (*see* Figure 11.3).

5. The trading area

The trading area is the area of the market drawn upon by the individual shop or
small store. Most of the main influences on catchment area size would apply to
the individual trading area, tempered by the localized factors affecting the site,
such as:

(a) Relationship of the site to the main shopping centre and thus to the catchment area.

(b) Accessibility of the site.

(c) Strength of business interception, e.g. it is strong if the site is on a pedestrian
walkway.

(d) Cumulative attraction (amount of pull the centre has as a whole).

(e) Compatibility (amount of associated business from sympathetic trades).

(f) Competition, depending on:

(*i*)   location
(*ii*) size and type
(*iii*) character and strength.

(g) Inherent factors in the shop itself, including ability to carve out, retain and build up a viable share of available trade.

6. Sources of information

The retailer can gather much useful site and location data from the following sources: local authorities, estate agents, the press and other published data.

7. Local authorities

The local government organization in each area will provide information through various departments.

(a) **Planning department**. Structure plans and written statements describe the present and future shopping environment, backed by maps of relevant areas.

(b) **Electoral office**. Electoral rolls, which are detailed lists, show numbers and names of voters at each address in a town or city. Ward and parish maps help a researcher to make an up-to-date head count for very small geographical areas. These figures may be grossed up to include under-18-year-olds by use of local data on the average number of persons per household.

(c) **Rating office**. Valuation registers show addresses and rateable values of all commercial properties, including shops, in an authority area. Sometimes the type of trade is included. Rateable value is a reasonable guide both to the general prosperity of the area and to that of individual shops. Some researchers have found a correlation between it and retail turnover.

(d) **Clerk's office**. The administrative office in each authority may be able to furnish street plans and other useful textual and statistical information (including council minutes) for the retailer.

(e) **Other official sources**. The local building inspectorate and the library may be able to give further information.

8. Estate agents

Commercial property agents not only put vendors and potential buyers in touch with each other but can often supply local 'key' plans and research information.

9. Press

Both the local and national press can be of assistance.

(a) **Local newspapers**. These are often first with news of shopping redevelopment and they also carry advertisements for properties for sale or to let.

(b) **National property journals.** The *Estates Gazette* and *Property Week* carry news of developments primarily for multiple traders who are particularly interested in the display and semi-display advertising for shop properties in important centres.

10. Other published data

Much information with emphasis on local and national shopping conditions has been published.

(a) **Census of Population.** This decennial count of persons in Great Britain and Northern Ireland gives much valuable demographic information including ward populations, ethnic origins, place of work and socio-economic groups.

(b) **Registrar General's estimates.** Published annually, these show up-to-date estimates of population in the local government areas.

(c) **Family Expenditure Surveys.** Published annually, these give the expenditure per family on a wide range of foods, consumer durables, semi-durables and services.

(d) **Shopping Centre and Retail Directory.** This lists retail ownership and various trade categories.

(e) **Commercial sources.** Many companies supply specialized information of interest to retailers. For example, CACI pioneered the use of demographic data for consumer targeting. Other companies providing specialized services to retailers are Experian, Verdict Research, AC Nielsen and many more.

11. Information required

Five main factors are of importance, namely existing shopping provision, local geography, make-up of local population, economic background and transportation.

(a) **Existing shopping provision.** This includes:

(*i*) shops that are in direct competition to the particular trade under study, with their addresses, estimated turnover and the class of the trade (e.g. 'up-market' merchandise) all marked on a street plan

(*ii*) department, variety stores and major multiples that all help the area's attractive power

(*iii*) general notes on the apparent prosperity and atmosphere of the shopping 'centre' and surrounding area

(*iv*) numbers of pedestrians at various points marked in figures on the street plan (pedestrian counts)

(*v*) position of pedestrian crossings, traffic lights and crush barriers that should be marked on the town plan.

(b) **Geography.** This consists of :

(*i*) topography – whether any hills, rivers, etc. influence shopping flows

(*ii*) positions of motorways and other arterial roads, factories, offices and housing areas; they should be marked on the map, along with locations of competing shopping centres.

(c) **Population figures.** These are broken down by:

(*i*) age groups – large numbers of young or old people, for example, may put different demands on the shopping system

(*ii*) socio-economic groups – showing numbers in each type of occupational group, giving a clue to spending power

(*iii*) ethnic groups – where there are concentrations of ethnic groups this shows possible requirements for different types of food and other merchandise

(*iv*) employment groups

(*v*) changes in population totals and density over the past ten years.

(d) **Economic background.** This comprises:

(*i*) numbers of customers per retail establishment and numbers per trade, locally, regionally and nationally

(*ii*) average turnover per shop in the trade under study, locally, regionally and nationally

(*iii*) retail expenditure per head, per trade, regionally and nationally; this can be calculated from the Family Expenditure Survey

(*iv*) daily newspaper circulation area and readership, and other local media data.

(e) **Transport facilities**

(*i*) *Private.* Position and size of present and future car parking layout in the study area, with the convenience of road systems taken into account (e.g. traffic management/pedestrianization schemes), and local car ownership per household.

(*ii*) *Public.* Lines of bus routes (marked on maps), bus stops, service frequencies, fares and any changes of route.

Determining the sales potential of different catchment/trading areas

12. Quantifying the total market value

The steps to be taken are as follows.

(a) Assess the number of households or the total population within the area (*see* the Census of Population).

(b) Gross up the population by an expenditure factor appropriate for the trade or trades under consideration (*see* the Family Expenditure Survey). The population expenditure factor = estimated total sales of goods and services under study.

(c) Adjust for inflation.

(d) Adjust for segmentation variable (e.g. age group, sex, etc.).

13. Index of saturation

As well as the value of the market in a given area, the degree to which that market is already served will be a major factor in determining the potential for a new store. The index of saturation is a way of comparing opportunities in different areas in terms of market value and competitor activity.

$$\text{Index of saturation} = \frac{\text{(Customers in area) (Expenditure per customer)}}{\text{Retail selling space allocated to product or product group}}$$

14. Growth

Another important factor determining the potential of an area is the extent to which growth is occurring. For example, the building of new housing estates, etc.

Choosing the area that would fit best

15. Objectives

Having assessed a variety of catchment areas it is important to choose an area that best provides those characteristics desired by the retailer. For example, Asda has put much effort into developing stores in the South of England. They were originally strong in the North but the South was identified as the area for growth because of its relative lack of superstores.

Choosing a specific site: types of site

16. City centres

Such centres in the middle of major towns offer a full range of retail outlets to the shopper, from convenience shops through durable shops to shops of a high degree of specialization in some of the most important centres. Department stores are also found in this type of shopping complex. These centres are often visited weekly by families by bus or by car. Increasing use of cars has created severe problems of congestion in these centres. These problems are being tackled in four main ways as follows, by:

(a) The provision of adequate public transport and the incentive to use it.

(b) Building adequate car parks and access roads.

(c) Pedestrianization (excluding cars altogether from the main shopping centre).

(d) Restricting the development of a town centre and concentrating on the provision of other types of shopping (e.g. in suburban centres).

These approaches are not mutually exclusive and in particular **(a)** and **(c)** may form complementary approaches in a given situation.

City centre locations offer a variety of environments from the 'planned shopping centres' which offer climatically controlled, traffic-free shopping, to the high street locations with lower rents but problems of traffic congestion and exposure to the elements.

These centres will usually serve a population in excess of 250,000.

17. District centres

This type of centre is found in the suburbs of large cities. It is also known as a secondary shopping centre, while the type discussed in **16** is known as a main or primary centre. The population served might be 50,000–60,000 but could be as low as 10,000.

Successful district centres demonstrate the following attributes:

(a) A complete range of convenience goods and a choice of stores for all these goods.

(b) A proportion of the more popular comparison goods shops and service outlets.

(c) Sufficient support population to ensure a high level of prosperity and efficiency.

(d) Easier and quicker accessibility to the district centre from every part of the catchment area than to any competing centre.

18. Neighbourhood centres

These centres are small clusters of 2–20 shops and are found in suburbs as complements to the district and town centres. They are normally very integrated with their markets and have support populations of 2,000–3,000 up to 10,000. As a result they are very biased towards convenience shopping and depend more on 'walk-in' trade than on car-borne shoppers. Shops in such centres are often used for 'topping-up' purchases (i.e. shopping trips made between main trips).

19. Corner shops

These are found in abundance in most urban areas of the UK and date back to a period of low personal mobility and long working hours. Today many of them have become general shops and their attributes are those of the independently owned shop (*see* Chapter 2: 2–5). Urban renewal has drastically reduced their numbers but they now appear to have stabilized and are often quite successful when converted to convenience retailing with longer opening hours.

20. Factors altering shopping provision

Newer, better organized edge-of-town or out-of-town centres have taken more and more trade away from corner shops and older town centre shopping centres. The factors involved are:

(a) **Changing customer requirements**. This is due to a shorter working week, larger real disposable incomes and higher car ownership and usage, which has made out-of-town shopping far more accessible and attractive.

(b) **Redistribution of population**. The demolition of inner-city areas has caused the population to move outwards to the suburbs.

(c) **Redevelopment of town centres**.

(d) **Demolition due to road construction or slum clearance**. Road and urban renewal plans have often 'blighted' shopping centres, i.e. have caused a 'no hoper' attitude on the part of shopkeepers and shoppers alike, driving both away from the doomed centre.

(e) **New roads**. Fast, new dual carriageway ring-roads have often cut off housing from their traditional shopping centres and made it easier for shoppers to gain access to the out-of-town centres.

21. Off-centre stores

Some discount operators have taken warehouses and old industrial buildings on the periphery of town centres. These are low-cost locations and the benefits are being passed on to consumers in the form of lower prices. Some local authorities are still wary of such practices, however.

22. Free-standing superstores

Hypermarkets and superstores are still being built in the UK on sites that are on the edges of urban areas. A great deal of antagonism from local authorities is still seen towards this type of development due primarily to problems caused by increased traffic and also the loss of green-belt land. However, they are generally successful and thus the large multiples have poured money into their development. From a base of 400 in 1986 the number of superstores has now increased to over 1,200. Superstore operators like Tesco have highlighted two points that should be particularly considered in connection with this type of retail development:

(a) Very large retail units can, through economies of scale, pass on the benefits to the customer in the form of lower prices.

(b) Superstores should be considered on at least a county planning basis and not just with regard to localized factors.

23. Out-of-town shopping centres

Innovated in the USA, the first out-of-town shopping centre was the Country Club Plaza, Kansas, which was opened in 1923. The Metrocentre (Gateshead) opened in 1986, and Meadowhall (Sheffield), Merry Hill (Dudley) and Lakeside (Thurrock) are other successful British examples.

The main reasons for the development of out-of-town shopping centres are:

(a) Increasing suburban populations.

(b) Increasing real income.

(c) Central area decay due to:

(*i*) movement of affluent consumers to the suburbs, leaving the less-well-off consumers in the inner city areas

(*ii*) the tendency of retailers to follow purchasing power

(*iii*) the inability of successive governments to cope either politically or financially with the problems

(*iv*) the decline of public transport.

(d) High level of car ownership.

(e) Traffic congestion in towns and cities.

The arguments against out-of-town shopping centres, particularly the large regional ones, are:

(a) The green belt or rural areas should be preserved at all costs.

(b) Diversion of trade out of the towns could imperil urban renewal programmes and might seriously damage trade in smaller towns. (Local authorities, which often have a reasonable representation of small shopkeepers on their councils, sometimes plead that their rate revenues would fall.)

Arguments for out-of-town shopping centres are:

(a) The green-belt argument is said by some to be somewhat spurious because the belt has often already been harmed by unplanned infilling and a variety of sub-industrial uses.

(b) Out-of-town centres cater specifically for those shoppers with cars who do not wish to shop in town centres because of the problems of congestion. Any restriction on out-of-town development goes against market forces which may result in the creation of more unplanned and less socially desirable features.

24. Retail parks

Another type of out-of-town shopping centre is the retail park. This is often a grouping of 'big shed' type operators such as DIY, furniture and electrical superstores out of the town centre, often on the edge of town and usually operating on discount principles.

The specific site

25. Factors in choosing a specific site

Factors that must be taken into account in choosing a specific site are:

(a) **Suitability.** Whether the site or building is physically suitable for the purpose. It may be too big, oddly shaped, lack rear-loading facilities, require extensive rebuilding or refitting and so on. Accessibility and parking facilities should also be considered.

(b) Rent or purchase price. High costs may make a unit quite uneconomic for certain trades or certain levels of turnover (*see* **29–31**).

(c) Compatibility. Whether flanking and nearby stores will help or hinder sales. Trade can be classified as:

(*i*) generative – attracting business direct from shoppers' homes
(*ii*) shared – with other shops in an associated selling situation
(*iii*) suscipient – impulse attractions on trips incidental to shopping purposes, e.g. as in shops in airport terminals.

(d) Interception. Whether the store is on a popular pedestrian route from car parks, bus stations, etc. to the shopping centre itself.

(e) Competition. Heavy competition nearby in certain retail sectors can be harmful, in others quite beneficial.

(f) Planned acquisition. Whether the site or the general area has been identified specifically by the growing company in its development plan.

26. Site research

In order to check out further the viability of a specific site the following considerations should be taken into account:

(a) Pedestrian and vehicular flow counts in the vicinity of the site for comparing with figures from apparently similar locations.

(b) Position of 'magnets' like department stores, pedestrian interruptors (vacant stores, non-retail uses) and all other influences on pedestrian flows not previously covered.

27. Estimating the turnover of a new retail unit

The most frequently used method of estimating sales of a new, enlarged or refurbished retail unit is to use the 'share of market' method.

Here an appropriate percentage of total catchment expenditure is assumed to be the potential. The percentage market share selected could be one attained at an existing store of similar size, site and location, dependent on approximately the same size and quality of the catchment area.

Competitor shares would be assessed with reference to:

(a) Size of net sales areas.

(b) Number of assistants.

(c) Number of checkouts/cash points.

(d) Range of goods.

(e) Pricing and promotional facilities.

This method is also known as the 'analogue' method when comparison is made with stores that have essential features in common with the proposed store.

Profit appraisal

28. Gross profitability

We have seen how turnover for a particular site can be forecast. But the retailer also needs to know what sort of return on the investment it is likely to receive. The first step in this is to estimate the gross profit (net sales minus cost of goods sold) likely to flow from the new outlet. This can be worked out by examining the following factors:

(a) **The product mix**. Although many multiple retailers try to achieve a standard product mix in each of their branches by taking prime locations in towns of a minimum size, the volume sales from each section or department in various branches may differ from one town to the next. This may be due to a variety of things such as the age and socio-economic groupings of families in the town, local ethnic or regional factors, which may affect tastes and therefore consumption patterns, the strength of local competition from other shops and shopping centres and so on.

(b) **Gross margins**. In order to estimate an average gross margin for a store, not only does the product mix have to be estimated (often this is done by comparison with other similar stores in comparable locations), but the average gross margin per section (if not per line) must be worked out.

Example

A small newsagent and stationery shop has a current turnover of £300,000 per annum; the gross profit contributions from each of seven main sections might look as shown in Table 11.1.

Table 11.1 Gross profit contributions for the sections of a newsagent's shop

Section	Product mix (% of total sales)	Annual sales (£)	Gross margin (%)	Gross profit (£)
News/magazines	20	60,000	33⅓	20,000
Paperbacks	15	45,000	33⅓	15,000
Stationery	25	75,000	30	22,500
Greeting cards	10	30,000	40	12,000
Toys	10	30,000	35	10,500
Confectionery	10	30,000	27	8,100
Tobacco	10	30,000	10	3,000
	100	300,000		91,100

Example continued

The average gross margin for the shop is

$$\frac{91,100}{300,000} \times 100 = 30.4 \text{ per cent}$$

Assuming a combined mark-down and shrinkage loss of 3 per cent of turnover, the gross profit is reduced by £9,000 to give a realized gross margin of 27.4 per cent.

29. Capital costs

The capital cost of a new outlet must also be worked out with reference to:

(a) Freehold or leasehold purchase.

(b) Building costs, if any.

(c) Fitting-out costs.

For example, assuming that there were no building works but shopfitting cost £25,000, total capital outlay including legal fees, estate agent's fees, initial stock and working capital could easily reach £100,000.

30. Operating expenses and net profit

The running costs of the unit must be taken into account in order to work out the net profitability of the operation. These costs come under headings such as:

(a) Wages and salaries.

(b) Rent and rates.

(c) Other accommodation costs (including heating, lighting and telephone).

(d) Other expenses including depreciation.

The following is a cost breakdown for the store under consideration (with annual sales of £300,000), at the same time summarizing the information so far:

	£	£
Gross profit	91,100	
Less: Mark-down, shrinkages etc.	9,000	
		82,100
Wages and salaries	33,000	
Rent and rates	21,000	
Other accommodation costs	7,500	
Other expenses	9,000	
		70,500
Net profit		11,600

The net profit after all expenses have been paid is £11,600, showing a net margin on sales of 3.9 per cent. Taking the capital outlay of £100,000 this net profit gives a return on capital employed (ROCE) of 11.6 per cent. Whether this figure is an attractive return or not will largely depend on the prevailing interest rates at the time. For example, would the £100,000 produce a similar or better return in a deposit account with a bank or building society?

31. Forecasting for the future

While it is very important to estimate sales and profitability for the first year of an outlet's operation, estimates must be made for the future so that these can be incorporated in the company's total budget projections. It is notoriously difficult to forecast, but it is usual to produce figures for a five-year planning period. A future cash flow estimate can thus be made to produce a long-term return on capital figure, using discounted cash flow techniques. These estimates are often made on the basis of 'today's' prices and therefore do not take inflation into account.

It is useful to illustrate the planned progress of an investment project by constructing a break-even chart. Figure 11.4 shows the projected sales over a given period of time, with costs broken down into the fixed element (e.g. rent), variable costs (e.g. wages) and showing the difference between total costs and sales revenue. The resultant earnings should progress from a loss situation through a break-even point to a steadily increasing net profit.

Figure 11.4 Retail branch break-even chart

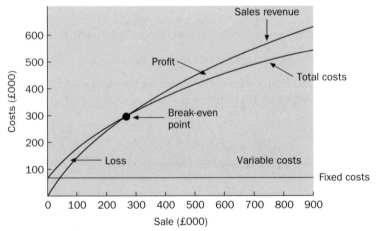

Progress test 11

1. What is the major determinant of the ideal store location?

2. Describe the three steps in determining the general area in which to locate.

3. What are the main influences on catchment area size and shape?

4. How can the sales potential of different catchment areas be determined?

5. Describe three types of shopping centres.

6. List the factors to be taken into account when choosing a specific site.

7. How can the turnover and profitability of a new retail outlet be estimated?

8. What is a break-even chart? Why is it useful?

9. 'The three keys to success in retailing are location, location and location.' What did the writer mean? Discuss the merits of the location of a local retail store in relation to its target market.

10. Discuss the merits of, and problems with, using price, merchandise or promotion to compensate for poor location.

12 Product decisions

Introduction

The most important element of the retail mix according to most retailers is the product. This is what customers require, why they visit a retailer and what generates profit. This chapter explores a number of aspects of product decisions, including ranging policy, own branding, turnover philosophy and sales forecasting.

Merchandise

1. What is a product?

A product is anything that can be offered to a market that might satisfy a need or a want. Therefore, our definition includes not only physical objects, such as washing machines and toothpaste, but also services, for example a haircut, a cleaning service, insurance, etc.

2. Benefits

The retailer must ask: What products should I offer? What benefits will these products offer my customers? Do these benefits match the requirements of the customer?

3. Terminology

Retailing has developed its own terminology and thus it is more usual to speak of merchandise rather than product, and of a merchandise philosophy as embracing such elements as variety, price/quality, branding and stock turnover. Similarly, the term 'merchandising' is often used in retailing but is a rather ill-defined term. To some it is simply the display of merchandise, while to others it is much broader. The most quoted definition of merchandising, attributed to Gordon Selfridge, is to have the 'right goods at the right time, in the right place, in the right quantity, at the right price'. Many readers will recognize this definition as also being one definition of marketing.

4. The aspects of merchandising

To most retailers the merchandising process covers the selection, purchase, stock-management and display of a range of products, the successful sale of which will achieve the marketing objectives of the business in terms of the so-called six 'rights' of merchandising, namely: type, quantity, price, quality, time and place. Broadly, then, merchandising relates to the problems concerned with maximizing sales and profits of products and services.

5. Types of merchandise

The type of merchandise offered by a retailer is probably the major determinant of the business the retailer is in, and the variety of merchandise will have a major impact on how the customer perceives the store. Thus a retailer may adopt a specialized merchandise policy and carry only a few related product lines (e.g. a shoeshop), or the retailer may choose a scrambled merchandise policy and offer a wide range of product lines (e.g. Asda).

6. Polarization

Retail polarization has occurred over the last few years with more stores pursuing each of the above policies and resulting in one-stop shopping on the one hand and highly specialized stores such as Tie Rack on the other.

7. Quantity of merchandise

Obviously the amount of merchandise ordered at any particular time must be related to the demand for it. Seasonal factors will thus be very important, along with whether the item is a 'staple' or a fashion good, and an eye must also be kept on the line's own stockturn related to the overall stockturn. Some multiple chains still order only a few hundred of a particular line and distribute two or three to each branch 'to see how it goes'. This often results in very fast sales in some branches and nil sales in others, making costly stock transfers or mark-downs necessary. Successful chains like Marks & Spencer use, say, 20 'pilot' stores in busy locations for new lines and extend allocation to other stores if and when the merchandise is successful.

8. Pricing merchandise

Prices have not only to be appropriate to the market segment aimed for, but must also produce sufficient gross profit overall to pay all selling costs and leave an acceptable net margin. A much fuller discussion of pricing policy is contained in Chapter 15.

9. Merchandise quality

Again, quality of merchandise (of which price is very much a function) must be related to the target market. The Harrods' merchandise mix could well be unrepeatable in any other location, while a cut-price food retailer would not necessarily flourish in a high-class suburban area.

10. Timing

The timing of the arrival of merchandise is largely related to seasonal factors. There is no use, for example, in a pharmacy receiving a supply of sunglasses in October!

11. Placing of merchandise

The concept of 'place' has two aspects in merchandise theory. First, the correct branches of a chain should be fed with the appropriate goods. Most multiples, for instance, grade their stores into five or six sizes which determines the merchandise ranges they are able to carry in normal circumstances. One retail chain sent a supply of paper panties to the Highlands of Scotland one autumn and, not surprisingly, the stock was all returned unsold some months later. Secondly, the location of the stock within a store is often crucial (*see* Chapter 19).

12. Ranging policy

The mix of merchandise required can be looked at in two ways:

(a) **Depth**. A 'deep' stock assortment describes a comprehensive selection of brands, sizes, styles, colours and prices within a particular generic class of product, e.g. specialist shops such as Just Jeans concentrate on providing a deep assortment within narrow merchandise variety. In-depth stocking leads to lower stockturns, compensated for by higher margins.

(b) **Breadth**. A 'broad' or wide stock variety describes a wide selection of different generic classes of product but with little choice in brands, styles, etc. within an individual line, e.g. an audio shop may begin stocking a few 'white' goods (refrigerators, washing machines, etc.) in order to broaden variety and increase sales. Stockturn may well be higher from a broad merchandise variety, but margins could be slimmer. Most retailers find it necessary to compromise in their ranging policy by optimizing both the 'depth' (assortment) and 'breadth' (variety) factors in order to maximize their profitability.

13. New products

Existing lines of merchandise may be selected on an ongoing basis. New lines are appraised by their:

(a) Appropriateness and compatibility with other existing lines and ranges.

(b) Growth potential (bearing in mind the life cycles of products).

(c) Availability and competitive conditions (including exclusivity).

(d) Profitability (including a monitoring of current sales trends of similar lines presently carried and their gross profitability).

14. Range rationalization

The objective of any progressive retailer should be to keep as far as possible an optimum range of product lines for sale. Points to note in this connection are:

(a) The Pareto rule is a mathematical calculation that shows that, for instance, roughly 20 per cent of the lines carried by a retailer account for about 80 per cent of the sales and/or gross profit. This is important for display purposes, but the slower-moving lines must be carried in order to offer a comprehensive range that will attract shoppers, by allowing choice and facilitating comparisons.

(b) As new lines are introduced there should necessarily be a parallel policy to reduce the numbers of old, less profitable lines.

(c) When slow-moving lines are cut out, more space is available for extending better-selling products (true not only of shelf space but stockroom area as well, which all helps to reduce costs).

(d) Not only can lines be pruned, but suppliers, too.

Own branding

15. Types of own branding

Own branding occurs when products are sold under a retail organization's house brand name and are sold exclusively through the retail organization's outlets. There are two basic types of own branding (or own labelling) which are as follows:

(a) **Integrated**. Here the retailer is integrated with its own manufacturing capability, e.g. in menswear or audio products, and the retailer has a greater control over quality, delivery, etc.

(b) **Independent contracting**. Here the retailer contracts a manufacturer to supply products labelled with the name of the retail company. This situation is particularly relevant in food products where companies manufacture to specification very large ranges for the major food retailers.

16. Significance of own branding

The market share of grocery own brands in the UK is now over 40 per cent. Most UK multiples regard 30–40 per cent of sales under their own name as about right, although Sainsbury's has carried it much further and Marks & Spencer is almost totally committed to a premium-priced own-brand policy. (Generic brands – the so-called 'own brands to the own brands' – are low-priced products in basic packs aimed at low income households. Tesco and other grocery supermarkets carry them.)

17. Advantages of own branding

(a) **To the manufacturer**. Overheads are more easily covered when production of regular brands has fallen off because of seasonal factors. Own-brand production can be slotted in to fit in with production schedules.

(b) **To the retailer**

- (*i*) Purchase prices can be significantly lower and therefore either margins can be increased or lower prices can be passed on to the consumer to stimulate sales.
- (*ii*) It allows the offer of a better price choice.
- (*iii*) It may allow better space utilization either through the rationalization of minor manufacturers' brands or by producing an improved stockturn.
- (*iv*) It allows better control over price, delivery and quality.
- (*v*) The retailer's own corporate identity can be strongly reinforced by a broad-ranging and aggressive own-brand strategy.

18. Disadvantages of own branding

(a) The strength of manufacturers' brands may be so strong through heavy advertising that the own brand may not be able to establish its own consumer appeal through its lower price.

(b) Carrying an extra line in a range may increase stock investment and, without minor brand rationalization, it could actually lower the stockturn. (For the electrical appliance retailer this could mean the extra problems of spares and service and for all retailers it could mean extra paperwork.)

(c) Minimum order sizes may be prohibitive for the smaller retailers.

(d) The success of own brands may squeeze out the smaller specialist brand, thus reducing consumer choice.

(e) The pressure on margins due to the price competition from own brands may force manufacturers to reduce investment in research and development and thus lead to fewer new products coming to the market.

Stock turnover/gross margins

19. Definition

Stock turnover is defined as sales in a given period divided by the average stock, and thus is a measure of how fast merchandise is sold and replaced (*see* Table 12.1). For instance, if sales in a particular period were £200,000 and average stock held was £25,000, the stockturn would be 8, i.e. 200,000/25,000.

The calculation may be done in cash terms or unit terms, i.e.

$$\frac{\text{Unit sales}}{\text{Average unit stock}}$$

Table 12.1 Average stockturns for various retail sectors

Trade	Average number of times stock is turned per annum
Food retailers	
Large grocers	18
Dairies	69
Butchers, poulterers	61
Fishmongers	140
Clothing and footwear retailers	
Footwear	4
Mens' and boyswear	5
Women's and girlswear	6
Durable goods retailers	
Furniture	4
Radio and electrical	6
DIY	6
Other kinds of retailers	
Bookshops	5
Chemists	8
Jewellery	2
Confectioners/tobacconists/newsagents (CTNs)	12

20. Methods of averaging stock

Stock levels can vary enormously from one month to another so it may be very important to average out stock. There are three methods of getting to a figure that will, when divided into sales, give a reasonably accurate stockturn figure. These are:

(a) The average opening stock and closing stock over a particular trading period, e.g. if opening stock was £17,000 and closing stock £23,000, average stock would be £20,000.

(b) The addition of opening, middle-period and closing stock divided by three.

(c) Stock at the first of each month divided by 13 if the year is broken down into four-weekly periods.

21. Turnover philosophy

The retail organization may adopt a high-volume, low-price merchandise philosophy which yields low margins but results in high stock turnover. The major multiple grocers work along these lines. Alternatively, a decision may be made to offer exclusive merchandise which would result in high prices, low volume and high margins but low stock turnover. The speciality delicatessen stores would be in this latter category.

22. Advantages of rapid stockturn

(a) It increases sales due to the rapid flow of new merchandise.

(b) It increases the return on the merchandise investment and allows the cash released to be invested, if required, in further stock. Some food retailing companies sell a great deal of stock within a few days of its receipt; if they take 30 days' credit from suppliers this means that they are getting further stock investment 'free', i.e. it is being financed by their suppliers and this investment situation is known as 'nil capital'.

(c) It reduces expenses like:

(*i*) depreciation
(*ii*) interest on working capital
(*iii*) insurance
(*iv*) space.

(d) It reduces the possibility of mark-downs.

(e) It reduces the incidence of returns out.

(f) It keeps stock clean and fresh and therefore more attractive to customers.

23. Limitations of rapid stockturn

(a) Possibility of lost sales due to out-of-stock position, particularly in fast-moving lines.

(b) Increased cost of purchases particularly in:

(*i*) carriage inwards
(*ii*) discounts receivable (which are effectively deducted from cost of sales) because possibly smaller average purchases are being made.

(c) Increase in certain expenses such as:

(*i*) correspondence
(*ii*) goods handling
(*iii*) clerical.

24. Methods of increasing stockturn

(a) The increase of sales without increasing average stock assortment proportionately.

(b) The decrease of stocks without interfering with sales.

(c) The increase of sales and at the same time reducing stock.

The need is to keep the inventory low in order to reduce stock-holding costs and increase the return on capital tied up in stock by:

(a) The reduction in the number of lines carried.

(b) A concentration on key stock items, e.g. the most popular.

(c) A reduction in size or colour assortments to meet only the most popular demands.

Sales forecasting

The sales forecast is an essential part of the planning process. Management requires an idea of the scale of the operation and predicted market developments in order to estimate the resources needed to capitalize on the opportunities presented and whether these resources will be available from profit.

25. The method

One method of producing a sales forecast is as follows:

(a) Construct a graph of sales for the corresponding periods over the last three to five years.

(b) Use a suitable statistical technique to establish a trend line.

(c) The basic assumption is that the trend will continue and a first approximation to the new season's or annual total is arrived at by extrapolation.

(d) An estimate is made of the extent to which external factors, i.e. those over which the firm has no control, are likely to affect the initial forecast in step (c). External factors include:

    (*i*)   government intervention, e.g. tax, interest rates, etc.
    (*ii*) changes in economic conditions, e.g. structural changes in demand which bring about factory closures or lay-offs and 'dumping' of cheap foreign imports
    (*iii*) changes in competition, e.g. opening, extension or closure of competitors' branches within various catchment areas or important competitive national sales promotions.

(e) Internal factors are those over which the business has control; they are now carefully considered and the forecast further modified in the light of a detailed evaluation of their profitable effect. These include:

    (*i*)   changes in promotional support
    (*ii*) changes in staffing or in selling methods
    (*iii*) refitting or redecorating
    (*iv*) any changes in the policy of the firm towards the expansion or restriction of sales not expressed in terms of (*i*) to (*iii*) above.

It is clear that the effect of internal factors can be much more accurately estimated than that of the external factors in step **(d)**.

(f) The result is now a total figure for the store, possibly broken down by areas, reached from the best information available.

(g) Total the sales of each month over the comparative period, e.g. all April figures, all May and so on.

(h) Express monthly sales total **(g)** as a percentage of the grand total of all the three years or so studied. This will give the percentage of each year's sales for which each month is normally responsible. (It may be necessary to make some allowances for inflation over a three-year period.)

(i) Apply the monthly percentages thus calculated to the forecast for the total for the year to give the monthly estimates.

26. Sales adjustment

Sales estimates are treated as budgets and revised often at monthly or fortnightly intervals as the year and its component seasons progress. Any major revision will have important effects on the merchandise plan, affecting both the level of stock to be carried and the allocation of purchasing power.

Progress test 12

1. What is a product?

2. What is merchandising? What are the main aspects of the merchandising process?

3. Define 'depth' and 'breadth' in the merchandise mix and give examples of retailers operating each of these ranging policies.

4. What is the significance of the Pareto rule in relation to ranging policy?

5. What are the advantages and disadvantages of offering own brands?

6. What is the significance of stockturn and how can it be increased?

7. How can sales be forecast? Is it necessary to adjust these throughout the year – why?

8. 'Goods well bought are goods well sold' is an old retailing adage. Compare and contrast the alternative merchandise ranging policies for retailers of sports goods.

9. Explain the importance of width, depth and consistency of merchandise mix to merchandise strategy decisions.

13 Buying

Introduction

Buying is the process of implementing the decisions dictated by the merchandise philosophy (*see* Chapter 12: **3**). This chapter explores the five major areas of buying: who buys; what to buy; how much to buy; from whom to buy; and when to buy.

1. The importance of buying

The vital significance of good merchandise buying in the retail context cannot be overstated. Stock is one of the largest forms of investment made by the retailer. Good stock selection is important because it:

(a) Ties up the optimum amount of capital.

(b) Reduces the amount of space taken up by stock.

(c) Provides an adequate choice for the customer.

(d) Enhances the image of the business and encourages repeat purchases.

(e) Increases the overall profitability of the business.

Who buys?

2. One individual or specialists

The buyer may be responsible for the purchase of a comparatively small range of merchandise or for several complete departments, depending on the size and type of the retail organization. The advantage of having one individual responsible for buying for the entire store is that consistency within the merchandise mix will be maximized. However, buying for larger stores will usually require specialists in order to do the job properly. By using specialist buyers' greater knowledge, control of merchandise can be developed and maintained.

3. Attributes of the buyer

A successful buyer should be able to:

(a) Recognize customer needs, even though customers themselves may be unaware of them.

(b) Know thoroughly the merchandise they deal with, keeping a balanced stock assortment.

(c) Be a good judge of quality.

(d) Be a good judge of resaleability.

(e) Be up to date in their knowledge so that they can pick up ideas for new and profitable lines quickly ('flair' is required particularly in textiles, toys and other fashion goods).

(f) Liaise effectively with suppliers, store management and other sections of the merchandising and marketing departments, e.g. advertising, sales promotion.

(g) Plan effectively in numerate terms.

4. Types of buying organization

Because of the way they are structured to service their chosen markets, different types of retail organization have developed their own modes of buying.

(a) **Department stores**. In the department store the buying and selling functions are often merged. A buyer/manager will not only control the sales operation in their chosen department but will buy stock for it as well. However, in some department store groups the responsibilities of buying and selling are divided between a central buyer and departmental (sales) managers.

(b) **Multiples**. The multiple chain invariably buys centrally with only rarely the branch manager being able to select lines for the local market.

(c) **Buying groups**. Buying groups provide competitive advantage by banding together dozens of individual retailers, giving them enough clout with suppliers to negotiate the same low prices as a large chain. For the independent retailer in today's highly competitive market, belonging to a buying group is almost essential for survival. Some groups handle collective billing but allow retailers to purchase and receive merchandise directly from suppliers. Others maintain their own warehouses and distribution channels. Whatever their arrangement, their purpose is the same: to reduce wholesale costs for small retailers, allowing them to increase profit margins and offer lower retail prices.

Price is not the only benefit that buying groups can provide for independent retailers. Most groups offer a range of other benefits as well, such as group advertising, industry updates, buying shows, market research and customer-loyalty promotions. Often, they enable small stores to purchase products that would not be available to them otherwise because of high minimum orders from manufacturers.

5. Separating the buying and selling functions

Most large multiple groups have set up quite separate buying and selling organizations, but partly through historical accident some department store groups still rely on departmental buyer/managers who carry out both functions. The advantages and disadvantages of separating these two functions are:

(a) Advantages

(i) The duties of buying and selling call for different qualities not always found in one manager.

(ii) A manager cannot effectively carry out both functions and delegation is not always the answer.

(iii) The buyer who is released from routine can travel further, study the market and sources of supply, visit trade fairs, etc.

(iv) Selling departments need no longer necessarily conform to arbitrary divisions of merchandise as purchased, but can develop and spread into related ranges. Range rationalization may be encouraged.

(v) Competent buyers are scarce and a buyer with no departmental duties can buy a wider range of merchandise to the benefit of store and customer.

(vi) Buyers can be centralized in buying offices where team work and liaison with the merchandise manager is helped.

(vii) Segregation of buyers eradicates the wasted time sometimes spent in protracted dealings with customers.

(b) Disadvantages

(i) It is difficult to ensure that the buyer will retain a really responsible attitude to the purchase of 'risk' merchandise.

(ii) Friction is likely to arise between the buyer and the sales manager, particularly where lines are unpopular or turnover declines.

(iii) To apportion responsibility, criticism or congratulation for results is difficult and may appear to be invidious.

(iv) The store may become too unwieldy in the proportion of managers to selling staff.

(v) Remoteness between buyer and sales staff can ensue, with first-hand customer reactions being irretrievably lost.

(vi) Valuable local purchasing arrangements may be overlooked by central buyers.

6. Central buying

(a) Advantages

(i) Better terms may be gained as a result of the very large orders placed with suppliers.

(ii) Central buyers are full-time specialists; they should therefore be able to place the best possible orders and obtain the best possible merchandise.

(*iii*) Because of increased buying efficiency there should be a greater proportion of fast-selling lines and stock should be turned over more quickly.

(*iv*) The central buyer is in continuous contact with the market and is in the
best position to purchase new lines quickly.

(*v*) Merchandise can be transferred from one store, where sales for a particular line are disappointing, to another where demand is heavier.

(*vi*) Under centralized buying there are no travelling costs incurred by buyers
from stores in going to visit suppliers.

(*vii*) Store selling can be organized by specialist department sales managers.

(b) Disadvantages

(*i*) There is some danger that local needs may be ignored, since merchandise
is bought in bulk for the group or chain as a whole. Although local differences
are small they do exist, for example in food and some fashion merchandise.

(*ii*) There are additional costs of warehousing and distribution as well as
maintaining the central buying office.

(*iii*) Sales staff may be unenthusiastic about selling merchandise that they
know is not quite what their particular customers need.

The buying plan

7. Importance of the plan

Any buying plan must be firmly based on the company's plans for the ensuing
period. Most buying plans are broken into monthly periods that accurately reflect
seasonal changes and are easily comparable with similar periods in previous years.
The plan must, however, be flexible enough to take into account the purchase of
new lines and any unforeseen changes which may occur in the trading pattern.
The major problems for the buyers are to know:

(a) What to buy.

(b) How much to buy.

(c) From whom to buy.

(d) When to buy.

What to buy

8. What to buy

For the buying of particular items the general guidelines are as follows:

(a) **Past experience**. With staple merchandise (non-fashion, long-term sellers)
the majority of sales will be made in the most successful lines of the recent past.
For merchandise with sales that change markedly with shifts in consumer taste,

e.g. fashion items, past experience is less useful. Buyers have to rely largely on their flair for knowing what customers will purchase. Buyers usually have to order in advance and, as fashions change very rapidly, they cannot always rely on fill-in orders, as by the time these are delivered the merchandise may be unfashionable. Too much stock means there is unsold merchandise at the end of the season, too little stock results in lost sales.

(b) **Current information**. A good deal of up-to-date information on customer demands can be gleaned from the normal accounting and control records of a retail business. The following methods are used:

(*i*)   EPOS data – electronic data captured at the point of sale provides extremely detailed information on sales by product, brand, size, etc.

(*ii*)   Store or loyalty cards, especially 'smart' cards.

(*iii*) Sales receipt duplicates.

(*iv*) 'Tallies' of sales, particularly of new lines.

(*v*)   Kimball (or other type) tags; these are punched tickets that are attached to goods (usually clothing) and give details of stock numbers, so that after swift processing a quick update of the stock position in a branch is possible.

(*vi*) 'Wants' slips (recorded customer requests for specific merchandise).

(*vii*) Customer complaints.

(c) **External sources of merchandise information**. These can be obtained from:

(*i*)   Organized comparison shopping of competitive stores (monitoring of in-store and window displays, plus their advertising).

(*ii*)   Suppliers.

(*iii*) Consumer research – retailers are becoming more and more involved in consumer surveys. These may be conducted at the store or in the home (*see* Chapter 7).

(*iv*) Trade fairs.

How much to buy

9. How much to buy

There are three approaches to the quantitative aspect of buying which, as previously stated, should rely on the sales forecast.

(a) **The open-to-buy approach**. This determines in cash the amount of purchases to make for a particular selling period. An authorized order becomes a commitment, and this reduces the available purchasing power (the open-to-buy or OTB) for the period for which it is timed. Continuous monitoring of current OTB and future commitments ensures that warning is given of overbought positions. This type of stock budgeting is called 'top-down' and forms an integral part of a company's financial stock control.

There are various ways to increase open-to-buy and these are as follows:

(*i*)   increase planned sales
(*ii*) increase planned mark-downs
(*iii*) reduce stock on hand by return or transfer
(*iv*) postpone outstanding orders to a later month
(*v*)   cancel outstanding orders
(*vi*) increase planned closing stock.

Example

Assuming that the trading year ends on 31 January, the sales forecast for the ensuing six months is £1.6 million, the required stockturn is eight times per annum and the anticipated gross margin is 25 per cent of selling price, the open-to-buy figures would be as in Table 13.1.

An average stock of £400,000 at selling value is planned to ensure a required stockturn rate of four in six months (4 × £400,000 = £1.6 million).

This table shows the total of estimated sales (£1.6 million) has been broken down into monthly targets so that the peak sales are planned for April and May and peak stocks are built up in March and April. The breakdown should be based on an examination of previous years' performances – the average contribution made by each month to the year's total. For example, total the February sales for the past five years and express it as a percentage of the five-year total. Then determine the contribution to be expected from February (in this case it is 10 per cent of the six months' forecast).

Table 13.1 Open-to-buy method

	Feb £000	Mar £000	Apr £000	May £000	June £000	July £000	Total £000
Sales forecast (at selling prices)	160	200	330	350	280	280	1,600
Planned closing stocks (at selling price)	400	600	500	450	300	250	
	560	800	830	800	580	530	
Deduct planned opening stock (at selling prices)	300	400	600	500	450	300	
	260	400	230	300	130	230	
Deduct average margin 25%	65	100	57.5	75	32.5	57.5	
Open-to-buy (at cost price)	195	300	172.5	225	97.5	172.5	

(b) **The assortment planning approach.** Here stock requirements are calculated on a unit rather than a cash basis. This system of calculating buying requirements is called 'bottom-up' because, unlike OTB, which deals with a blanket cash figure, assortment planning tries to build up the cash budget from the total value of all stock items budgeted for.

(c) **The sales-based ordering system.** Increasingly retailers are demanding shorter lead times and in the grocery sector in particular have developed sophisticated sales-based ordering systems. The sales-based ordering technique is used to control high turnover stock where the need for daily deliveries requires the use of sophisticated forecasting techniques. Based on the rate of sales (from point-of-sale data) as well as capacity, regression analysis is used to produce accurate forecasts of requirements. The systems are sufficiently flexible to be able to incorporate seasonality factors and promotions on individual lines.

10. Model stock plans

This aspect of stock planning is particularly important in clothing and fashion stores where customers naturally buy most in the middle sizes in the popular colours and in the medium price ranges. By careful sales monitoring it is possible to calculate what percentage of sales each size, colour or price is responsible for. Model stocking is a quantitative method of planning to buy that provides general guidelines on the size and composition of stock but does not specify the exact nature of the merchandise.

11. Bulk buying

Buying large amounts of stock has certain advantages for the larger retail store or chain able to afford it, but it also produces problems.

(a) **Advantages**

  (*i*)   Less possibility of run-outs at times of unexpectedly heavy demand.
  (*ii*) Minimum quantity discounts are possible, with higher discounts as the purchases become larger.
  (*iii*) Clerical work per unit ordered is reduced (i.e. it costs the same in clerical terms to buy one unit as it does to buy 1,000 units).

(b) **Disadvantages**

  (*i*)   Higher sales and stockturn are required to keep 'in balance'.
  (*ii*) Deterioration and pilferage may increase.
  (*iii*) Valuable storage space is tied up.
  (*iv*) Cash can be over-committed.
  (*v*)   Price mark-downs tend to occur with stock that is out of date.

From whom to buy

12. Types of supplier

(a) **Manufacturers and primary producers**. These will normally tend to be limited in the range of goods they produce and to vary considerably in the nature and extent of distributive services that they provide.

(b) **Wholesalers**. These carry stock at their own risk in either wide (general) or more limited (specialist) assortments. This category includes voluntary group wholesalers and cash-and-carry operators.

(c) **Importers**. These are usually linked in the range of merchandise carried and the extent of the services provided. They may specialize by type of goods wherever produced or by the products of a particular country or area.

(d) **Agents**. These intermediaries do not carry stock at their own risk. They include food brokers who look after the marketing of a manufacturer's or importer's products through grocery, chemist and CTN outlets. Some agents do not handle the goods at all and others may carry sample ranges but do not hold stock at their own risk. The range of merchandise carried and the services provided depend largely on their principals.

(e) **Other retailers**. The three main ways in which retailers act as sources of supply are:

  (*i*)   for 'specials'
  (*ii*) for finished goods that form part of a more complex product
  (*iii*) for bankrupt, damaged or discontinued stock.

(f) **Manufacturer-owned retail chains**. The problems of supply are somewhat reduced for companies like Thorntons confectionery because substantial percentages of the product ranges are self-supplied.

(g) **Government and semi-government sources**. A very broad spectrum of products comes from this source, examples being BBC and government publications, 'forces' surplus clothing, etc.

(h) **The public**. In merchandise fields such as antiques and second-hand items, the public remains an important source of supply.

In addition, sources of ideas for products can be obtained from exhibitions, trade journals, customers and so on.

13. Supplier selection

Existing suppliers may be retained because they have given particularly good service in the past, or because there is no identifiable competition. The factors taken into account when selecting a new supplier are:

(a) Prices – including extra trade discount for bulk purchases.

(b) Terms, e.g. length of credit, size of cash discount.

(c) Deliveries – fast and prompt delivery may be vital for retailers in high-volume sales situations.

(d) Service – general co-operation.

New suppliers may be found as a result of sales representatives' calls or from the supplier catalogues that are mailed to retail buyers. However, a good buyer should be actively seeking suppliers who can do a better job than current suppliers.

A list of suppliers should be available and kept fully up to date, showing lines supplied by each. Continuous comparison should be made between suppliers under the headings:

(a) Price comparisons, including discounts.

(b) Efficiency of delivery back-up.

(c) Level of service.

(d) Introduction of new lines.

This will aid the process of review of suppliers and lines, which should be a rolling process, so that strong suppliers may be rewarded with larger orders and weaker support discarded (unless sole sources of supply are involved).

When to buy

Merchandise should be purchased so that there will be sufficient in stock to meet consumer demand, bearing in mind seasonal factors and the need to keep down inventory levels to acceptable levels.

14. Ordering

Frequency and size of orders are matters influenced to a great extent by the type of merchandise concerned, i.e. whether staple or fashion merchandise. Important aspects of ordering are:

(a) **Price**. Although a buyer may be searching initially for the most competitive price available, any final price is likely to be affected by quantity discounts of various kinds.

(b) **Terms**. These largely involve discounts of two basic kinds:

  (i) *Trade discounts*. These are discounts allowed by suppliers from their catalogue price to trade customers only and may be quite substantial, perhaps 25 per cent. They provide a means whereby the retailer can cover costs and by which it can obtain a reasonable profit without too large an addition to suppliers' prices.
  (ii) *Cash discount*. Prompt payment for goods often ranks for a cash discount. Thirty to sixty days' credit is usual.

(c) **Deliveries**. It is important for a retail buyer to set and insist upon precise delivery dates. Where delivery is to be made in more than one consignment, the order should specify:

(*i*) the date on which the delivery is to commence
(*ii*) the date by which the delivery is to be complete
(*iii*) the proportions of the order that are to be delivered within stated intervals, e.g. 30 per cent in September, 40 per cent in October, 30 per cent in November, where necessary or desirable.

Other delivery instructions may include:

(*i*) method of shipment
(*ii*) address (for branch etc. deliveries)
(*iii*) agreed variations from standard carriage-paid terms
(*iv*) method of charging or returning containers.

15. Progressing the order

Once the details of price, terms and delivery have been agreed, the following factors are also important from the buyer's viewpoint:

(a) The order details should be written up as fully as possible immediately.

(b) If the order cannot be completely finalized on the spot it should be marked 'await confirmation', with the agreement of the supplier.

(c) It is good retail practice to require suppliers to acknowledge orders placed with them, especially those for forward delivery.

(d) Some form of follow-up should succeed this to see that delivery promises are being kept.

16. Buying control

The order, once authorized, is a commitment to buy. Commitments are either:

(a) Current, i.e. for delivery during the current period, or

(b) Future, i.e. for delivery in a subsequent period.

When a commitment is delivered and changed into stock it ceases to be a commitment and becomes a purchase. Open-to-buy (OTB) means the balance of stock between that already committed to or purchased and the budget for purchases for the period. Open-to-buy for the current period is therefore: planned purchases for the period, minus deliveries to date in the period, minus current commitments. For any future period it is: planned purchases for that period, minus future commitments for that period.

17. Buying adjustments

The adjusting of buying operations to the plan becomes automatic with the OTB system. As long as the OTB for any period is positive, the buyer may place orders for delivery in that period. When the purchase plan is fulfilled the OTB automatically cuts off. If deliveries are delayed, a check in the system should make allowances for the extra time that this will take.

18. The catalogue

Many retail firms have constructed a catalogue listing all the lines they purchase and from whom they are supplied. The catalogue can be used in the following ways:

(a) As an order form (for head office or for the individual branch).

(b) As a stocktaking list.

(c) For range control.

Progress test 13

1. Why is the buying function important?

2. What attributes does a successful buyer need?

3. What are the advantages and disadvantages of separating the buying and selling functions?

4. What are the advantages and disadvantages of central buying?

5. How does the buyer decide (*a*) what to buy, and (*b*) how much to buy?

6. Describe the open-to-buy method.

7. How does the buyer decide (*a*) from whom to buy, and (*b*) when to buy?

8. According to some retail analysts, it is essential for retailers to develop uniqueness in order to be successful. Many retailers have already established policies to achieve this aim. For example chain store boutiques and department stores rely on nationally promoted products to draw customers into their stores. Calvin Klein, Pierre Cardin, Yves Saint Laurent, and many other UK and European 'designer' products are sold at these stores. When designer labels were first introduced, they were found on distinctive products that offered the stores that carried them a competitive edge. Recently, however this edge has begun to evaporate because of the proliferation of outlets that sell designer labels at prices significantly lower than those of the larger stores.

   In the face of increased competition, how large a part should designer labels play in the merchandise mix of fashion-image speciality chains and department stores? (Assume the role of consultant.)

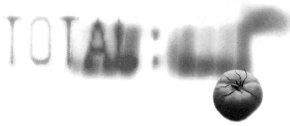

14 Stock management

Introduction

The purpose of a stock management system is to provide information on the amount of merchandise in stock and its condition. Specialized stock control software systems have significantly improved the retailer's ability to operate tighter and more rational stock control. This chapter considers systems of stock control, stock shortages and merchandise receipt and return.

Stock control

1. Aims

The importance of controlling merchandise has already been made clear. It involves the maintenance of a correct balance between the range carried and the sales to which it gives rise. The aim is to obtain as big a turnover as possible with the most economic inventory level. There is a clear indication that the rate of stockturn has a decisive effect on the net profitability of a retail business. If correct stock levels are not kept the problems that arise are as follows:

(a) **Too little stock**. The merchandise will not generate the full potential sales volume. The gross margin (and therefore the net profit) of the business will be restricted in the short run and in the long run the customer's perception of the business will change for the worse.

(b) **Too much stock**. Interest chargeable on the stock investment (which is part of the business's working capital) will reduce gross and thus net margins. In the longer term further reductions in gross margin may occur due to mark-downs.

The three main systems of controlling stock are unit control, financial control and combination control.

2. Unit stock control

This is a method of controlling stocks by physical units of merchandise rather than by cash investment. The merchandise characteristics of the stock are compared with those of the products bought in the period under review. The advantage this method has over others is that it can be used to monitor changes in the characteristics of merchandise being sold and is usefully allied to range creation (model stock-building). The stock is physically counted and often merchandise sub-groups are stocktaken on a rotated basis. This is not a full stock control system because:

(a) It cannot control the profitability of the inventory held.

(b) It therefore requires back-up by financial systems of control.

(c) It loses some of its usefulness if not screened by some system of market monitoring.

3. Financial stock control

As its title suggests, such a system uses cash limits for monitoring stock levels and may be used as an alternative or a back-up to a unit stock control system. This value approach works by comparing the total value of the stock from time to time with the value of the sales it has produced. It is still a common form of stock control, particularly among small retailers, and has two advantages:

(a) It is cheap to operate since the figures it uses are produced by the normal accounting operations of the business.

(b) Because it deals in money figures it can be used to regulate the gross margin attained or to be aimed at.

4. Combination control

As the name implies, this method is a combination of unit and financial control, and although it is more complex, most retailers would benefit from controlling both the financial investment in stock and the units in inventory.

Items that generate high profits or items that customers expect to be in stock should be controlled by the combination method because stock-outs will substantially reduce profits. Equally, very expensive items overstocked could create financial problems.

5. Stock control software systems

A number of suppliers provide specialized stock control software that captures data from a number of sources (for example POS data). The systems manage stock levels and process inventory receipts, shipments, returns and adjustments. They also provide extensive reporting functions to give detailed, current information about quantities, prices, item movements and sales history that is crucial for effective inventory management.

6. Periodic and perpetual inventory control

Inventory control may be carried out periodically (*see* **7** below) or on a continuous basis (*see* **14** below).

7. Periodic inventory

One method of keeping track of inventory is to count the stock on hand once, twice or more times per year on a specific date. It is a costly and time-consuming procedure and, although suitable for accounting purposes, periodic inventory control is rarely sufficient for decision-making purposes.

8. Methods

The three main ways by which stock may be observed and recorded are:

(a) Stocktaking.

(b) Stock check.

(c) Stock calculation.

Although all three methods lay different emphasis on particular aspects of observation and recording, the objective is the same: the maintenance of a correct balance between stock levels and sales. Too much cash unnecessarily tied up in stock can severely reduce the profitability of a business.

9. Stocktaking

This process involves the counting and valuing of every item of stock at a given time. It is therefore the most comprehensive and, if properly carried out, the most accurate of the three methods mentioned above. Physical stocktaking is initially done for strictly merchandise control reasons and consists of:

(a) The breakdown of stock into component parts of the range (i.e. lines and merchandise sub-groups relating to size, style, colour, price line, etc.) to assess its composition.

(b) Stock rating by age to find how long products have been in stock in order to depreciate them.

(c) Current valuation – the taking of the cost or market value, whichever is the lower – irrespective of the original cost.

Other reasons for stocktaking include:

(a) Valuing the stock asset for final accounts purposes, including depreciation and tax.

(b) Finding true stockturn rates.

(c) Isolating fast and slow-selling lines.

(d) Finding true stock losses.

(e) Finding the true gross margin.

(f) Ascertaining agreed figures for insurance purposes.

Physical stocktaking by staff has the additional benefit of familiarizing staff with the merchandise.

10. Preparation for stocktaking

By preparing for a stocktake, interference with customer service can be minimized to a great extent by:

(a) Resorting the stock by subcategories of merchandise to aid counting.

(b) Checking goods for missing tickets or other information sources.

(c) Clearing up all outstanding queries from suppliers, including debits.

(d) Locating and identifying all goods allocated to the department that are, for whatever reason, not physically present.

(e) Making appropriate arrangements for dealing with customers' own goods.

(f) Fixing cut-off dates for invoices, transfers, price changes, etc. that affect the value of stock.

(g) Briefing staff.

(h) Requisitioning supplies and equipment.

(i) Pre-counting case lots and similar quantities which are then 'frozen' until after the take.

(j) Preparing a layout plan showing how the stocktake is to be operated.

11. Main methods of stocktaking

(a) **Cost-price method**. For goods that have a short shelf-life and consequently low stocks, like produce, items are counted at buying (cost) price. This method is a very accurate trend recorder. The disadvantages of this method are:

   (i) it may involve searching through many old invoices which can be time-consuming
   (ii) because the gross margin cannot be calculated in this way there is no way of estimating unknown stock losses, e.g. through pilferage.

(b) **Selling-price method**. Current retail selling prices are used here and this method is popular in trades where large stock variety makes control difficult, e.g. DIY. The advantages of this method are:

   (i) it points out both high and low profit lines
   (ii) it is a good indicator of unrecorded stock losses because known stock losses, e.g. breakages, can be built in; the largest cause of hidden stock loss is, of course, pilferage
   (iii) it allows an interim gross profit percentage to be estimated without taking physical stock.

The main disadvantage is that, because individual invoices are not consulted, the margin used is an average.

(c) **Cost and selling methods**. By using the modifying factors described previously to obtain 'cost or market value', we find the difference between current selling prices and the true cost value of the stock to the company, thus giving a book figure for current stock at selling prices. Therefore the stock can be stated both at current selling and true cost values. The advantages of the cost and selling method are:

(*i*)   *Accuracy*. The only limitation on the accuracy of the book stock figures is the amount of the shortage. This leads to (*ii*) below.

(*ii*) *Shortage control*. Any shortage found after an accurate calculation must be due to shrinkage (here it has advantages over the estimated gross margin system).

(*iii*) *Pricing control*. All initial prices and subsequent changes must be recorded, yielding valuable data for pricing and mark-down control.

(*iv*) *Margin control*. Initial margins are calculable, therefore controllable.

12. Stock check

This is a simplified or less comprehensive form of stocktaking that has as its object an assessment of the selling qualities of the stock rather than its true value. It is frequently confined to quantities, price lines and the qualities of the assortment, e.g. colour, size, style, etc.

13. Stock calculation

This method can give a very close approximation to the value of stock carried at any given time by a consideration of the stock actually found at the last stocktaking and the additions thereto and deductions therefrom which have subsequently been made (*see* cost and selling method in **11(c)** above).

14. Perpetual inventory

The perpetual inventory system aims to provide information on a continuous basis by monitoring merchandise movements into the store (deliveries) and out of the store (sales).

The perpetual method provides up-to-date information which can be used both for accounting and managerial purposes. The main disadvantage is the cost of operating such a system due to its complexity.

Although it is possible to operate such a system by hand using documents, it is the introduction of computerization, particularly EPOS, which has really made the method feasible (*see* Table 14.1).

15. By hand

The tag system has been used for some time, mainly by clothing retailers, whereby a tag attached to the garment contains information of product, style, size, colour, etc. This information is read from the tag which is removed when the item is sold, the computer then producing the appropriate inventory reports.

Table 14.1 Stock movement printout

Movement code	Movement	Quantity
00	Opening stock	1,572
01	Purchases	370
02	Purchases returns	−55
03	Part exchange purchases	37
04	Transfers in	15
	Total in	367
10	Sales	412
11	Sales returns	−43
12	Transfers out	27
13	Free replacements	56
14	Stock written off	13
	Total out	465
00	Closing stock	1,474

16. Information technology

Perpetual inventory is one of the advantages of introducing specialized stock control software systems. One of the most common methods used for data capture at point of sale is the use of optical scanning to read bar codes. Very detailed information on the item can thus be held by the computer to produce many different reports, including the amount of inventory for that item at any time, the disclosure of overstocked items, slow-moving lines and those items that fall below a pre-set reorder level. The store computer can be programmed to transmit orders automatically to a central warehouse computer for delivery the following day, or directly to the supplier.

17. Stock valuation

Where possible, financial stock control should be linked to unit control so that both commercial and financial management enjoy the benefits. On introducing specialized stock control software, the opportunity should be taken to value stocks at cost rather than retail price. The latter is the traditional method of bookkeeping in retail companies, but where variable gross margins apply (either as a result of different mark-ups or selective price cutting) stock valuation at purchase cost price is the only way of determining the true margin earned on each item sold. As each new delivery of a stock item is made, its new value at cost is added to the value of existing stock and a new average cost price is struck. This is known as weighted average cost value of stock, because the cost price used to value stock is being successively weighted by the size and purchase price of each new delivery. This method is probably the best type of stock valuation because it shows the up-to-date earned margin on sales.

Two other stock valuation methods are commonly used. These are LIFO and FIFO.

18. LIFO

With LIFO (last in, first out) the cost of the last merchandise bought is used to calculate the cost of goods sold. However, in periods of high inflation where prices are rising rapidly this method would result in calculated profits lower than those actually achieved.

19. FIFO

With FIFO (first in, first out) the cost of the first merchandise bought is used to calculate the cost of goods sold. This system tends to lead to calculated profits higher than actually achieved, which of course could be disastrous if the discrepancy was large.

Stock shortages

When the total value of stock found at physical stocktaking is less than the book value (calculated for the same date expressed on the same basis) there is a stock shortage, i.e. an excess of book stock over physical stock. Stock shortages are of two kinds – real (physical) or apparent (clerical).

20. Physical shortages

Real shortages occur when goods are lost to the business in one of a number of ways:

(a) **Theft**. This may take the form of shoplifting (thieving by the public), pilfering (thieving by the staff) or 'sweethearting' (thieving by the collusion of a member of staff and a member of the public; for example, when goods are sold by staff to their friends at below the true retail price).

(b) **Loss**. When stock is loaned or transferred it sometimes 'disappears'. Although this can often be attributed to negligence rather than dishonesty, the result is the same.

(c) **Breakage or spoilage**. Glass and china may be accidentally broken, textiles may be ruined by stains and so on. If the damage is detected it is possible to make an adjustment, possibly through obtaining a supplier's credit.

(d) **Physical shrinkage**. Some merchandise normally sold by volume, length or weight tends to lose some fraction of these properties, sometimes under good storage conditions if kept too long. For instance, bacon loses moisture and thus weight (additionally, during the cutting and preparation of provisions, small pieces are often lost), perfume evaporates and textiles may shrink.

(e) **Over-issue**. Goods that have to be weighed or measured and small articles that have to be counted at the point of sale are subject to this form of shortage through carelessness or inexpertise. The growth of pre-packs has reduced this shortage factor somewhat.

(f) **Under-supply**. When, through faulty checking at goods reception, a smaller quantity of goods is accepted than is actually invoiced and paid for, a shortage is created.

Unexpected physical shortages are popularly known as either 'shrinkage' or 'leakage'.

21. Clerical shortages

Apparent shortages arise from any one, or a combination, of the following causes:

(a) Error in the count or valuation at physical stocktaking.

(b) Error in the extension or totalling of stock sheets.

(c) Error in the elements entered into the book-stock calculation, e.g. failure to credit sales or add back in customer returns.

(d) Error in the book-stock calculation itself.

22. Minimizing shrinkage

Shrinkage, as a percentage of sales, is typically 1–3 per cent. This is a huge loss – often approaching the level of net profit on sales. Internal losses can be minimized by better recruitment procedures, i.e. ensuring that staff are trustworthy, while shoplifting is minimized by prosecution of all shoplifters and tight surveillance and security systems.

Merchandise receipt and return

23. Centralized and decentralized receiving

Multiple retailers must decide whether they require suppliers to deliver goods to their branches (direct delivery) or to a central warehouse operated by the retail organization. This decision will depend on many factors but there is a strong trend towards centralized receiving, with the retailer carrying out much more of the delivery to branches formerly carried out by suppliers or third-party carriers.

24. Direct delivery

Some multiple chains still have suppliers' invoices routed to a central accounts section at head office and have goods delivered direct to their branches from manufacturers. Copies of buyers' orders are sent to each branch, giving allocation and the delivery data. The branch keeps these outstanding orders on file and checks the detailed description on receipt. The endorsed order is sent to the head office accounts department. The sum of all such copy orders confirming receipt should agree with the total invoice (debited at selling price). Of course, many independent shops still receive direct deliveries from confectionery and other food firms, but this is at the instigation of the supplier rather than (as in the multiple's case) of the retailer.

25. The advantages and disadvantages of direct delivery

(a) **Advantages**

(*i*)   Elimination of central warehouse costs.

(*ii*) Saves valuable time in unpacking, marking, repacking and transport of goods to branches.

(*iii*) Lessens the risk of deterioration of goods by double-packing.

(b) **Disadvantages**

(*i*)   The retailer could lose substantial quantity discounts for bulk purchase and delivery to a single warehouse address.

(*ii*)   A less balanced and less up-to-date allocation to branches is possible if manufacturers deliver direct.

(*iii*) Good quality control is more difficult outside the central warehouse system.

(*iv*)   Each branch may have to have its own price-marking machines, with the extra cost that entails.

(*v*)   Returnable cartons and other empties may remain in branches for too long.

(*vi*)   The need for confirmation of deliveries in different parts of the country can slow up invoice processing.

(*vii*) A central warehouse can keep back a certain proportion of a delivery to answer subsequent calls from branches to replenish depleted stocks.

26. Incoming merchandise

The receiving process is concerned with record keeping, inspection, marking and storage. The important points concerning the receiving section organization are as follows:

(a) Admittance only of properly authorized consignments.

(b) Speedy notification of the arrival of goods.

(c) Preliminary inspection of containers and outers for apparent signs of damage or pilferage (at this stage an internal check is impossible and carriers' notes should be marked 'damaged' or 'unexamined').

(d) Facilities for the collating of consignment documents and invoices with copy orders so that correct payment can be made.

(e) Facilities for the inspection of the merchandise itself, possibly by the buyer.

(**f**) Protection of the merchandise from loss or damage while it is under reception control.

(**g**) Return of chargeable containers.

(**h**) Prompt forwarding or handling of claims for loss or damage in transit.

(**i**) In appropriate cases, transport to the marking area, stockrooms or the selling area.

(**j**) Accuracy and speed at all times (goods in the pipeline cannot earn money).

The above list is particularly applicable to large stores that often have a receiving department. In a multiple's branch, although the bulk of this procedure might be followed, reception is made in the stockroom itself.

27. Receiving goods

The basic principles behind organization for the receipt of goods are the same for every establishment and are:

(**a**) To ensure that the goods conform to the buyer's order.

(**b**) To ensure that the goods conform with the charge made for them (copy order and invoice must be compared at the same stage).

(**c**) To expedite the speedy transmission of goods to the point of sale.

28. Inspection

Packages should be opened quickly after receipt for the following reasons:

(**a**) If the goods are in any way short or damaged, the notification of a claim on the carriers must be made within three days, followed by a fully detailed claim within ten days of receipt.

(**b**) The goods may be perishable or fragile.

(**c**) In order to maintain a steady flow through the marking process and to avoid bottlenecks.

(**d**) To expedite passing the invoice for prompt payment and full discount.

(**e**) Selling departments are probably awaiting the goods.

29. Stock checking

There are three methods of checking merchandise. These are:

(**a**) **Direct check.** Comparison of contents with the delivery note.

(**b**) **Spot check.** Random sampling.

(**c**) **Blind check.** Listing and checking without the benefit of a consignment note.

30. Rejection of incoming merchandise

The legal position with regard to the acceptance or rejection of merchandise is given in the Sale of Goods Act. In retailing terms, legitimate grounds for rejecting incoming merchandise and recovering damages if a loss has been suffered are:

(a) Where goods have been bought by sample, failure to come up to the sample.

(b) Where goods have been produced to a written specification, failure to meet that specification.

(c) Where goods have been bought as complying with a minimum specification, e.g. a British Standard, failure to comply with that specification.

(d) Where general standards exist, the supplying of imperfect or sub-standard goods.

(e) When the price, style, colour or any other merchandising characteristic is 'not as ordered', provided that the requirements have been clearly stated.

(f) When there is the wrong quantity or the goods are incomplete (as in the case of goods bought in sets).

(g) If there is a late delivery, provided that a definite delivery date has been specified and agreed to by the supplier.

Marking

31. Object and methods

The object of marking is to record merchandise information on the article itself or on its immediate container. The information may be for the use of:

(a) Staff (e.g. when stock control information is needed).

(b) The customer (e.g. when the price is marked on the items displayed).

The type of merchandise, the information to be recorded and the method of presentation will all determine the method and media of marking. Standard methods include:

(a) Swing tickets.

(b) Pin and clip-on tickets.

(c) Gum tabs (often automatically stuck on).

(d) Pressure and heat-adhesive labels.

(e) Direct marking media, e.g. rubber stamps, fibre-tip markers.

Marking can be done centrally or in the branch.

32. Centralized marking

Centralized marking, as done by some manufacturers for clients or in central food preparation plants, has the following advantages and disadvantages:

(a) Advantages

    (*i*)   There is increased efficiency from specialist workers.
    (*ii*) Opportunities for use of mechanization (speed, accuracy) are available.
    (*iii*) Close control over operation is made possible.

(b) Disadvantages

    (*i*)   Problems occur with matching the peaks and troughs of receiving activities.
    (*ii*) A certain inflexibility creeps in.

33. Decentralized marking

The advantages and disadvantages of decentralized marking are:

(a) Advantages

    (*i*)   Goods are got quickly to the point of sale.
    (*ii*) Processing can be undertaken piecemeal in cases of urgent demand.
    (*iii*) Idle staff are utilized during slack periods.

(b) Disadvantages

    (*i*)   Legibility may be poor without mechanical aids.
    (*ii*) Unauthorized or unreported price changes are possible.

Once again the widespread use of EPOS systems has led to a decline in individual item price marking, with the consequent saving of time and costs.

Storage

34. Requirements

The need for stockroom space varies from one retail trade to another and between various methods of retailing. Normally goods cannot all be sold as soon as they are received or be kept on display from the time they come in until the time they are sold. The need for this kind of space would be determined by:

(a) Seasonal peaks in sales, e.g. Christmas.

(b) Frequency of deliveries.

(c) Receiving and checking areas.

(d) Goods awaiting customer collection or return to suppliers.

35. Design

Stockrooms should be as conveniently located as possible to selling areas but should not take up valuable selling space. The following aspects should be taken into consideration:

(a) **Location**. Whether this is behind, above or below the sales area depends on the type of building and the type of retail organization concerned. The larger the store, the more important the location.

(b) **Size**. The dimensions should be determined by the rate of the stockturn, the sales level and the bulkiness of the goods merchandised.

(c) **Space ratios**. The ratio of stock space to selling space depends on the type of trade and the method of retailing, and will vary from below 1:10 to 50:50. The introduction of systems such as just in time (JIT) is reducing this yet further.

36. Layout

A stockroom should be used as efficiently and as infrequently as possible. The important factors in layout are:

(a) **Use of space**. Wall areas should be used to the maximum, with free-standing racks allowing sufficient aisle width for trolleys and bulky items. Full use of floor-to-ceiling height should be attempted.

(b) **Accessibility**. All stock should be as accessible as possible and the faster-selling items should be nearest to the sales area.

(c) **Grouping**. Lines should be stacked so that they follow the same pattern and layout as the store. This will naturally involve grouping allied products together (the only exception may be the really bulky or fast-selling lines).

(d) **Space allocation**. Enough space should be allowed, and kept, for the usual stock level of each line.

(e) **Identification**. As far as possible, lines should be kept in outer packs or cases, each properly marked with the contents.

(f) **Rotation**. Old stock should be moved into the sales area before new stock. This reduces deterioration and good stock-keeping can quickly identify the causes and take action.

(g) **Reception**. An adequate space for handling, checking and unpacking the goods as they are delivered is required so that the new goods are kept apart from the old stock until the reception procedure is completed.

(h) **Security**. All lines should be placed in visible positions if possible and lighting should be adequate. For high value items, like tobacco and small electrical appliances, some form of cage or lockfast store may be necessary.

(i) **Stocktaking**. Many of the points outlined above will aid the counting of lines during stocktaking.

Progress test 14

1. What is the primary aim of a stock control system?

2. What are the three main ways of controlling stock?

3. Describe the three ways of observing and recording stock: (*a*) stocktaking, (*b*) stock check, and (*c*) stock calculation.

4. What are the advantages and disadvantages of the perpetual inventory system?

5. What are the main reasons for stock shortages and what procedures can be used for dealing with them?

6. Describe the advantages and disadvantages of direct delivery.

7. What are the advantages and disadvantages of centralized and decentralized price marking?

8. What are the main requirements for the design and layout of a stockroom?

15 Pricing

Introduction

Price is for some retailers the most important element of the retail mix. For others, such as convenience stores, the main customer benefit is not the low prices but the convenience both in terms of location and hours of trading. This chapter considers the factors influencing pricing decisions, methods for setting prices and pricing tactics.

1. Price and profit

Price has traditionally been determined by the cost of goods and then adding a bit to cover profit. This, however, is no longer a reasonable approach in today's highly competitive market. Pricing terminology is loose; below are definitions of various terms.

Terminology

2. Cost of goods sold

The cost of goods sold is the amount that the retailer has paid the suppliers for goods actually resold. It is by far the largest expense incurred by a retailer who makes a profit by adding on the margin from which all expenses may be paid; the net profit left must be large enough to service and replace the capital and thus keep the retailer in business. Cost of goods sold includes:

(a) The invoice cost of all the goods that have moved out of stock in the period whether by sale, transfer or such shrinkage as theft, loss or breakage. This cost figure includes trade or quantity discount but not normally settlement discount.

(b) Value added tax, which is passed on at each stage of the transaction to the final consumer.

(c) Certain expenses involved in bringing the goods to the point of sale or into saleable condition. These may include:

(*i*) carriage inwards
(*ii*) buyers' travelling expenses directly connected with purchasing the goods
(*iii*) net alteration and workroom costs.

(d) Depreciation on goods remaining in stock at the end of the period.

(e) Transfers from other departments or branches.

The cost-of-goods-sold formula is therefore as follows:

Opening stock (at cost or market value whichever is the lower)
Add purchases and additions (as detailed above)
Less closing stock (valued on the same basis as opening stock).

3. Gross margin

The difference between net sales and the cost of goods sold. (Also referred to sometimes as gross profit.)

4. Percentage gross margin

The gross margin expressed as a percentage of net sales.

5. Mark-up

The amount added to the cost of goods to give the required retail selling price.

6. Percentage mark-up

The mark-up expressed as a percentage of cost.

7. Net profit

Net sales less net cost of goods sold less operating expenses.

8. Net sales

Gross sales less returns and allowances.

9. Mark-down

A reduction on the normal retail selling price. For example, 100 slow-moving items normally selling at £10 each are reduced to £7.50 in order to sell them quickly. The mark-down is £250 for the lot.

10. Margin levels

Gross margins tend to be high on comparison goods like furniture that have a low stockturn, in order to cover stocking costs. Conversely, lower margins are charged on convenience and faster turning products.

Factors influencing pricing decisions

As suggested earlier, the cost of goods is only one factor influencing the pricing decision; others are discussed below.

11. Target markets

The pricing decision should very closely heed the requirements of the target market. If that need is for the best possible price 'deal' then low prices would be offered. If exclusivity, service and status were required, higher prices would be in order. For example, some exclusive fashion retailers refuse to mark down slow-moving lines for fear of compromising their exclusive image. Instead they might sell their merchandise on to another retailer.

12. Competition

Analysis of the competition's pricing strategy will determine what pricing strategy a retailer may adopt in order to compete effectively.

13. Company objectives

The pricing decision must be consistent with the overall company objectives. For example, if the company wishes to pursue aggressive market share growth then lower prices may be required (penetration pricing); if on the other hand early cash recovery of investment is required this objective may dictate higher pricing (skimming).

14. The role of price

The role of price in the retailing mix should also be determined. If the price is perceived as a key element in the consumer's purchase decision, then price will be used to establish a differentiating role, e.g. Argos. If on the other hand price is not seen as so important, other elements of the mix may be emphasized, e.g. convenience stores.

15. Other factors

Intermediaries may well influence the pricing decision. Financial institutions may alter rates of interest, suppliers may put up their prices, trade unions may demand higher wages or the government may change the legal framework.

Setting prices

16. Cost-orientated pricing

The most basic method of setting the retail selling price is to add a standard mark-up to the cost of buying in. The problem with this approach is that it takes no account of competitor prices or demand for the product, both of which could be a crucial determinant of whether a line sells or not.

17. Demand-orientated pricing

There are several ways in which retailers may set prices according to the anticipated demand for products or services:

(a) **By customer**. Price discrimination is determined by the retailer's assessment of what an individual customer might be willing to pay. Typically, the price of a secondhand car can be negotiated and the eventual selling price will depend to some extent on the negotiating skill of the customer.

(b) **Version**. The price of an item in a line of products will be determined by the demand for that particular model. For example, the mark-up on a small portable colour TV will be considerably less than that on the top-of-the-range large-screen TV.

(c) **Place**. The retailer has to serve the needs of its local market place. Even the large multiples that operate to a national price list will make allowance for local factors such as strong local price competition or historical pricing tradition.

(d) **Time**. When a product or service is purchased may determine its price. The typical example is hotel accommodation, which is more expensive during peak periods.

18. Competition-orientated pricing

Retailers price according to the price charged by the competition. Most stores price at or near competitor prices especially in a homogeneous market. For example, there is a going rate for petrol and thus most retailers of petrol will charge very similar prices. In other areas, particularly where there is considerable product differentiation, the retailer has much greater scope for emphasizing other elements of the retail mix and thus price above the competition. Stores with high volume, low overheads or both are able to price below competition.

19. The multi-stage approach

The recommended method for setting retail prices is to take into account cost, demand and competition in a multi-stage approach as follows:

(a) **Select the target market**.

(b) **Determine the floor price**. This would usually be the cost of goods but would bear in mind the promotional value of loss leaders or clearance lines.

(c) **Determine the ceiling price**. The ceiling price is determined as the price charged for the same item by direct competitors. This price can be increased in order to promote an exclusive image or where additional customer services are offered. However, this ceiling price provides a reasonable upper limit unless the retailer has a retail mix strategy that allows it to transcend that limit.

(d) **Mark-up**. Having identified a range of possible prices it is now necessary to apply a mark-up to cost of goods which will be consistent with the profit objectives. Thus many retailers have a target mark-up to be achieved within a department or section but which allows some variation of mark-up on individual items.

(e) **Adjust and select specific price.** Many retailers end the pricing process with the mark-up stage, but it may be necessary to adjust this price – to fine-tune to be consistent with store image or policy or to adjust for consumer preference. For example, in determining the specific price the retailer should operate a consistent policy with regard to price lining, odd/even pricing, multiple unit pricing, complementary goods and fixed versus flexible pricing.

Pricing tactics

20. Price lining

Price lining is the setting up of a reduced number of distinct selling prices within a line of merchandise, goods being marked at these price points and at no others. The practice is particularly prevalent among multiple clothing retailers. With many types of merchandise, customers tend to group themselves into fairly narrow buying zones. The lower the unit price and the greater the frequency of purchase, the narrower and more sharply defined will these zones be. Normally one, two or three prices can be incorporated within the zone limits, depending on their breadth. For example, a retailer may decide that ties will be priced at £9.99, £15.99 and £25, even though there are 30 ties in the range and each one has a different buying-in price.

21. The basic price zones

(a) **The promotion zone.** Promotional merchandise is priced within this low price zone, which may be responsible for generating 15–45 per cent of the total sales volume.

(b) **The volume zone.** This mid-price zone is aimed at the typical customer and will produce at least 50 per cent of the sales volume.

(c) **The prestige zone.** Even very price-orientated retailers will carry a few of these higher-priced lines, which will be responsible for generating 5–15 per cent of the total sales volume of their business.

22. The advantages of price lining

These are as follows:

(a) **Sales volume**

    (*i*)   This can be increased by the provision of larger choice at each price point.
    (*ii*) More effective block displays and advertising through line concentration.
    (*iii*) Less confusion by customers on prices.

(b) **Gross margin**

(*i*) Increased sales from smaller stocks mean a higher stockturn rate and fewer mark-downs.

(*ii*) More possibilities of bulk buying with better discounts.

(*iii*) Possible reduction in number of suppliers, so reducing direct buying expenses.

(c) **Buying**

(*i*) Starting at the selling price level, price lining trains buyers to 'buy backwards'.

(*ii*) Reduction in numbers of suppliers allows closer relationships to develop with the remainder.

(d) **Pricing**

(*i*) Restriction of choice between prices makes it easier to determine the optimum selling price for a line.

(*ii*) Price co-ordination between related lines and between associated departments is simplified.

(e) **Control**. With fewer lines to watch the buyer should find it easier to keep stocks balanced to sales on a unit basis.

(f) **Expenses**

(*i*) In so far as cost-to-sell is a function of time, it will be reduced by quicker selling.

(*ii*) Marking expenses may be reduced.

23. Odd/even pricing

The use of odd prices like £2.99 or £499.95 is said to give the impression of lower prices. Certainly it is widely used in retailing and, despite inconclusive research evidence, it probably works. The opposite, even pricing, e.g. £470, is designed to give the impression that price is not the most important factor when considering the purchase decision; for this particular item prestige would be tarnished by the use of odd pricing methods.

24. Multiple unit pricing

Providing a discount for purchase of two or more units can encourage customers to buy more than they normally would. The technique is therefore useful in helping increase stockturn and in keeping out the competition for longer (while the customer has stocks).

25. Complementary goods

The sale of one item may be related to the demand for another. Thus the sales of normally-priced items may be boosted by a special promotion or price deal on another. For example, the sale of ladies shoes and handbags is related, and shirts and ties are considered complementary goods. Grocers may sell bread at a loss (as a loss leader) to stimulate sales of other related grocery products.

26. Fixed/flexible pricing

Most retailers operate a fixed-price policy when the price marked on an item is the only price acceptable to the retailer. However, in certain sectors it is traditional to operate a flexible pricing policy and for negotiation to take place to determine the final price. Flexible negotiation is typified in the retailing of cars, and most consumers would expect to haggle over 'big ticket' items such as furniture or possibly large electrical goods.

Price adjustments

27. Introduction

Although price lining allows some flexibility, in times of rapidly changing prices upward or downward adjustment may be necessary. If the share of sales in the volume zone falls below 50 per cent there is a clear indication that adjustment is required either up into the prestige or down into the promotion zone.

28. Mark-downs

Mark-downs are reductions in price to reflect current values. They help to:

(a) Maintain 'clean stock' and get rid of out-of-date merchandise.

(b) Create open-to-buy for fresh flow of merchandise.

(c) Foster customer goodwill.

29. Use of mark-downs

Mark-downs are made for various reasons, such as to:

(a) Encourage customers to respond more satisfactorily to a line (these are called 'correctional' mark-downs).

(b) Sell off shopworn goods, remnants and broken lots or out-of-date, end-of-season merchandise ('operational' mark-downs).

(c) Increase sales by giving customers the incentive of lower prices ('promotional' mark-downs).

(d) Correct errors in buying, in pricing or in selling (another example of the 'correctional' mark-down).

30. Mark-downs due to buying errors

Various types of errors in buying can be made and often they have to be corrected by price reductions. Buying errors include:

(a) Overbuying due to:

(*i*)   lack of planning for demand
(*ii*) failure to buy experimentally in small quantities first
(*iii*) buying more than the current stock requirement.

(b) Wrong buying, e.g. of styles, colours, sizes, fabrics. Other wrong buys can be of novelty goods or merely through poor recording or analysis of records.

(c) Failure to anticipate reductions in wholesale prices.

(d) Poor timing, e.g. buying too early or too late or because goods are received too late for sale.

(e) Failure to take advice.

(f) Individualistic or 'pet' buying.

(g) Failure to examine incoming merchandise for defects.

31. Mark-downs due to pricing errors

These include:

(a) When the initial price has been set too high.

(b) When the initial price has been set too low, causing suspicion in customer's minds.

(c) Failure to check competitors' prices.

(d) Deferring price reductions too long.

(e) Making the initial mark-down too small.

32. Mark-downs due to selling errors

On the sales floor, price reductions may have to be made due to:

(a) Failure to show and display merchandise properly.

(b) Merchandise displayed in the wrong location.

(c) Failure to inform sales people of the target customer market.

(d) Failure to encourage sales people to show old and new lines together.

(e) Poor stock-keeping.

(f) Careless handling.

(g) High pressure or careless selling.

33. Operational and uncontrollable causes of mark-downs

Other reasons for price reductions include:

(a) Lack of 'weeding out' slow and unprofitable lines.

(b) 'Display' items kept on display too long, thus becoming discoloured and dirty.

(c) Weather conditions, e.g. very wet summers may seriously affect the sale of light summer clothing like T-shirts.

(d) Economic conditions, e.g periods of recession hit sales of consumer durables and the more expensive foodstuffs.

34. Promotion policies leading to mark-downs

Deliberate promotion policies may also lead to price reductions as when:

(a) Price competition has to be met.

(b) There are special sales of regular stock, e.g. to counter low sales during times of economic recession.

(c) There are frequent sales of promotional merchandise, e.g. to counter seasonal troughs in demand, such as in January and in the summer.

(d) Ranges are maintained until later in the season to prolong goodwill.

(e) High initial mark-up policy is coupled with big mark-downs, e.g. as in some boutiques.

(f) Mark-downs are taken prematurely, e.g. to move stock out quickly.

(g) There is a policy of carry-over to the new season.

(h) There are multiple pricing policies, e.g. two for the price of one.

35. Timing of mark-downs

Mark-downs may be taken either early or late:

(a) Early price reductions occur when sales slow down or fail to take off, e.g. clothing stores having a sale just before Christmas.

(b) Late price reductions occur, for example due to an end-of-season clearance.

36. Effect of price cutting on gross profit

If a retail company is to expand, gross profit must be increased by generating a greater sales volume or by higher retail prices or by better buying. In terms of sales volume, a price reduction can result in a sufficient increase in unit sales for gross profit to be increased. This situation is explained by the concept of price elasticity of demand, which is the relationship between the price at which a product is sold and the quantity demanded by shoppers. It is therefore important to permit, indeed to encourage, pricing at those points at which the product of the individual margin and the unit sales volume is greatest, provided that any increase in expenses is less than the increase in margin.

37. Price increases

Much customer dissatisfaction can be caused if prices are increased after the merchandise goes on the shelf. However, when the buying-in price of an item rises rapidly the retailer must consider the replacement cost of inventory. Perhaps the most common reason for price increases is the cancellation of mark-downs. In order to minimize customer dissatisfaction the original price label should be removed completely. Price increases after goods have been put in stock should be the subject of very close control by merchandise management, particularly with regard to the following:

(a) Details of price changes should be submitted in writing for sanction before being put into effect.

(b) Unauthorized remarking of goods.

Margins

38. Control and monitoring of margins

(a) All suppliers' invoices should be extended and totalled at retail price with a record kept of the cost and retail values of each invoice.

(b) All invoices received should be totalled and the initial gross margin calculated. Warning of deviations from the planned overall margin can thus be spotted quickly and either adjustment can be made or, if this is impracticable, some assessment of their effect on the overall result is possible.

39. Improving the gross margin

Because the size of the mark-up may condition the size of the eventual price reduction, it is important to look to ways of improving the gross margin. These methods include:

(a) Selling at higher prices by:

    (*i*)   the acquisition of exclusive goods so price comparison is difficult
    (*ii*) elimination of odd prices
    (*iii*) selling a larger proportion of the higher mark-up goods already stocked by advertising, incentives to sales people and better display.

(b) Reducing the price reductions by:

    (*i*)   reducing mark-down losses
    (*ii*) reducing merchandise shortages
    (*iii*) reducing or eliminating discounts to special groups.

Progress test 15

1. Define the following terms: (*a*) cost of goods sold, (*b*) gross margin, (*c*) mark-up, and (*d*) net profit.

2. What factors determine the selling price of an item?

3. Describe the steps in the multi-stage approach to pricing.

4. What are the advantages of price lining?

5. Give four reasons for mark-downs.

6. How can price be used to improve margins?

7. Many retailers have adopted the principles of price lining. Evaluate this tactic with particular reference to the current economic climate and the recent success of the discount operators.

8. Discuss the role of price in the retailing mix. Choosing three local retailers as examples, check for consistency with other elements of the retail mix and recommend changes as appropriate.

16 Advertising

Introduction

A retailer could stock the most attractive merchandise priced very competitively and have a convenient location but still fail to attract customers if it did not communicate with them. This chapter considers how much to spend on advertising, the media available and what message to use.

Communication

1. Retail communication

The process of communicating with the target market is known as retail communication and is accomplished using one or more of the following:

(a) **Advertising.** Paid-for non-personal communication to present and promote products, services or ideas.

(b) **Personal selling.** Person-to-person communication for the purpose of making sales.

(c) **Sales promotion.** Short-term incentives to encourage an earlier or stronger market response and stimulate purchase or sale of a product or service.

(d) **Public relations.** Non-paid-for commercially significant news or editorial comment that might stimulate demand for a product or service, or promote understanding of the organization.

(e) **Sponsorship.** Financial or material support of an event, activity, person, organization or product by an unrelated organization or donor.

(f) **Direct marketing.** The provision of information and the aquisition and retention of customers by contacting them directly without the use of an intermediary. This includes such methods as direct mail, telemarketing, e-mail, text messaging and interactive digital television.

2. Retail communication mix

The extent to which each of the above is used will depend on the retailer's objectives. MFI, for example, is heavily involved in advertising to the consumer through newspapers and magazines. Marks & Spencer uses relatively little media advertising in its retail communication mix but relies more on word-of-mouth advertising and personal selling (through well-trained sales assistants). It can be argued that other elements such as the merchandise itself, price and location should be included in the definition of the communication mix because they too communicate something to the target audience. Within this broader view we would also include atmosphere and layout and customer services (these will be dealt with later). We will first examine the four conventional promotion elements: advertising, personal selling, sales promotion and public relations.

Retail advertising

3. Objectives

There are two principal objectives in retail advertising:

(a) **Short term**. To stimulate 'traffic building' within days of the appearance of an advertisement, usually by means of a specific merchandise or promotional offer. This is called promotional advertising.

(b) **Long term**. To increase the number of customers in the target market who automatically think of the advertised store as the right choice for the classes of merchandise that are on sale, i.e. including the store in the 'evoked' set. This is called corporate advertising.

These objectives are achieved by informing, entertaining, persuading, reminding or reassuring as part of the overall communication function of advertising.

4. Promotional advertising

Many retailers use promotional advertising in newspapers, magazines, etc. to sell specific items. The advertising will often incorporate an illustration of the merchandise and the price; however, there has recently been a significant increase in corporate advertising, particularly among multiple retailers.

5. Corporate advertising

Corporate advertising is used to project an image of a company and create a favourable impression of it. It has been used for some time outside the retail industry and classic corporate campaigns have been developed by British Airways and NatWest. More recently Sainsbury's has attempted to project a 'quality image' using TV personalities to extol the quality of food products now available at Sainsbury's. Thus advertising can be used to project an image or 'face' of the company to its various outside contacts, whether they be consumers, staff, suppliers, trade associations or government agencies.

6. Trends

Media advertising by retailers has grown remarkably in recent years. Retailers feature strongly in the top 100 of the largest advertisers with DFS, Sainsbury's, Tesco, Boots, McDonald's, B&Q and PC World each spending over £30 million per year.

The key to this growth was the abolition of resale price maintenance in 1964 that stimulated price competition and pushed the retail outlet into the forefront of the marketing battle. In the grocery field in particular, a few large multiple groups dominate sales and compete furiously with each other.

Advertising is the prime weapon in this battle, particularly as suppliers pay much of the advertising costs anyway, because retailer advertising in both food and durables is mainly geared to drawing attention to special offers on individual brands.

The extra money they receive is regarded by retailers as an addition to the discounts and general below-the-line deals they negotiate with suppliers.

How much to spend

7. Advertising spend

Large multiple grocers typically spend between 0.2 and 0.4 per cent of retail turnover on advertising. MFI typically spends 5 per cent of turnover on advertising, whereas Marks & Spencer spends relatively little. How then can the retailer decide on the right advertising appropriation? The recommended method is known as the objective and task method and put simply is the estimation of the cost of achieving the defined advertising objectives. Alternative methods commonly used but not recommended are the percentage of sales method or setting the advertising spend purely on the basis of competitor spend.

8. Objective and task method

Having defined the advertising objectives (for example, to increase awareness of the store by 20 per cent), it is necessary to determine the different media strategies available for achieving that objective and costing them out. Thus it may be decided that the objective could be achieved using either local radio or local newspaper advertising or a combination of both. The cost of advertising in various media is obtained either directly or through *BRAD* (*British Rate and Data*). The resulting figure should be checked to determine whether it is reasonable both in terms of a comparison with competitor advertising spends and as a percentage of sales. If the appropriation seems either too high or too low a double check with objectives should be carried out along with a justification for the figure.

What media to use

9. Media

The main types of media used by retailers are TV, newspapers and magazines, commercial radio, posters, cinema and the internet. Some retailers also make extensive use of catalogues, leaflet drops and mailings. Once again, the decision on which medium is best for a particular retailer will depend upon the objectives.

10. Newspapers

The UK is well served with a large number of local newspapers, which are extensively used by retailers to reach a well-defined geographic segment. Alternatively, the national press is available for regional or national coverage and choices can be made on which newspaper to use to reach particular segments (e.g. socio-economic groups). The advantages of newspaper advertising are flexibility, immediacy, selectivity and relatively low cost.

11. Magazines

Once again, the advertiser has a wide choice of magazines aimed at specialist groups, men's magazines, women's magazines or local magazines. The major advantages of magazines for advertisers are very good selectivity, good reproduction (allowing high-quality colour reproduction) and long life. Disadvantages would include longer lead times and higher relative costs (on a cost per thousand readers basis).

12. Commercial radio

Commercial radio has seen significant growth in recent years and is now a mature advertising medium with most of the UK population listening at some time during the week. The 250 local and four national independent radio stations cover the whole of the UK population. The advantages for retailers are selectivity, flexibility and relatively low cost (especially compared to TV). It is flexible in that advertisements can be changed regularly due to low production costs. Also high frequency of advertisement transmission can be achieved in a short space of time – especially useful to advertise special events. The main disadvantage is that because the message is audio only it is more difficult to attract the listeners' attention and get the message across.

13. Television

Independent commercial television in the UK is controlled by the Independent Television Commission and is available as follows:

(a) **Terrestrial television**

    (*i*)   ITV1, split into 14 regions
    (*ii*) Channel 4
    (*iii*) Channel 5
    (*iv*) S4C, the Welsh language channel
    (*v*)   GMTV
    (*vi*) Teletext
    (*vii*) Freeview Digital Terrestrial Television (DTT).

(b) **Cable television.** Reaches over 4 million UK homes, the two main operators being NTL and Telewest.

(c) **Digital satellite television**. Dominated by Sky TV, which reaches about 7 million UK homes. Digital satellite television was launched by BSkyB on 1 October 1998 offering 200 channels and the promise of more to come.

Thus it is possible to advertise on a local or national level. As an example of cost, it is possible to have a 30-second advertisement on Border TV for less than £1,000. The same advertisement shown in all ITV areas would cost over £150,000.

Thus commercial television offers a tremendous opportunity for the retailer either at national or local level. The major advantages are the dramatic impact through the use of sight, sound, movement and colour; the large audiences that are instantly and simultaneously accessible and a relatively low cost per thousand; the enhancement of the retailer's prestige and credibility; and the image of stability and substantiality that it fosters. The disadvantages of television are the high total cost (production costs can be high although the use of video technology has reduced these); the fleeting message that it delivers, with no chance for the viewer to take in detailed messages; and a possible lack in selectivity – it tends to be a mass medium.

14. Direct mail

This is the sending of advertising messages directly to customers through the mail. The target market is selected by the advertiser through the use of mailing lists and is therefore highly controlled and can result in minimal wastage. It is particularly suitable for new businesses or new merchandise offers, especially when linked with the use of coupons or catalogues. The advantages are that it is a personalized medium, flexible and an efficient way of reaching a target audience. Many people do not like direct mail, often throwing it away without reading it, so making the conversion to sales ratio low and thus cost per sale can be high.

15. Telemarketing

Telephone selling can be done in two ways:

(a) **Inbound**. This involves direct responses by consumers to TV or radio commercials, usually through 0800 and 0808 (freephone) numbers.

(b) **Outbound**. Here companies telephone consumers in their homes using database information, e.g. for selling double glazing. Like direct mail, many people object to such unsolicited telephone calls.

16. The internet

Spending on internet advertising in the UK has risen by nearly 20 per cent per year since 2000 and in 2002 online advertising spend overtook the spend on cinema advertising. More professional sales teams, improved research and the increasing amount of time consumers spend on the internet have all contributed to the sharp rise. Bigger brands have started to turn to the Web because they can track the effectiveness of their advertisements more easily.

Over 80 per cent of internet advertising spend is on banner ads which work by redirecting the user to another page when the banner ad. is clicked on. There are many examples of retail companies using this form of advertising. John Lewis and Phones 4 U have mounted successful campaigns on the Ask Jeeves website and most of the top internet sites such as MSN, Yahoo! and Lycos feature advertising as a means of generating income.

17. Posters

Posters are a popular medium with retailers because they can be used to reach a well-defined target market (especially a geographic segment).

There are 100,000 stationary roadside poster sites in the UK. In addition there is an extensive network of panels available on buses and taxis in most UK regions and on the London Underground.

18. Cinema

There are approximately 3,200 screens in the UK and advertising can be bought on an individual screen basis or nationally. The medium is particularly effective for reaching the 15–24 age group.

19. Media selection

Having identified the alternative media it is necessary to determine which combination provides the most effective way of delivering the advertising message. This can be an extremely complex process, given the many alternative media available. Specialist media planners are employed by advertising agencies to undertake this onerous task but the individual retailer can use a common-sense approach to arrive at a decision. Factors to be considered in media selection are:

(a) **Reach**. The number of people to be exposed to an advertisement in a given time period.

(b) **Frequency**. The number of times the advertisement is exposed to an audience – complicated messages may require greater frequency.

(c) **Target audience media habits**. For example, a sports retailer may decide that advertising in the sports section of the local newspaper is an effective way of reaching the target audience.

(d) **Merchandise**. The product itself can affect the selection of media. For example, products requiring demonstration to highlight benefits may be advertised on TV. Similarly, a retailer may feel that the quality of a line of furniture can best be communicated using the better colour reproduction available in magazines rather than newspapers.

(e) **Message**. A complex message or one containing a lot of technical data may not be effectively communicated using the transient media of TV or radio.

(f) **Cost**. Although the cost per thousand may be less using a TV advertisement, the total cost may be prohibitive. Therefore the cost must be related to the retail communications budget.

20. Media scheduling

Deciding when the advertisements are to appear is known as media scheduling. This is particularly important for the retailer due to the frequent and dramatic seasonal and weekly sales variations. Many retailers take a high proportion of weekly turnover on Friday and Saturday, thus advertising is often scheduled for Thursdays and Fridays. Similarly, Christmas is a peak selling time and the pre-Christmas advertising burst is typical. The most appropriate method of determining these scheduling decisions is to relate them to the advertising objectives, target market and to ensure consistency with the other elements of the retail mix.

What message to use

21. Purpose

The purpose of any advertisement is to inform, persuade or remind. However, the primary purpose of a particular advertisement will be determined by the advertising objectives. This should therefore be the starting point for deciding on the content of the advertisement. If, for example, the prime advertising objective is to stimulate potential customers to visit a new retail outlet, then informative advertising would predominate and the content of the advertisement would be heavily biased towards providing information in a straightforward and rational manner.

22. Content

The content of an advertisement is usually a mixture of words (copy) and illustrations in a particular configuration (layout). Occasionally advertisements appear that are entirely copy. They are usually designed to provide information only and to appeal to the rational nature of buyers. However, humans are far from being totally rational creatures and we require sensory, social and ego satisfaction rewards. Thus advertisements will use both copy and illustration to persuade customers that their needs can be satisfied by visiting a particular store or purchasing a particular product. Consider the appeals presented in the following examples:

'Don't just book it, Thomas Cook it'
'Exclusively for everyone'
'Every little helps'
'United colours of Benetton'
'Stamping down on prices'

An advertisement should be appealing by being desirable, exclusive and believable: it must generate the desire to act within the reader. If possible, in a highly competitive field, a unique selling proposition (USP) should be stressed as something exclusively available at a particular store. Finally, the appeal must be credible.

23. Copy techniques

The following are some techniques that have been found to work:

(a) **Headline**. Bold headlines create impact and stop readers in their tracks.

(b) **Tag lines**. Memorable slogans are often used at the end of an advertisement, e.g. 'Finger lickin' good'.

(c) **Repetition**. Repetition aids learning and can be used within an advertisement and/or as a repetition of the whole advertisement over a period of time.

(d) **Colloquialisms**. These help to give warmth or local credibility, e.g. 'Is that alright Fyuz'.

(e) **Rhyme**. Rhyming words aid recall, e.g. 'The family store where your pound buys more'.

(f) **Alliteration**. This is another form of repetition – the first letter of sequential words are repeated, e.g. 'The wonder of Woolworths'.

24. Agencies

Retailers have tended in the past to feel that they know their own business best and there has been some suspicion of advertising agencies and the importance of their contribution. Most current retail advertising is much more like direct marketing than product advertising because its effects can be measured with some immediacy by the till. But now the trend is for retailers to use advertising agencies more intensively and many have already taken on the sophistication of successful manufacturers in their use of central media buying, creative consultancies and so on.

Progress test 16

1. What are the six main methods of retail communication?

2. What is meant by the retail communication mix?

3. Explain the difference between promotional and corporate advertising.

4. How does a retailer decide how much to spend on advertising?

5. Describe the main types of media used by retailers.

6. What are the factors to be considered in media selection?

7. Is the use of advertising agencies by retailers likely to grow? Why?

8. Dixons spends in the order of 4 per cent of turnover on advertising. Marks & Spencer spends far less. Why should this be so? Marks & Spencer is as profitable as Dixons – does this indicate that Dixons should spend less on advertising?

9. Outline and discuss the key decision areas involved in designing and implementing an advertising campaign for a department store.

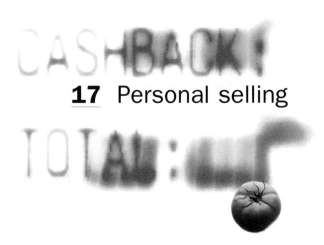

17 Personal selling

Introduction

Sales assistants, who form the bulk of the stores workforce, can make a tremendous difference to the customers' image of a store. This chapter considers the role of the sales assistant in dealing with a variety of customer types and their buying behaviour.

The sales force

1. Definition

Personal selling is person-to-person communication for the purpose of explaining, informing and demonstrating in order to make a sale. The personal selling process is designed to help sales staff match merchandise benefits to customer needs. It is therefore vitally important that the retailer develops an overall sales force strategy.

2. The role of the sales force

The first decision with regard to the sales force is whether to employ one or not. In many retail situations customers prefer either self-service or self-selection. In this way, customers have come to expect, for example, self-service in supermarkets and petrol stations – this method is consistent with the overall image of cutting frills to allow the most competitive prices to be offered. Situations where assistance in making the purchase decision would be expected are when:

(a) The item is made to the customer's particular requirements (e.g. made-to-measure clothes).

(b) The product is technically complex (e.g. cameras).

(c) The product is expensive.

(d) Flexible pricing is practised and negotiation on price, etc. is the norm (e.g. cars).

3. Decline of personal selling

In recent years many retail sectors have moved away from personal service towards self-selection and self-service. The reasons given for this are:

(a) High cost of good sales staff.

(b) Customer waiting time at peak periods tends to be longer than in a self-service store.

(c) Inflexibility of the personal-service mode that makes transfers of staff more difficult.

(d) Generally lower-quality staff because of lower level of wages for retail sales assistants.

(e) The popularity of the self-service type of retailing for many other reasons, e.g. greater sales potential, customer preference, etc.

4. Sales force objectives

Once the role of the sales force and its emphasis within the retail communication mix have been determined, it is necessary to determine specific objectives. Sales force objectives must be set in relation to sales turnover. Salespersons can be responsible for providing information, persuading, accepting payment, wrapping, handling complaints, in-store displays, etc. Alternatively, salespersons may be required only in transaction processing, such as checkout or cashier duty. Although it may be considered that little personal selling is involved here, this final part of the buying process is crucial and a bad experience at the checkout may provoke a customer not to shop at that store again.

5. Sales force size

Determining the size of the sales force to service customer needs adequately should take into account:

(a) The role and objectives of the sales force, i.e. in terms of workload and responsibilities.

(b) The customer arrival times – it will be necessary to deploy more sales assistants at peak times.

(c) The length of time to service each customer.

(d) The average sales to each customer – it may be necessary to balance the cost of using more sales assistants to reduce queues against the value to the customer of doing so. For example, customers may prefer to wait in a queue in order to buy at the most competitive prices, than have no wait but at the cost of higher prices.

The size of the sales force can be critical to retail profitability. Salaries typically run at between 4 and 10 per cent of sales turnover and can account for as much as 60 per cent of operating expenses. Where net margins for some retailers are as low as 4 to 5 per cent (e.g. multiple grocers) it can be seen that mistakes in determining the sales force size can have a dramatic effect on net profits.

Customers

Chapter 9 explored consumer buying behaviour in terms of the buying process, the buying participants and the factors affecting choice. Some of these aspects are reconsidered below within the context of the selling process.

6. Why consumers buy

It is useful to know the general motivations that help encourage people to buy: it may help the sale and therefore the shopper. The fundamental motives are as follows:

(a) **The satisfaction of physical needs**. This includes far more, of course, than the basics of food, drink and clothing.

(b) **Recreation and comfort**. Greater discretionary income coupled with increased leisure time have caused a boom in recreational products and services.

(c) **Imitation**. Advertising bases much of its appeal on the need for many consumers to imitate those they admire or whose tastes they consider superior. Cosmetics and clothing are two particular areas of imitation – or 'aspirational marketing'.

(d) **Exclusiveness**. Some consumers require prestige and are willing to pay high prices for durables or clothing to underline their self-proclaimed leadership.

(e) **Family affection**. A good deal of money is spent on children and the strength of 'pester power' should not be underestimated.

(f) **Other motives**. Consumers are also brought into retail shops by motives that include health, habit, curiosity, novelty, possession and pride.

The salesperson who recognizes these motivations can modify the presentation of information to appeal to the motivations of that particular customer.

7. What customers buy

The motives for buying may be constrained by other factors which will influence choice, as follows:

(a) **Source**. Some sources have strong selling appeal, e.g. Swiss watches, Japanese cameras.

(b) **Economy**. Price is almost invariably an important factor and not just with the lower income groups. Customers balance price with their subjective idea of value.

(c) **Performance**. An article is sold for what it does, as well as for what it is.

(d) **Durability**. Many people are prepared to pay more for articles that are likely to last longer without replacement. This is important in the case of consumer durables but less so for clothing.

(e) **Low running costs**. What may be cheap to buy may be expensive to use, but a total saving can be made over a long period if a customer can be assisted in choosing a quality item that is economical to run, even if the cost is a little higher at the outset (e.g. printers).

(f) **Maintenance facilities**. An article that is expensive at the outset may be designed for cheapness and ease of maintenance while a less expensive article may not. Additionally, a comprehensive after-sales service by the supplier is often a powerful influence on customer choice.

8. Customer types

The points of attraction in goods that appeal to customers must be used by the retailer, keeping in mind that what attracts one shopper may deter another. It is important to 'weigh up' the customer quickly and to recognize their main characteristics so that the right approach can be made. Basic customer 'types' are as follows:

(a) **The 'just looking' customer**. This type of customer may well be browsing or comparing prices and qualities and should be left alone until signs of interest are shown.

(b) **The decisive customer**. Such customers present few difficulties to sales staff because they have already made up their minds about what they want to buy. They should be served as quickly as possible while at the same time ensuring that the product will deliver what the customer requires of it.

(c) **The uncertain customer**. This type of customer requires lots of reassurance, based on the assistant's extensive product knowledge as required.

(d) **The silent customer**. Without clues to the customer's opinions about merchandise, demonstration may be necessary, with the customer free to handle merchandise so that their intentions can be gauged.

(e) **The talkative customer**. Time spent in conversation with a customer could mean lost sales elsewhere. Tact and firmness are required to bring the customer back to the merchandise and its selling points.

(f) **The disagreeable customer**. This type of customer should simply be shown the merchandise and be given the chance to do most of the talking.

(g) **The opinionated customer**. The opinions offered, even if they are factually incorrect, should rarely be challenged, but the correct information should merely be provided as part of the conversation.

(h) **The suspicious customer**. Suspicion is sometimes produced by a disappointing purchase made in the store previously. This should be allayed and the confidence of the customer built up again. This can be achieved by an apology, an offer to exchange a faulty article or, if appropriate, a full refund.

The progress of the sale

9. Prospecting and qualifying

The selling process, particularly for expensive items, may actually begin well before the customer comes anywhere near the store. The search for potential customers (prospects) to convert into customers is known as prospecting. This may be achieved through advertising, leaflet drops, recommendation from current customers, obtaining lists of potential customers, etc. This list of prospects must then be filtered to provide a list of definite prospects – this process, known as qualifying, involves trying to determine such things as the individual's financial position: can they afford the item? Does the prospect really require the item and have they authority to buy?

10. The pre-approach

Before the salesperson approaches a potential customer, a good deal of preparation and information gathering is necessary. This includes much information on the products and their particular benefits as well as facts about local competitors, prices, etc. In addition the salesperson should have received sales training to allow customer types and their motivations to be spotted.

11. Making contact

The customer's first impression of the salesperson is important. A smile is important, but the salesperson should be civil not servile.

The most common approach phrase used by sales personnel is 'Can I help you?' and the most common answer is thus generated automatically 'No, I'm just looking'. To overcome this automatic rejection the approach phrase should be modified by the salesperson commenting on the merchandise the potential customer is viewing, e.g. 'That camera is the latest in the range and is on special introductory offer at present'.

Alternatively, a more specific service approach than 'May I help you?' would be 'Have you seen the special introductory offer on the new cameras?' With experience salespersons can modify their approach phrases to avoid becoming (and sounding) too mechanized.

12. Finding out customer needs

Sales staff must know customer needs before they can know they are selling the right merchandise. Much of the information relating to the customer, such as economic standing, family size, specific reason for purchase, may come out through observing and conversing with the customer.

13. Selling the correct goods

Important points at this stage of the sale are as follows:

(a) If the most appropriate item is not in stock, the salesperson may be able to offer a satisfactory substitute, but this must not be pressed on the customer.

(b) In a substitution situation or where the customer is amenable to purchasing higher-priced items in a range, 'selling up' is a possibility.

(c) One of the key sections of the salesperson's presentation is the selling of the benefits of the article.

(d) It may be that at some point the customer's objections have to be overcome. A clever salesperson can spot the negative response and use it as part of their presentation – or even turn it into a selling point!

(e) Some positive points for salespersons:

    (*i*)   present the facts slowly; they are new to the customer
    (*ii*) emphasize the selling points of the article that appeal most to the customer
    (*iii*) encourage questions from the customer; this could lead to a multiple sale
    (*iv*) give the customer the opportunity to 'try' the merchandise
    (*v*) handle the merchandise with care; this shows how valuable it is.

(f) Some negative points:

    (*i*)   items should never be demonstrated on top of other merchandise
    (*ii*) technical language should not be over-used
    (*iii*) a salesperson should never mislead a customer; honesty builds goodwill
    (*iv*) never criticize any items – this may either lose a sale or reduce the firm's goodwill.

14. Closing the sale

(a) As with the initial approach, timing is essential, e.g. the sale must be concluded before interest wanes.

(b) The customer must feel that the buying decision has been their own.

(c) At this point the salesperson may be asked about credit, servicing, alterations and so on; it is essential to be as fully conversant with these matters as with the products and recognize these as buying signals.

(d) The goods are wrapped and the money is taken.

(e) The correct time to make a related sale is when the merchandise is being wrapped.

15. Related selling

Once the customer has made a first purchase it may be quite natural for them to make a second, complementary one, e.g. the purchase of a car wax may suggest a further purchase of a chamois leather. Suggestions should be specific, however, and not the general 'Do you require anything else?'

16. Customer leaves the store

The customer's visit might finish with the salesperson showing them to the door, thanking the customer for their custom and expressing the hope that they will revisit the branch or store in the near future. In most cases today, however, this rather leisurely leave-taking is impossible because of the volume of custom that successful stores need to attract in order to survive.

Importance of the salesperson

17. Salesperson's attributes

To be successful in the personal selling situation, the salesperson needs the following attributes:

(a) Retailers aim to recruit staff whose appearance and manner is consistent with the store image, i.e. salespeople with whom the customers can identify.

(b) The salesperson must be a good communicator, who can set up a rapport easily with the customers and has the ability to be flexible.

(c) A pleasant and courteous manner is most important, but avoiding the danger of being obsequious.

Progress test 17

1. Give three examples of retailing situations where personal selling would be expected.

2. What factors should be taken into account when determining the size of the sales force?

3. What is meant by prospecting and qualifying?

4. Does the selling process end with 'closing the sale'? If not, why not?

5. What are the main attributes of a good salesperson?

18 Sales promotion and public relations

Introduction

Because of the sheer volume of advertising these days and the continuing need to attract customers' attention, many retailers are focusing more on sales promotion and public relations. This chapter considers the different types of sales promotion, public relations and sponsorship.

1. Meaning of sales promotion

There is often confusion over the term 'sales promotion' because it has been used in the past and still is used by some to mean anything that attempts to increase or promote the level of sales. This definition would include advertising and personal selling, so this old definition of sales promotion is very broad indeed. A more narrow and precise definition is preferred and therefore sales promotion is now thought of as those promotional activities other than advertising, personal selling and public relations that stimulate consumer purchase.

Media advertising is often classed as 'above the line' expenditure while sales promotion is 'below the line'. Typical sales promotion tools would be coupons, samples, competitions, etc.

2. Objectives of sales promotion

(a) **Stop and shop.** Customers passing the store, who had no intention of going in, can be encouraged to enter by a sales promotion in store, e.g. wine tasting.

(b) **Shop and buy.** Having persuaded customers to enter the shop, they must now be encouraged to buy by presenting the merchandise in such a manner as to create the desire to purchase, e.g. money-off vouchers, trade-in allowances.

(c) **Buy bigger.** During the buying process customers can be persuaded to buy either a larger quantity of the same goods or to buy other products in addition, e.g. 'Buy one get one free' (Bogof), cash-back offers.

(d) Repeat purchase. The final aim is to persuade customers to return again and again to the store, trading on the goodwill and loyalty that previous purchases have, hopefully, instilled, e.g. store 'club' cards, or continuity programmes such as collecting a dinner service.

Therefore sales promotion efforts are usually designed to support other communication activities. For example, advertising may be used to generate awareness and desire but sales promotion may be used tactically to overcome any resistance to purchase by offering a (short-term) incentive to create a quicker sales response.

3. Ways to increase sales using sales promotion

The methods of increasing sales without necessarily incurring extra costs, such as increased staffing or sales area, are as follows:

(a) Increase the number of transactions by:

(*i*) using sales promotion methods to get more people into the store
(*ii*) improving point-of-sale incentives to buy.

(b) Increase the size of the average sale by:

(*i*) promotions on high margin goods
(*ii*) getting more goods sold by offering incentives to buy more, e.g. (multi-pack) pricing.

Sales promotions can emanate from two sources: suppliers or the retail company itself.

Supplier-originated sales promotions

4. In-store activities

There are many types of suppliers' promotions that affect in-store activity:

(a) Price-off pack. For example '10p off' printed or banded on the pack.

(b) Premiums. Small gifts either in, or occasionally attached to, the pack, e.g. plastic toys.

(c) Self-liquidating premiums. Cheap promotions primarily concerned with obtaining good in-store display. The customer writes to the supplier for the gift, enclosing pack tops plus money. The gifts are likely to be bought in bulk by the supplier, giving it the benefit of large discounts, thus making the bought-in unit price low enough to be covered by the profit on all extra sales made.

(d) Personality promotions. Some manufacturers use TV personalities to promote their products, but their appeal may be declining because so many companies now use them. To avoid overexposure some firms now use personalities select-ively, e.g. in certain parts of the country.

(e) **Competitions**. These are often printed on the packs with the advantage to the supplier that the budget is known in advance, with the requisite number of prizes ordered from suppliers.

(f) **Co-operative promotions**. For example two or more branded products shar-ing (and funding) a joint in-store promotion, e.g. garden peat and packet seeds.

(g) **Sampling**. The giving away, often in-store, of product samples, sometimes with a demonstrator present, e.g. Swiss cheese, Cyprus sherry.

(h) **Coupons**. Price-off coupons are printed on the packs or in store handouts, usually allowing a substantial saving on the next purchase of the brand. The effectiveness of this type of promotion can be significantly reduced if the store allows the coupon to be redeemed for quite different goods – this is called 'malredemption'.

(i) **Cash-back**. Customers have to send pack tops back to the manufacturer and, although initially attractive, may be loath to in practice due to the hassle; this reduces the cost of the promotion, as a result of low 'redemption rate'.

(j) **Multi-packs**. Two or more packs are attached and sold for a better price than buying the items singly. Occasionally a 'stretched' version of the pack obviates the extra shelf space required. Popular in toiletries and drinks.

(k) **In-store salespersons**. An example would be 'demonstrators' used in the electrical 'white goods' market. To work well there probably has to be a further inducement offered, e.g. reduced prices. This promotion is used selectively, normally in supermarkets, department stores and electrical goods stores.

It will be seen that the retailer has to be organized for the promotion, e.g. the collection and redemption of coupons, reorganizing shelf displays and store layout.

5. Point-of-sale display material

Most manufacturers produce sales-aid material for placing near the products themselves. Examples of these are:

(a) **Special fittings**. For example paperback publishers' racks, battery stands.

(b) **Showcards**. Designed to stand on or fit round the products, e.g. washing machines, pens.

(c) **Leaflets and product labels.**

(d) **Demonstrators**. Sometimes demonstrators are used in this context, as are authors in bookshop signing sessions.

Many retailers use the display material from suppliers very selectively due to the danger of producing a cluttered and unco-ordinated retailing environment. In some cases, particularly the large multiple groups, manufacturers and retailers will collaborate to produce mutually acceptable point-of-sale display material.

6. Trade incentives

These are normally of the following kinds:

(a) **Cash discounts or straight cash handouts**. These are given by manufacturers to encourage volume sales, period stock building, display and cut-price offers to consumers.

(b) **Special credit terms**. These support special promotions and are often aimed at the bulk retail buyers.

(c) **Goods in lieu of cash**. For example one extra free item for every ten purchased by the retailer.

(d) **Staff incentives**. These are payments made by the manufacturer to store management and staff for reaching particular targets. Obviously these are agreed prior to the start of the promotion by the retail company and may form part of a much larger supplier–retailer promotion package. This type of incentive does offer the promoter an opportunity to motivate the people who actually come into contact with the public.

7. Direct promotion to the public

As part of its below-the-line effort, the manufacturer may make use of direct promotions to consumers' homes such as couponing or free samples. This relies heavily on access to up-to-date information, i.e. databases (*see* Chapter 26).

8. Pack design

Because so many products are prepacked and because there is such a fight for shelf space, pack design is important to the retailer who may decide to accept or reject a pack just on the basis of its design rather than its contents, e.g. because of its dimensions or its 'stackability'.

Retailer-originated sales promotions

9. Window displays

Shop windows today have largely become bigger and backless and show much of what is going on in-store. However, department stores and certain types of multiple chains, like jewellers, booksellers and chemists, keep windows for particular products and seasonal or special event promotions. For example, a new line in toiletries may be given a mass window display to itself; Christmas and Easter displays encourage shoppers to enter the store (*see* Chapter 19), by displaying 'special offers' or items 'on promotion'.

10. In-store displays

These can be of various kinds:

(a) **Mass displays**. For example in dump baskets or at ends of gondolas.

(b) **Multiple product promotions**. These are when two or more complementary products are sold together in an integrated display, e.g. food and wine from Italy.

(c) **Demonstrations**. For example sampling, product demonstration, fashion shows.

11. Price promotions

These may occur for short periods on a selected number of lines, e.g. the 'super savers' in supermarkets. Some firms prefer to advertise their 'permanent store-wide discounts'. Many retailers, particularly in the clothing sector, have annual or half-yearly (or even more frequent) sales where slow movers, bad buys, cheap 'bought-in' lines and deteriorated stock are sold off.

12. Store loyalty cards/trading stamps

Trading stamps were a particularly popular sales promotion device of the latter half of the 20th century. They were often used to even out trade over a week, e.g. 'double stamps on Tuesdays', or to promote particular lines, as well as being a general incentive to shop in that particular store rather than its competitors. Customers would collect stamps given out with each purchase to be redeemed at a later stage for gifts. Trading stamps have now largely been replaced by the stores' own loyalty cards, although versions of the trading stamp concept remain e.g. Air Miles and the Nectar Card. (*See* Chapter 26 for a discussion of loyalty cards and database marketing.)

13. Competitions

Many retailers use competitions as a sales promotion device. These can be particularly successful if linked to a promotion theme. For example, Woolworths' 'Back to school' competition linked to its 'Back to school' leaflet distribution requesting completed entries to be taken to the local Woolworths' store and posted in the box provided.

14. Free gifts

Electrical retailers, for example, have offered small electrical appliances such as low saturation items like liquidizers as 'free' gifts to consumers buying large ticket items like cookers and washing machines.

15. In-store display material

Most retail companies produce, or have produced for them, window posters, point-of-sale display material, printed tickets and other 'software'.

16. Personality promotions

Following the lead of the manufacturers, some retail chains have paid TV personalities to take part in their advertising, store openings and so on.

17. Joint promotions with other retailers

As in the promotion of the food court in managed shopping centres.

18. Incentives to sales staff

These take the form of:

(a) Competitions between salespeople or between branches with cash or merchandise prizes.

(b) Use of 'premium' money or bonuses paid to salespeople for the sale of particular lines, usually high margin.

Public relations

19. Public relations

Public relations (PR) is the deliberate, planned and sustained effort to establish and maintain understanding between an organization and its publics. The role of public relations is to obtain favourable publicity for the organization, build a good image and handle adverse comments, rumours or stories. This is often achieved (in larger companies) by the public relations department, which will plan a campaign to communicate the right message to the right people. It is important to understand the concept of 'publics' in the public relations definition. An organization's publics will consist of customers, shareholders, employees, government, suppliers, the local community and the media. Therefore, it may well be necessary to produce information in different forms to appeal to these different publics or indeed to provide different information for different publics.

20. Example of PR objectives

Examples of information that a large food retailer might wish to project in order to maintain understanding are:

(a) **External**. This is a group that:

  (*i*)   is a major and influential force in the food marketing and distribution scene
  (*ii*) has substantial financial backing
  (*iii*) has considerable buying power
  (*iv*) in its commercial operations is aggressive, tough and progressive – but also reliable and fair.

(b) **Internal**. This is a group that:

(*i*) is a large well-developed business with plenty of opportunities
(*ii*) is interested in personnel development
(*iii*) provides a good total remuneration package
(*iv*) deals firmly but fairly and sympathetically with the staff.

It is interesting to note that a number of retail groups have recently begun spending on 'financial public relations', which is largely aimed at the City. This has reflected a growing concern by companies as to the performance of their share prices and the consequent value (market capitalization) the City puts on their share issues.

21. Publicity

Publicity may be defined as information appearing in the media concerning products, services or companies and secured as editorial material rather than paid-for space.

22. Purpose

The purpose of providing publicity material to the media is to promote brands, products, people, places, ideas or companies. In providing information through editorial space greater credibility results as the audience is less likely to be sceptical of editorial than space that has been paid for by an advertiser.

23. Forms

The most common forms of publicity material are:

(a) Press releases or news items

(b) Photographs

(c) News conferences/speeches

(d) Videos.

Publicity is often thought of as free advertising but it is far from this. It is not free because although the cost of space may not be paid for there may be considerable cost in producing publicity material. To be truly effective, publicity must be planned and managed professionally.

24. Sponsorship

Retail organizations of all sizes and types are spending increased sums of money on sponsorship of sport and the arts. A once minor area of PR, sponsorship is fast becoming an important form of promotion in its own right. Sponsorship does seem to offer the retailer a way of being perceived as giving something back to society and thus fostering a good corporate image. Sainsbury's is one of the largest sponsors of the arts in the UK and Benetton is well known as sponsor of a highly successful Formula 1 motor racing team.

Progress test 18

1. What is the meaning of sales promotion? Give four examples of sales promotion tools.

2. What trade incentives are normally provided by manufacturers?

3. Describe three types of retailer-originated sales promotions.

4. What is publicity?

5. What are the most common forms of publicity material used by retailers?

6. Describe the advantages of sponsorship as compared to media advertising.

7. In the late 1990s Tesco launched its Computers for Schools promotion. 13,000 items of equipment including 3,000 computers, 600 printers and 9,400 software packages were given away to 8,000 schools nationwide. The promotion was based on a voucher collection system, with one voucher being given for every £25 spent in a single transaction. The promotion has been repeated every year since, and in later years the number of vouchers offered for each transaction has been increased.

    Evaluate this method of promotion and comment particularly on objectives that it might achieve for Tesco.

8. Ian MacLaurin, former Chairman of Tesco, contends that publicity is more important than advertising. Comment on whether you would subscribe to this view in relation to UK retailing.

19 Atmosphere and layout

Introduction

As a means of establishing a competitive advantage most retailers now pay a great deal of attention to their stores' design. This chapter considers the store exterior, interior, layout and displays.

Store image and atmosphere

1. Store image

This can be defined as the customer's perception of the store and its attributes. As such it is a composite of the following dimensions: merchandise, store location, promotion, pricing policy, service, store clientele and store atmosphere and layout. These dimensions are lumped together by the customer in order to simplify matters to produce a store image. When asked to describe a store's image, customers will respond using terms such as honest, dependable, exciting, etc., as well as describing the physical facilities such as cleanliness, convenience or ease of parking.

2. Atmosphere

This is a major component of store image and can be defined as the dominant sensory effect created by the store's design, physical characteristics and merchandising activities.

The components of the store that collectively produce the store atmosphere are the store exterior, general store interior (e.g. flooring, walls, lighting), layout and displays. The sensory reaction they produce within an individual can be considered in terms of sight, touch, taste, smell and sound.

3. Design

Design has become increasingly important in retailing in recent years, not only in the development of company logos and graphic styles, but also in developing a total retail concept to appeal to particular target groups. Habitat was the first of a new breed of design-led retailers. Terence Conran opened his first Habitat store in 1964 with the basic philosophy of providing well-designed products at reasonable prices and in a comfortable environment. In 1982 he applied the same principle to the retailing of clothes and Next was born, offering stylish collections of co-ordinated clothes exquisitely presented. Since then many retail groups have used design consultancies to redesign stores to create a particular atmosphere and thus achieve a differential competitive advantage.

4. The right atmosphere

The right atmosphere starts with the definition of the target market and identifying their requirements. For example, customers buying expensive ladies' fashions would expect an 'expensive' atmosphere – deep pile carpets, top-quality fixtures and fittings, etc. The atmosphere of the store should be entirely consistent with the desired store image and the other elements of the retail mix.

Store exterior

The first impression a potential customer has of the store is generated by the store exterior. It should therefore be designed to project and be consistent with the desired store image.

5. The store's position

The primary concern with regard to position is how visible the store is. Ideally a store should be positioned so that it is clearly visible from the major routes (pedestrian or vehicular) passing the site. Compatibility with surrounding stores and the surrounding area is desirable, as is the provision of easy access to the store either by the provision of car parking facilities and/or the exclusion of vehicular traffic to permit safe, convenient conditions for pedestrians.

6. Architecture

Architectural style can indicate the size and prestige of the retailer's operation. The use of certain materials (e.g. marble) can also affect image. The overall size of the outlet is important, but width (particularly for window space) is often more important than the height or depth of the building.

7. The store's sign

The fascia serves to identify the store and attract the customers' attention. The store's sign may be used to identify who the retailer is (e.g. McDonald's), what is sold (e.g. Tie Rack), where the retailer is located (e.g. Nottingham Hi-fi) or when they are open (e.g. '7–11').

8. The shop front

The three basic shop-front configurations are:

(a) **The straight front**. Here the shop front runs parallel to the street or pavement with possibly a small recess for the entrance.

(b) **The angled front**. This creates a more attractive and interesting front and funnels or directs customers into the store. It also helps provide a better viewing angle and can reduce glare.

(c) **The arcade front**. Basically, this is a straight front configuration but with several recessed windows or entrances, thus providing the shopper with several protected areas for window shopping and creating an attractive and relaxing atmosphere.

9. The store entrance

The store entrance should be designed to encourage the customer into the store. The major factors to consider are the size of the entrance and flat-entry surfaces. Some retailers have dispensed with windows, thus opening up the whole of the shop front as an entrance – this is possible in a covered shopping centre but does involve increased security risks.

10. The window

Apart from the overriding aim of image-building the conventional window has functions such as:

(a) To show a representative sample of merchandise sold in the store.

(b) To display promotional or seasonal lines.

(c) A mixture of (a) and (b).

The window, whether it is arcaded or a 'picture', is important in helping to persuade the customer to enter the store initially. Many retailers have dispensed with normal window displays and use the window to allow the customer to view the entire store and its contents. Retailers selling small items such as jewellery, however, still rely on window displays, usually set off against a window back.

11. Basic principles

The basic principles of window display are similar to in-store display principles and are as follows:

(a) Like products should be grouped together in the window.

(b) Featured lines should be placed in prominent positions in the windows, just below eye-level.

(c) Window display height in a backless window (and these are preferred by most retailers today except in jewellery and other small item stores) should be between average waist and shoulder level so that customers can see into the store. Tall products, such as upright freezers, should be displayed to the sides.

(d) Window displays should not be too deep. The window should allow potential customers to look into and see the whole store.

(e) Where window space allows, mass displays of individual stock items such as a promoted line are valuable interest catchers.

(f) If windows are used as part of the positive effort of attracting customers into the store, displays should be changed regularly to keep up the customers' interest. This has the added advantage of rotating window stock that might otherwise become faded.

(g) Electrically driven turntables, which hold stock, can attract attention. The colour of displays should also be eye-catching, e.g. the use of red and green at Christmas time.

(h) All stock and window fittings, such as shelving, should be clean.

(i) Windows should be well lit, particularly for evening window shopping.

The advantages of window displays are that they can be inspected after the store has closed and, unlike press advertising, actual merchandise is used.

Store interior

12. Design

The general design of the store interior must be consistent with that of the exterior, thus the colour and design aspects of floors, walls and ceilings must present the right image. For example, it is common practice for food-selling areas to have white marble-effect flooring to give the impression of cleanliness, whereas fashion-selling areas will normally be carpeted or have wood flooring to enhance the quality/plush image.

13. Other considerations

The basic objective of the retailer is to minimize costs while maximizing sales and customer satisfaction. The store interior can contribute to this objective by providing the appropriate fixtures and equipment, lighting, dressing rooms, lifts or escalators and aisle widths to allow comfortable shopping.

Layout

14. Definition

The layout of a store is the arrangement and location of fixtures, fittings, equipment, merchandise, aisles and non-selling areas such as checkouts and dressing rooms.

15. *Grouping of sections*

In such retail sectors as DIY, grocery and electrical, stock can be divided into a number of sections which form mini-departments of the store. For example, in DIY stores such sections could be: gardening, home decoration, kitchenware, etc. In electrical retailing the convention is to split the store into 'brown' (TV/audio) and 'white' (major domestic appliances) goods and then to further subdivide the sections, say, into home laundry, refrigeration, TVs, videos, etc. This logical approach helps customers and staff to find sections quickly.

16. *Allocation of in-store space*

The amount of floor space required for customers will depend on the type of trade, the lines carried and the type of service offered. A balance should be struck between customer, selling and non-selling areas. The amount of customer space required will depend on whether certain factors are present, namely:

(a) Need for customer browsing, e.g. at greeting card racks.

(b) High percentage of comparison goods, e.g. furniture that requires a lengthy selling time.

(c) Need for chairs and tables for 'signing up' procedures for hire-purchase or rental agreements.

The allocation of space for the different merchandise groups should be based on a profit productivity approach, i.e. providing selling space on the basis of profit per square foot. For example, a merchandise group contributing 5 per cent of total profits could be allocated 5 per cent of the sales floor area. However, this initial calculation may have to be modified in the light of other requirements, e.g. the need to provide variety and choice and a proper assortment of merchandise.

17. *Ways to maximize the use of space*

(a) Devote as much total space to selling activities as compared to storage or non-selling functions.

(b) In prime shopping locations consider assigning non-selling activities to other areas where rental costs are much lower.

(c) In the designated selling space eliminate all non-selling functions, e.g. clerical work areas.

(d) Use vertical as well as horizontal space (but keep the store image intact).

(e) Replace inefficient fixtures with modern, open, volume-selling fittings.

(f) Analyse sales and profit per square foot of selling space and relocate departments taking into account:

   (*i*)   seasonal changes where appropriate
   (*ii*) unprofitable departments, which should be cut back or dropped altogether and more promising sections extended
   (*iii*) the meeting of set minimum acceptable sales/profits targets per square foot.

Figure 19.1 Layout of a CTN store

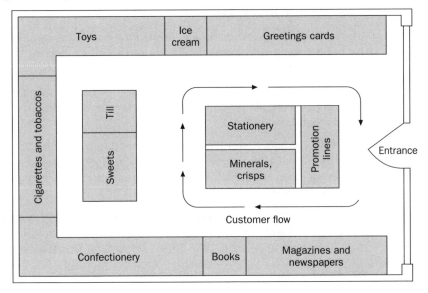

18. Different retail sector approaches

(a) A typical DIY store will place high-demand lines such as nails and screws towards the back of the store so that customers are forced past other high-profit impulse lines such as kitchen utensils and gifts.

(b) In confectioner/tobacconist/newsagent (CTN) stores newspapers are normally located near the door because their sales peak is in the morning and evening and customers shopping only for these items can be served quickly. Rear space is used for 'browsing' lines like toys, while impulse lines like sweets are positioned next to the till (*see* Figure 19.1).

(c) Footwear stores, where most of the stock is in the window or round the walls, allow a large part of the space to customers, chairs and fittings.

(d) Stores that sell large consumer durables, such as major electrical appliances and furniture, display much of their stock so that it is free-standing. Therefore the customer circulation area is the same as the display area.

Laying out a store

The three main factors to be considered here are:

(a) Fixtures and fittings.

(b) Merchandise.

(c) Customer circulation.

19. Fixtures and fittings

These take four main forms:

(a) Wall fixtures consisting usually of shelving but sometimes made up of hooks (for bagged stationery items), browsers (for records or greeting cards) and other specialist types of fitting, some of which can be used free-standing.

(b) Free-standing gondola (walk-around) or browser units, again with shelving (often adjustable). Many shelves have slotted edges so as to carry price labels for the merchandise displayed.

(c) Special containers and stands such as wire dump bins and 'spinners' (circular free-standing racks that may be rotatable) for lines displayed as a special promotion, or manufacturers' display units specially designed to carry their own particular product.

(d) Refrigerated cabinets of various designs for the sale of frozen foods, meats, fish, provisions and produce. These can be placed against the wall or free-standing, and it is important to keep these lines close to their preparation areas.

20. Merchandise

The arrangement of fixtures and fittings will be guided by the type of merchandise sold. The merchandise is positioned in particular ways to aid customer selection and therefore stimulate sales. The following points should be noted:

(a) Principal merchandise sections should be prominently labelled by clear overhead signs.

(b) All merchandise sections should be accessible to the customer.

(c) All merchandise must be clearly and correctly priced (either on the merchandise or on the shelf edge).

(d) The general rule on merchandise location is to use the best-selling position for goods providing the greatest profit (i.e. gross margin × rate of sale), not goods carrying the highest profit margins. Best-selling positions include ends of gondolas and wall units.

(e) 'Everyday' purchases like canned fruit, vegetables and soups should be placed near the entrance to start the customer buying.

(f) Merchandise can be categorized into three broad types, and this will radically affect their locations in-store:

- (*i*) *Demand lines.* These often consist of staple merchandise that is bought almost automatically, e.g. bread, milk.
- (*ii*) *Browser lines.* These are products that remind customers, by their presence on open display, that they should buy them, and which need space to allow customers to make an unhurried selection, e.g. greetings cards.
- (*iii*) *Impulse lines.* The customer purchases these lines without any prior intentions, e.g. confectionery.

(g) Careful placing of basic demand lines helps to draw customers to all parts of the shop. High-profit-margin, impulse-purchase lines should be placed alongside them.

(h) Promotional displays should be controlled in size and number so that clutter is avoided, and neither should they be located immediately inside the store entrance nor immediately opposite a fast-moving line. Customers tend to miss badly sited displays.

(i) Heavy and bulky goods, e.g. bread, cereals and drinks, should be placed near the end of the in-store 'journey'. Positioned earlier they could fill the basket too quickly. This is also true of fragile goods, which might break.

(j) Displays (except for seasonal lines) should not be changed too often as this tends to annoy the customers.

21. Customer circulation

The following points should be noted:

(a) In self-service stores there is a tendency for customers to 'follow the walls'. Merchandise display techniques mentioned above can encourage wider circulation.

(b) Free-standing units should not be set together in a long line but should show gaps so that customers can move across the store and not be 'forced' round.

(c) Aisle widths should be great enough to allow two trolleys to pass in comfort and to allow access by wheelchair users. Some supermarkets have aisles of up to 2–3 metres in width. Circulation space at the front of the store should be adequate to avoid congestion.

(d) Research can be used profitably to lay out stores scientifically and to have particular regard to customer circulation behaviour.

Figure 19.2 shows different kinds of layouts. The grid layout, often used in super-markets, aids and directs customer flow and is designed to enhance efficiency. The boutique layout arranges the sales floor into partially separated areas to create an unusual and interesting shopping experience. The free-flow layout encourages browsing and is used most by clothing stores.

Display

The manner in which merchandise is exhibited or presented to the customer is a vital element of the selling process.

22. In-store display

Once customers are past the window line they are usually within the store and the effect of good display continues to be important in catching a customer's eye.

Figure 19.2 Examples of layout

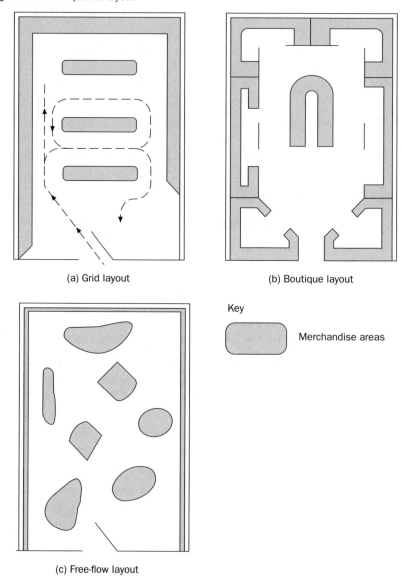

(a) Grid layout

(b) Boutique layout

Key

Merchandise areas

(c) Free-flow layout

(a) A logical arrangement helps to sell the stock:

    (i)   like products should be grouped together in displays

    (ii) within the store, a logical arrangement of categories of stock should be attempted ('adjacencies')

(*iii*) the position of stock within the store in some retail sectors is largely dependent on seasonal requirements, e.g. raincoats and umbrellas should be in prominent positions in the winter to encourage impulse buys.

(b) Displays with impact attract customer attention and they may also use space economically.

(*i*) mass displays of identical products can increase sales substantially: the eye appeal of massed packs can be enormous and this type of display is almost essential for small, promotional lines

(*ii*) displays should not be too tidy and symmetrical – a certain amount of planned disarrangement can encourage the customer to buy

(*iii*) point-of-sale material can often help increase sales but an excessive amount (of suppliers' messages) can confuse and take up valuable selling space – this type of promotional material also tends to creep over stock and windows, obscuring the real message of the product.

(c) Accessibility of merchandise:

(*i*) products should be as accessible as possible to the customer: merchandise handled is merchandise half sold (the security aspect must not, of course, be forgotten)

(*ii*) in some stores, like toys and electrical stores, some merchandise should be working and self-demonstrable

(*iii*) products should be displayed in proportion to their sales and stockturn

(*iv*) there is no point in featuring lines for which only a few items are in stock

(*v*) main aisle widths in non-food stores should be a minimum of 1 metre so that two people can pass in comfort

(*vi*) stockrooms should be neatly laid out, as far as possible on the same lines as the shop itself – this will speed service

(*vii*) best-selling lines on wall fixtures should be displayed just below eye-level, medium sellers on the bottom shelving and slower lines at the top: this is how the human eye travels normally over shop stock – again, block displays of similar items on a shelf should travel vertically, not horizontally ('vertical blocking').

23. Shelving

The methods of displaying goods for maximum accessibility to the customer may vary with the nature of the goods themselves. The basic method is the use of shelving, whether on walls or gondolas, and adapting the shelves within the whole unit to different purposes, rather than using special equipment. The advantage of this system of arrangement is that a neat orderly presentation of goods is made, which does not create confusion in a customer's mind. At the same time long lines of shelves showing a monotony of cans and packages are broken up and become much more interesting for inspection, while vertical blocking aids comparison and selection with optimal efficiency.

24. Other in-store checks

Other important factors that the store or department manager should cover, preferably before trading starts each morning, are:

(a) All lines carried by the store should be on display (not just in stock) and correctly ticketed where appropriate.

(b) Damaged goods should never be on normal display but may be sold off at a discount in a 'bargain corner'.

(c) Clutter and the 'bazaar effect' should be avoided.

(d) Stock should be regularly cleaned and dusted along with the shop, its fascia and fittings, from window line to the rear of the sales area.

(e) Displays of any product should be built so that they remain steady. Breakages can cost money and lose customers.

25. The objectives of merchandise display

To summarize the importance of window and in-store display we can say that its objectives are:

(a) To interest customers in merchandise and to draw them into the shop to enquire further.

(b) In particular to focus the customer's interest on those goods that the company's marketing plans are currently concentrating on selling.

(c) To make it as easy as possible for customers to find and examine the goods they want.

(d) To make it as easy as possible for the sales assistants to demonstrate and sell the products.

(e) To enhance the company's image and reputation.

Most multiples send out detailed computer-generated 'planograms' to their branches, which provide detailed layouts and illustrate how displays should look. All this helps to standardize the look of a multiple group's stores.

Allocation of selling area space

26. Basic practice

Selling area space is at a premium in most retail outlets, particularly those that depend on high sales volumes. In an attempt to optimize the selling area space used with its cost, space for individual lines is allocated as far as possible in line with their contribution to sales and profitability. The extension of space allocated to popular lines will, up to a point, increase their sales, and the opposite is often true when space allocation is reduced.

27. Importance of correct shelf allocation

The correct use of limited space within retail outlets is very important because it:

(a) Improves profitability (experiments have shown a 20–100 per cent increase in sales and profitability due to correct allocation).

(b) Helps to optimize the use of space with its costs.

(c) Helps give maximum exposure to market leaders.

(d) Makes adequate use of space on the basis of customer requirements for heavier-demand lines.

(e) Reduces out-of-stock shelf positions.

(f) Feeds back information to the buyers as to what lines are fast or slow movers.

(g) Makes shelf filling more concentrated and less frequent.

(h) Allows variety reduction with the use of Pareto analysis (the 80:20 rule) and the automatic elimination of slow movers.

Some words of caution:

(a) Experiments have shown that the effects of varying the number of identical facings (items) on a shelf display affect volume lines only.

(b) The theory and practice of extending display space to increase sales does not work in the case of slow-moving merchandise.

(c) Changes in sales can also occur when volume lines are displayed at varying shelf heights.

28. DPP

The allocation of space by computer analysis is now commonplace. The market-leading space management package is Spaceman which is produced by Nielsen Logistics. This is often linked to the concept of direct product profitability (DPP), that is establishing the individual contribution to profitability of each product by identifying costs of shelf space and transport, overheads and person-hours. The idea is to optimize the return for each type of merchandise as far as possible by matching its profitability against its space allocation. Space is reallocated by switching space to those products with the highest DPP. Profit for the firm should therefore be maximized. The main problems associated with this type of analysis are that its value in maximizing profit could be severely reduced by the costs of mounting and maintaining such a system, and the need to ensure that an adequate choice of merchandise is offered to the customer.

Progress test 19

1. Compare and contrast store image and atmosphere.

2. What should the store's sign communicate?

3. What are the three main types of shop front?

4. What are the important points to note in window display?

5. How should selling space be allocated in order to maximize sales and profitability?

6. What three main factors should be considered in determining store layout?

7. Detail the factors that are important in general in-store display.

8. How should display space be allocated?

9. Over the last few years many specialized design groups have flourished through providing design services to retailers. Equally, many retailers believe it is necessary to refurbish stores much more frequently than in the past. Examine why this should be so, and discuss the relationship between store layout and 'atmosphere'.

10. 'Store image' is a major influence on store selection. Identify those components that go to make up store image and, using a local retailer as an example, suggest how atmosphere and layout affect store image.

11. How might an understanding of (a) light and colour, (b) display techniques, and (c) store movement patterns be used by a practising retail manager? Illustrate your answers with examples from current practice.

12. Critically assess the application of DPP to merchandise planning decisions with particular reference to assortment and variety.

20 Customer service decisions

Introduction

The store environment offers the opportunity for the delivery of either excellent or poor customer service. This chapter considers additional services the retailer can offer, as well as exploring customer dissatisfaction and handling complaints.

1. Primary and complementary services

Retail organizations offer goods and services to the consumer for personal use. Some organizations concentrate on providing a service, for example, banks, insurance companies and estate agents, and they are known as primary service retailers. Many retailers, however, concentrate on selling physical products and offer services as a back-up. These complementary services, such as delivery, credit, installation, alteration, etc., are not essential to the retail operation but are often used strategically to provide a competitive advantage and enhance the retail offering.

2. Level of service

The extent to which a retailer provides consumers with additional services associated with purchasing a product or service will be determined primarily by the target market (and its expectations) and the retailer's objectives with particular regard to store image. The type of merchandise is also a major determinant of service requirements. For example bulky or heavy items often require the retailer to offer a delivery service. Also to be considered when setting the level of service would be the location of the store, competitors and the resources of the firm.

Credit

3. Types of credit

The provision of credit to customers by retail organizations has now become very common, particularly for costly items like large electrical products, furniture, cars and even clothing. In order to compete, most companies in these particular sectors, even discounters, offer some form of credit. The main types are detailed below.

4. Monthly account or charge account

This type of account is operated typically by department stores and normally there is no additional (interest) charge to the customer as long as accounts presented are paid promptly. If they are not, the retailer has to provide the extra credit, which is costly, and therefore effectively reduces gross margins (these tend to be higher to support the normal credit lines).

5. Budget account

Many stores, particularly in the clothing sector, offer this type of account, which enables the customer to buy goods on credit up to the value of perhaps 12 times the monthly payment. These accounts are often of the revolving credit type, so that when payments are made, new credit is increased to the same amount. A small charge is usually made, often a percentage of each purchase value.

6. Payment out of income

Forms of credit of this type are used for the purchase of goods such as clothing and travel goods for which hire-purchase facilities are not usually available. They normally require a down-payment and the balance to be paid over a 6, 12 or 24-month period, with an appropriate service charge made to cover administration and not infrequently to make an extra profit.

7. Hire-purchase

This is still a popular method of purchasing durable goods on credit. In case of default on payment, the retailer has the right of repossession under certain conditions because the goods are not sold outright, only hired to the customer until the debt is extinguished (unlike credit sale agreements). The retailer, instead of financing the hire-purchase debt, seeks support from a finance house. Although the customer's total debt may then be funded by an outside organization, the retailer still takes payments, repaying the finance house from this income. For some retail and television rental companies, these repayments can be a substantial form of short-term funds flow, collection costs being minimal.

8. Credit cards

Many financial institutions now offer credit cards, with most operating under the Visa or Mastercard payment system. They provide credit facilities to retailers who accept the cards and the retailer normally pays between 2 and 5 per cent of the value of the sale as a service charge. The retailer also pays a sum to join the scheme, with the amount depending on how many stores are owned.

Because of the cost to the retailer of offering these third-party credit cards, many larger retailers now operate their own in-house credit cards. These operations have uses in addition to the credit facilities. Since much information is gathered on individual customers on the application for credit and subsequent use of the card, this may also be used for promotional purposes (e.g. direct mail).

9. Advantages and disadvantages of credit to the retailer

(a) Advantages

- (*i*) Turnover is higher.
- (*ii*) Higher value purchases are encouraged.
- (*iii*) A better defined target market may be attracted.
- (*iv*) Customers become 'regulars'.
- (*v*) Buying becomes easier, e.g. by telephone.
- (*vi*) Goodwill is increased.

(b) Disadvantages

- (*i*) Additional capital is needed for funding the debt and this may have to be borrowed and interest will have to be paid.
- (*ii*) Extra overhead costs are incurred such as in keeping customers' accounts and preparing monthly statements.
- (*iii*) Some losses from bad debts have to be faced.

10. Credit policy

There is no point in operating credit unless it generates a sufficient increase in profits to cover interest charges on borrowed capital, administration costs and bad debts. The retailer has to think whether the capital could be used more profitably in other ways.

11. In-house credit control

The three main aspects to control are:

(a) **The application.** Customers selected for credit lines should be thoroughly vetted as to their financial standing and ability to pay in full. An application form usually has to be filled in and the vetting of the customer may be carried out by a credit status agency, such as Experian.

(b) **Authorization.** Identification of authorized customers is made possible by the issue of store credit cards. A system of credit sanction allows customers to purchase further goods on credit if the credit control department finds that their accounts show a credit balance.

(c) **Speed of payment.** To keep the capital invested to a minimum it is essential to send out accounts regularly, e.g. monthly. Slow payers should be sent polite reminders and if payment is very late (say over three months), without a good reason, the firm may have to threaten (and eventually take, if the threat is not effective) legal action.

12. EFTPOS

In 1987 Barclay's Bank launched its Delta card and the other major banks launched their Switch card which allows electronic funds transfer at the point of sale (EFTPOS). Customers pay when their personal debit card is scanned by the in-store terminal and their accounts are instantaneously and automatically debited. Although many retailers initially rejected the scheme due to its high cost compared to cheque clearance, the system quickly grew in popularity due to the convenience it offered the customer (for example, in simplifying checkout procedures), and is now widely used and expected by many customers.

Alternative service offerings

13. Hours

There is an increasing tendency for many types of store to stay open for longer hours. Once again, this is in response to the customers' requirement for convenience. With more and more women working it has become necessary for grocery stores to stay open longer in the evening. Many DIY operators also operate outside the traditional nine to five, six days a week in recognition of the fact that their customers want this type of product outside normal working hours. Ultimately, the retailer's decision on opening hours depends on the target market. Many small 'convenience stores' have increased turnover by up to 50 per cent by extending opening hours to the 'eight 'til late' type of format and some stores are now open 24 hours a day.

14. Delivery

The provision of a delivery service is essential for certain types of merchandise such as furniture or large electrical durables such as washing machines. For others it can provide a competitive advantage and enhance the retail offering by providing time and place convenience. Some fast food operators (e.g. Domino's Pizza) have chosen to offer a delivery service as one way of setting themselves apart from the competition.

There can be considerable problems associated with the provision of a delivery service and it is essential to set up a system to handle them. Perhaps the greatest issue is minimizing cost, particularly in situations of considerable variation in demand. Also, when customers purchase products they want immediate possession. If a delivery service is provided customer dissatisfaction can be caused if delivery is not on time or the product is damaged in transit. Delivery problems are also caused if the customer is not at home on the agreed delivery date – some retailers try to minimize this by phoning the customer before delivery. Certain types of merchandise will require more than delivery and the retailer should determine whether to offer an installation service either free or for a small additional payment.

15. Alteration and repairs

These may be offered either as part of the customer service facility or as an income-generating service in their own right. For example, many clothing retailers offer minor alterations at no charge but will also offer to alter garments some time after the initial sale for a fee. Similarly, electrical appliance retailers will arrange for free repair of items within the warranty period and charge outside of warranty on a full profit-making basis. The provision of extended guarantees can also be a useful way of generating customer satisfaction and increasing revenue.

The decision to offer an alteration and repair service does not automatically require an in-house facility to be set up. These services can often be subcontracted to a third party, although this may lead to loss of some control and longer service time.

16. Wrapping

It is interesting to note that US consumers expect their purchases to be wrapped whereas in the UK few retailers offer a full wrapping service. Some UK supermarkets offer help with the loading of groceries into the shopper's bag but very few retailers offer the gift wrapping service featuring bows and ribbons that is commonly available for an additional fee in US stores.

Handling complaints

17. Complaints

Even in the best run establishments there will be occasions when a customer is not completely satisfied and has cause to complain. It is here that the truly successful retailer will stand above the competition by converting a dissatisfied customer to a satisfied one who will return. With the high costs of marketing in today's highly competitive retail scene it is less expensive to resolve a current customer's problem than to win new customers.

18. Causes of complaints

Major causes of complaint are products not being in stock (especially when advertised), unsatisfactory performance of products or unsatisfactory repair or service. Many complaints are easily resolved but require a procedure to deal with them.

19. Complaint-handling procedure

Minor complaints may be handled by the sales assistants but customers will often appreciate the attention of a higher level of employee. In larger stores a customer service department will handle complaints. Whatever the appropriate complaint-handling procedure, it should be clear to both employees and customer where to go to complain and who to speak to. Standard procedures should be adopted and all employees informed of them.

20. Returns

A customer who returns merchandise that was found to be damaged or broken when unpacked is obviously entitled to return it and demand a replacement or refund. However, there are other circumstances that are not quite as clear-cut and require some extra thought by the retailer. If the retailer is offering a high level of customer service a liberal returns policy would be appropriate; for example, offering a replacement because of a customer's 'change of mind' or making a mistake in thinking an item would match or fit in with another product they already own. Marks & Spencer has operated a liberal returns policy for many years which has resulted in a good deal of extra business in the form of buying gifts, with customers knowing that if the item is not suitable the recipient of the gift could return it (in perfect condition) for replacement.

Returns or refunds are normally offered only on the production of a receipt but here common sense must prevail, e.g. a customer who received an item as a gift will not have a receipt.

21. Product adjustment

Retailers can satisfy most complaints about damaged or unsuitable products by exchanging them, but complaints about poor quality should be handled very carefully for fear of damaging the store image. Therefore, higher quality products should be offered as a replacement with an appropriate price adjustment if necessary to protect the reputation of the store as not selling 'shoddy' goods.

Complaints about products not being in stock can be dealt with by agreeing to stock the product, explaining why the product is not stocked and offering an alternative or directing the customer to a store that does stock that product.

22. Price adjustments

Since it is not always possible or practicable to exchange or adjust a product (e.g. an electrical durable delivered to the customer's home), the retailer can often satisfy the customer by offering to reduce the price. A price reduction is often an effective way of demonstrating to the customer that the store is making a special effort to correct a problem, and it is usually possible for the retailer to make a claim upon the manufacturer.

New services

Retailers should constantly monitor their service levels and compare them with competitors. Today's sophisticated consumers have moved beyond the search for lowest possible prices and are demanding higher service levels. New services are being introduced, copied by competitors and then replaced, upgraded or abandoned in the constant battle for competitive advantage.

Progress test 20

1. What is the difference between primary and complementary services?

2. What is meant by the level of service?

3. Describe the main types of credit.

4. What are the advantages and disadvantages of credit to the retailer?

5. Describe four customer services, other than credit, that many retailers offer.

6. Describe a good complaint-handling procedure.

7. Why should retailers constantly monitor their service levels?

8. Provide examples of customer services that retailers have offered in order to gain competitive advantage. Recommend a customer service strategy for a specific department within a department store. Should this service level be higher or lower than operates in other departments?

Part three

Administration

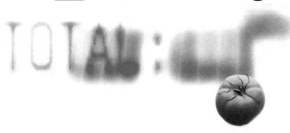

21 General management

Introduction

This chapter considers what management means to retailers and other businesses, key interpersonal skills and how retail managers can use their skills.

1. Retail management

Historically management in the British retail sector has not been noted for its effectiveness. The same could fairly be said of British industry as a whole, but retailing labours under a number of drawbacks:

(a) The sector generally is more product- than people-focused, a situation not helped by the centralization that multiple retailers have imposed upon their structures.

(b) Because it is operationally biased, retailing tends to be short-termist and lacking in strategic vision.

(c) Traditionally the sector is seen as a young person's game, offering 'holiday' jobs in low-paid, low-skilled occupations with few prospects of promotion and personal development. Staff turnover, as a result, averages 30 per cent.

(d) Strategically, retail has been criticized. John Richards (for many years one of the City's leading analysts) has followed such well-known retailers as Ralph Halpern, Gerald Ratner and George Davies. He said he has seen a recurrent pattern of retail entrepreneurs 'creating something wonderful which they subsequently smash to bits'. Financial Times People column 02.05.03

The outcome of all this is that many retail staff may feel disengaged. This means that they are demotivated; they 'leave their brains in the locker room'. Such revelations are totally counter to received knowledge in management today. A host of ideas have flowed from business schools and consultants over the past few years purporting to offer general solutions to the big question, 'What makes people work?' However, a few leading retailers have adopted some of these ideas and the benefits seem now to be evident – as in the case of Tesco.

2. The nature of management

A simple definition of management might be 'causing resources to be used in an effective way to meet organizational objectives'. According to the management guru Peter Drucker, the seven tasks of managers are that they must be able to:

(a) Manage by objectives.

(b) Take more risks and for a longer period ahead. Risk-taking decisions will also have to be made at lower levels in the organization.

(c) Make strategic decisions.

(d) Build an integrated team, each member of which is capable of managing and of measuring their own performance and results in relation to common objectives.

(e) Communicate information fast and clearly. They have to be able to motivate people and must be able to obtain the responsible participation of other managers or the professional specialists and of all other workers.

(f) See the business as a whole and integrate their functions with it.

(g) Relate the product and industry to the total environment, to find what is significant in it and what to take into account in their decisions or actions. And, increasingly, the field of vision of tomorrow's managers will have to take in developments outside their own market or country. Increasingly, they will have to see economics, political and social developments on a worldwide scale and to integrate worldwide trends into their own decisions.

3. Skills needed by managers

According to work carried out for Boyden International, the recruitment consultants, the skills that managers need to do their jobs properly are administrative, decisional (problem-solving), communication, motivation and self-motivation skills.

(a) **Administrative skills**. Administration can be defined as the setting up, use, maintenance and development of systems of forecasting, planning, control, organizing, co-ordination and delegation. Consultants on both sides of the Atlantic agree that the most important administrative abilities are:

    (*i*)   planning and organizing in advance of events
    (*ii*) delegation
    (*iii*) following-up to check that instructions have been understood and executed.

(b) **Problem-solving skills**. In order of importance these are:

- (*i*) judgement – reaching appropriate conclusions from available data
- (*ii*) problem analysis – grasping the source, nature and key dimensions of a problem
- (*iii*) decisiveness in making a choice between various possibilities
- (*iv*) being innovative in tackling problems
- (*v*) application of abstract reasoning so as to formulate general principles from observed occurrences.

(c) **Communication skills:**

- (*i*) active listening
- (*ii*) being able to engage in dialogue (rather than a monologue) when talking with another person or in a small group
- (*iii*) speaking one's ideas with poise, relevance, persuasiveness and clarity
- (*iv*) effective writing.

(d) **Motivation skills**. These involve the ability to influence other people. In order of importance, these are:

- (*i*) leadership – directing the behaviour of others towards the achievement of common goals by charisma, insights or the assertion or will
- (*ii*) the creation of an impression of self-assurance and so commanding respect
- (*iii*) the demonstration of sensitivity to the needs and feelings of others
- (*iv*) assertiveness – taking a forceful approach.

(e) **Self-motivation skills**. These include:

- (*i*) drive – the ability to make sensible decisions under conditions of stress
- (*ii*) consistently high standards of goal execution
- (*iii*) initiative – being the first to start
- (*iv*) perseverance
- (*v*) adaptability
- (*vi*) willingness to take risks
- (*vii*) self-reliance
- (*viii*) a positive attitude to self-development.

Store managers require these skills in the following sequence of importance: communication, motivation, problem-solving and administration. We now discuss in more detail the key interpersonal skills required by operational managers.

Communication

Communication skills are vital for managers. Communication is a two-way process where a message is sent that is intended to be understood. Understanding is the minimum response and this response may develop into an activity or feedback. This produces the two-way effect from the communicator to the audience.

Communication in an organization goes upwards, downwards and laterally. There is also an inward and an outward communication to and from the external environment. At a deeper level, communication is often designed to motivate and through this to change behaviour.

4. Channels of communication

There are four media through which communication can be made: verbally, in writing, visually and by body language.

(a) **Verbal or oral**. This is most effective in face-to-face situations like interviews and meetings. The communicators are able to 'edit' what they say as they go along by noting the limb and facial responses of the audience as well as their spoken reactions; this is not to say that the spoken communication should not be prepared beforehand – this is essential for all types of communication. One problem with a spoken message is that there is usually no record of it.

(b) **Written**. Again if this is personalized it can be very effective. Some people would rather believe what they read than what they hear – such is the power of the written word. This makes it important to pick the correct words when writing a report or a letter. A major problem with written communication is that there is not the immediate feedback that there is with many oral forms.

(c) **Visual**. This includes TV, poster plans, charts and so forth. Visual communication can be very effective for large groups of people who may have some common characteristic, e.g. they all work in your company. But visual communication is rather impersonal and lacks immediacy and relevance to individuals. It acts instead as a support to other media.

(d) **Body language**. Face and body movements, which are often unconscious, give people away. Although we may be able to control what we say and, indeed, say things that we do not mean, our body language sometimes gives the lie to our words. This form of, often involuntary, communication is most important in meetings and interviews.

5. Barriers to communication

There are four basic barriers to good communication:

(a) **Bad communication method**. The transmitter or communicator of information may be bad at speaking in public. We've all seen the poor person who gets tongue-tied or who uses the wrong words and so on. Public speaking is an art and it has to be learned. Messages should be clear, understandable, accurate, complete, useful and brief.

(b) **Faulty perception**. The audience or the receiver of information often have their own ideas as to what is being said. Our perception is the way we organize the sense information (e.g. what we see, hear, etc.) to make it useful to us. Our experience in the past helps form the way we interpret what is said to us – and quite often we don't want to know! We screen out ideas and thoughts that we do not understand or that are unpleasant to us, and so it is important that the communicator knows the audience well.

(c) **Status difference**. In large, bureaucratic organizations everyone knows their place. Junior staff may fear their seniors and senior staff may use their formal positions to bully more junior people. This barrier is enormously difficult to remove.

(d) **Organizational weakness**. Sometimes the structure of the organization has not been designed well. There may be gaps in communication between departments or over-long lines of communication. Sometimes there are parts of the organization that are overloaded with information so that really important things are missed. Such weaknesses need what is called a communications audit or check on the ways in which messages move within the system and how effective it is.

6. Solutions to communication barriers

(a) Training is the way to solve a manager's inability to communicate. Literally hundreds of report writing and public speaking courses are run in the UK each year.

(b) Feedback needs to be established with the person receiving the message. Has it been received and understood? A few questions from the communicator will soon establish this.

(c) In communications, listening is generally the most important skill. A few tips from a US study:

(i) listen for ideas as well as facts, i.e. do not be overwhelmed by the latter, but ask yourself 'Why am I being told this?'
(ii) judge content not delivery
(iii) listen optimistically even if you are bored
(iv) do not jump to conclusions
(v) concentrate on evaluating what the speaker is saying and react appropriately using body language or speech
(vi) keep an open mind and your emotions under control.

(d) Much more informality in the management style of the organization may be essential. Unfortunately this could mean the sacking of the chief executive!

(e) After carefully auditing the effectiveness of communication it is essential to bring the system together so that it becomes and remains a well-organized, interactive structure.

Motivation

Motivation can just mean 'doing more than you are paid for'. There is a clear link between good people management practice and high levels of job satisfaction and loyalty. Managers need to understand this link and therefore appreciate the ideas behind motivation. We examine here three theorists: Maslow, Herzberg and McGregor.

7. Maslow's hierarchy of needs

Maslow's theory of motivation has two major components:

(a) Maslow attempted to identify the major needs that human beings have – the needs that form the basic rationale for the ways in which people behave.

(b) Maslow claimed these needs could be placed or seen in a hierarchy of importance – indicating that in most circumstances the lower level needs have to be at least partially satisfied before a person will pursue a higher level need (*see* Figure 21.1).

The needs Maslow identified are:

(a) Physiological needs. The requirement for food, water, shelter, etc. Until these basics are obtained, other needs are unimportant. (These are also called basic needs.)

(b) Security needs. The need for stability, longer-term safety, future satisfaction, etc.

(c) Social needs. The requirement for the companionship of others. This is met by membership of a range of formal and informal groups. (These are also called love or belongingness needs.)

(d) Status needs. The feeling of making a valuable contribution to a group, which is seen as useful by those who belong to it. (These are also called ego or esteem needs.)

(e) Self-fulfilment needs. The need to utilize and develop the full range of capabilities and potential that a human being possesses.

Two important qualifications need to be made at this stage, as Maslow's approach to motivation is often regarded in a rather rigid way:

(a) Although it was intended to be seen as a hierarchy of needs, it should not be interpreted as claiming that people will only start thinking about higher

Figure 21.1 Maslow's hierarchy of needs

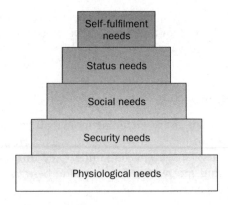

level needs if the level of need they are presently concerned with is completely satisfied. For example, one's security needs may never be completely satisfied, but this does not mean that this situation will prevent a concern with the 'higher order' needs of status and self-fulfilment.

(b) Maslow's work has sometimes been regarded as a general view of motivation to work. This is incorrect – Maslow's theory can be used to identify some of the means by which companies can meet the needs of their employees and to help answer the question 'What makes workers work?'

8. Herzberg's two-factor theory

Building on Maslow's work, Frederick Herzberg based his research on interviewing large groups of accountants and engineers. He asked them what they liked or disliked about their work. The things they disliked most were what Herzberg called hygiene or surface factors. These had to do with the job environment but not the job itself. They included:

(a) Pay and working conditions

(b) Company policy

(c) Physical environment.

If these factors are poor, said Herzberg, they lead to job dissatisfaction, but if they are improved they only reduce the level of demotivation and do not positively increase motivation to work.

The managers interviewed said that the things they liked most were aspects of the job itself. These included:

(a) Achievement

(b) Increased responsibility

(c) Interesting and challenging work.

These job factors were satisfying and motivating if they were present in a job.

Recent research by Investors in People UK shows that salary levels are not the biggest factor that influences the choice of job. Graduates planning careers were polled and 93 per cent said that joining an organization that focuses on training and development was important.

9. Job enlargement

Following on from Herzberg's studies, the ideas of job enlargement have been applied to the design of jobs. There are two kinds of job enlargement:

(a) **Horizontal job enlargement** (usually just 'job enlargement') occurs when two or more functionally linked jobs at the same level of responsibility are merged. It is the opposite of job specialization and aims to make jobs more interesting, e.g. in a bank a clerk might input figures from documents into a computer and at intervals take the processed documents to the central filing section.

(b) **Vertical job enlargement** (usually called 'job enrichment') occurs when two or more functionally linked jobs at different levels of responsibility are merged. This kind of job design increases the challenge of jobs. For instance, machine operators in a factory may be given the responsibility of checking the quality of their outputs. It has sometimes been said that 'one person's job enrichment is another person's job impoverishment' and so job designers must be careful to see that such schemes do not cause redundancies. Redesigned jobs usually have to be paid more money as compensation for the change in work methods. Some of this extra payment could, of course, be financed from productivity savings. No job design system should be seen to be producing redundancies because of the demotivating effects this would have on a workforce.

10. McGregor's theories

Douglas McGregor proposed two theories: 'X' and 'Y'. These are both assumptions, which managers may or may not hold about their workers:

(a) **Theory 'X'** suggests that workers actually avoid work and responsibility and can only be motivated by crude 'carrot-and-stick' methods.

(b) **Theory 'Y'** suggests that workers look upon work as being as rational as rest and play. They want more responsibility and the chance to participate. They are motivated more by job content factors than by those external to the job.

Of course, in real life, workers are likely to exhibit traits from both theories at particular times. The importance of McGregor's work is its relationship with leadership theories and the assumptions they make about people, e.g. autocratic managers see workers through the 'X' prism.

11. Focusing on people

The way managers can motivate others is rather like marketing – finding out peoples' needs and motives and then providing a solution that fits them. This requires the manager to spend time by observing but, above all, by talking to individual members of staff to find out where their skills, knowledge and attitudes lie. The manager needs to know what the individual's proven skills, knowledge and attitudes are. This data may come from interviews, tests, observations, questionnaires or, preferably, a mixture of all four – a skills audit. Individuals are often unsure of their relationships with others and with the organization as a whole. Individual skills, knowledge and attitudes are not always apparent. They may be deliberately hidden or they may be latent and therefore unknown to anyone, including the individual themselves.

Most individuals are ego-driven, which means that they want at least to be regarded as useful if not important. Therefore it is vital for the manager not only to gain individual's confidence but to pass confidence over to them. Unfortunately many managers still do not appreciate the importance of the human resource in terms of the cliché that 'everyone is different'. Managers often treat people as a homogeneous resource that can be applied to tasks without reference to differences and, indeed, see time spent on building up detailed information on individuals as being a waste of time. But the manager, to be successful in achieving goals through other people, needs to give each subordinate confidence. In the retail sector today a new focus on people is seen as having positive business advantages. Evidence of this can be found in some of the job titles springing up at head offices. For example, Sainsbury's has a head of talent, Tesco a director of learning and at W.H. Smith there is a people director.

12. Motivational methods

One approach to motivating staff is to try to instil confidence in them in three ways: confidence in their job, confidence in themselves and confidence in the team with which they work.

(a) **The job**. Individual employees need to believe that their job has value. They need to understand the context of their job and its contribution to the effectiveness of the whole organization. This encourages them to think about their job and how execution can be improved. They will tend to do this more if they know that their contributions will be noted and recognized but, deeper still, many individuals get an ego-trip over their own cleverness and how it marks them out from supposedly less clever employees.

Staff often watch and listen to managers, probably to detect some slip-up or other which then makes them feel superior. Managers needs to lead by example: they are always on show. Managers who nip off early or who have the smell of alcohol on their breath are not giving a good example because the watchers will accept that as the norm and will tend to think 'If they do it so can I'. The admission from staff members that they 'only run the baling machine in the store' suggests that they feel that their job is inferior. They do not realize that if the baling is not done the store would soon be submerged in unwanted cardboard boxes. They need to be made to feel wanted and important. The importance of the job must be put over.

(b) **The individual**. People need to have confidence in their value as individuals. The reason why so many otherwise intelligent employees are often openly frustrated is that they lack challenge. It is vital for managers to identify such individuals and to encourage them to volunteer their skills for the general good of the organization. This is not only good for the organization but good for the individual.

Again, individuals need praise. It is often said that when things go wrong subordinates 'get the bullet' but when they do something in an excellent manner it often receives no response at all.

Managers need to probe beneath the surface when it comes to the problem of the 'lazy' worker. Particularly when usually reliable employees begin to exhibit bad working habits, there is a need for a manager to ask what is wrong – to show concern about what personal or domestic difficulties are causing problems in their work.

(c) **The team**. People need to have confidence in their value as a team. Managers often reflect their own inadequacies by blaming their staff. Effortlessly, they victimize or show favour and this further demoralizes employees who, at least formally, are members of a section or department. The manager must help group members to feel part of a team. One-way communicators who rely on directives cannot expect the members of their department to think like a team. Only when two-way open discussions between all group members and the manager occur can this happen. Briefing the team together can encourage two-way flows of ideas and feelings. Blending people together and encouraging them to support each other can then get the team to work together.

Management techniques

13. Managers and the environment

Retail managers along with others face today the most turbulent environment for probably 70 years. Political, economic, sociocultural and technological change has rarely been so dynamic and this must stretch the skills, knowledge and attitudes of managers to the limit. The phrase 'the only constant is change' has become a cliché but it means that the techniques discussed in this section must be applied as effectively as possible by managers. It is a truism that while the techniques may be efficacious, their application often leaves something to be desired. This in turn suggests that managers must be adequately and continuously trained to meet the challenges of constant change. The idea of the learning organization, referred to in Chapter 4, is crucial, particularly for firms in the most fast-changing trades such as mobile telecommunications retailing.

14. Key management techniques

(a) **Balanced scorecard**. With a growing recognition that financial measurement techniques alone were insufficient for adequate performance monitoring, the 'balanced scorecard' approach has been developed. This typically includes measures in each of four areas: financial, customer, internal business processes and learning and growth. Some organizations add a fifth area, which reflects their mission.

(b) **Benchmarking**. Here companies compare and measure policies, practices, philosophies and performance against the best performing organizations in the world, with a view to emulating them.

(c) **Downsizing**. Although the term 'downsizing' is often associated with job losses engineered for the purpose of cost saving, it can also mean a movement closer to customers and employees. The current belief is that large companies have to act like small companies. Wal-Mart attempts this at unit level, although it is the largest retailer in the world. Downsizing can also be carried out by break-up and demerger (*see* Chapter 3).

(d) Empowerment. This means allowing individual employees to use their own initiative to make a difference while providing them with the resources to do so. The concept is connected with downsizing where if delayering occurs (taking out management levels in a hierarchy) the wider spans of control created need empowerment to support them. Managers are in effect giving more delegated authority to their subordinates. Empowerment is also connected with TQM (*see* below).

(e) Total quality management (TQM). TQM is much more than the processes described in ISO9000 and is a 'way of being'. In this respect it is rather like the marketing concept with which it has been associated. Put simply, TQM is a four-process approach to market focus:

(*i*) *Set the objectives*. These must meet or if possible surpass customer expectations. Information on these may be drawn from customer relationship management (CRM) sources or general consumer research.

(*ii*) *Create a plan to meet the objectives*. Here employees need to participate both as empowered individuals and as a team.

(*iii*) *Set up feedback monitoring systems*. These compare actual results with the objectives and help the team to take appropriate corrective action.

(*iv*) *Involve top management*. The board of directors must be seen to be supportive of the TQM programme. TQM is also supported by staff suggestion schemes based on the idea of 'continuous improvement' in quality. Marks & Spencer receives 150 staff suggestions for improvement each week.

Progress test 21

1. Explain some of the special problems that affect the retail sector.

2. List, in order of importance, the skills that store managers need to deploy.

3. Discuss some of the solutions a consultant might suggest after an audit of a retailer's communications problems.

4. What factors do you think motivate shop staff to work?

5. How do you think job enlargement could be applied to a retail store?

6. Explain how a retailer could use a total quality management programme to improve its performance.

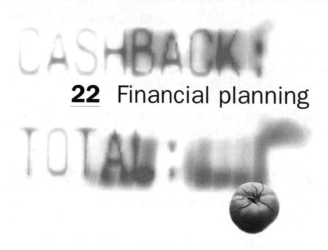

22 Financial planning

Introduction

Profit is essential for the survival of any business activity. This chapter explores aspects of profit planning, budgetary control and financial measures of retail performance.

Profit planning

1. Profit

The retailer must set profit objectives or targets to be reached in a particular time period. Generally, profit objectives will be determined in conjunction with sales targets, but bearing in mind that the profit generated should be compared to that which might be achieved by investing the capital employed in the business in an alternative (and perhaps less risky) manner.

2. Sales revenue and costs

Since profit is the surplus after deducting the cost of goods sold and expenses from the sales revenue, then a sales forecast is often the starting point for profit planning. Sales forecasting was dealt with in Chapter 12; for a new business the sales forecast is usually calculated by the market share method, but for established businesses it is very much easier since historical data is available for extrapolation. Similarly, costs can be estimated for the given sales volume from historical cost data or industry norms.

3. Improving profit

The profit estimated from the above procedure should be compared with profit objectives and ways of improving profit should be considered. Essentially these will fall into two categories: increasing sales and reducing costs.

4. Increasing sales revenue

This can be achieved by a number of methods; for example, by increasing promotional activity such as advertising or personal selling. Improving customer service helps to stimulate sales, as will adding other products or services. Changing prices can also lead to increased sales revenue.

5. Reducing costs

There are many expenses involved in running a retail operation and these need to be carefully monitored and controlled. Wage costs are one of the most significant and may be reduced by better scheduling of staff. Reduction of stock levels can also reduce costs, as could a reduction of service level. The relationship between cost, sales and profit should be fully understood. Break-even analysis can be useful to show how the classification of fixed and variable costs helps determine the impact of changes in sales on profits (*see* Figure 11.4).

Budgetary control

6. Meaning of budgetary control

This is the name given to the technique of planning and measuring a firm's operations usually in cash terms for a specific period. Unlike the quarterly, six-monthly and annual financial accounts, which are a historical record of a firm's performance, the budgets attempt to forecast the activity of the firm and to chart progress as it occurs, so that action necessary to deal with the changing situation can be taken. Budgeting shows what is happening in the firm and the management's task is to discover why it is happening and to do something about it.

7. Advantages of budgeting

(a) Helps to ensure the most efficient use of a firm's resources and helps to prevent waste.

(b) Reduces risk and helps ensure profits.

(c) Replaces guesswork, to a large extent, by facts.

(d) Acts as a target-setting agency.

(e) Pinpoints areas for investigation and corrective action in good time.

(f) Permits 'control by exception' so that only variances from the forecast need be brought to the management's attention.

(g) Fixes responsibility within the organization for the achievement of targets.

(h) Engenders co-operation and co-ordination within the firm.

8. Disadvantages of budgeting

(a) May stifle 'over-achievement', which may result in stiffer targets being set in the future.

(b) Over-elaboration or inflexibility can produce a situation where the budget becomes an end in itself and not just another management tool.

9. Types of budget

In retailing there are normally three main types of budget produced:

(a) **The operating budget**. Made up from three other budgets: the sales budget, the merchandise budget and the expense budget.

(b) **The cash budget**. Relates to receipts and payments of money.

(c) **The capital budget**. Covers capital expenditure.

These budgets are interrelated and forecasts in one sphere may depend upon what occurs in others.

10. The sales budget

The core of the sales budget is the sales forecast. Because it affects other forecasts, such as cash flow, it is important to refine it as much as possible – paying particular regard to the following factors:

(a) **Comparability**. Exceptional or non-recurring events (e.g. local sales, branch closure for refitting) should be excluded. The calendar year presents a problem (e.g. different numbers of Saturdays in one month compared with the same month in the following year) so that most retail firms work on 13 four-weekly periods or on a quarterly basis (5 weeks + 4 weeks + 4 weeks).

(b) **Modifications**. Modifications may affect either a single trade (e.g. changes in consumers' tastes for particular types of furniture) or the economy as a whole (e.g. lower volume of consumer offtake due to a recession) or local circumstances (e.g. higher unemployment due to closure of factories).

(c) **Data sources**. The main data sources are:

   (i) *Internal information*. This details turnover for the past period and a trend of sales over the past three or four years may be taken. The use of moving annual totals and other moving totals and averages will highlight trends. Note should be taken of newly extended or modernized branches.
   (ii) *External sources*. These include the indices of value and volume sales experienced by broad categories of retail trades, for example Mintel or Keynote Publications. These indicate sales levels at current and constant prices since it is most important, particularly in times of high inflation, to make allowances for increased prices that may mask changes in volume. Some sector's trade associations produce their own data on product offtake, such as in the consumer electrical and car industries.

11. The merchandise budget

This is as realistic a forecast as possible of the cost of goods sold, i.e. the cost of the merchandise for the expected sales volume.

12. The expense budget

This is concerned with expenditure planned for the coming period, specifically in connection with generating the forecast level of sales.

Expenses are classified into fixed, variable and semi-fixed:

(a) **Fixed expenses**. These do not vary with the volume of the business, e.g. rent and rates.

(b) **Variable expenses**. These alter in proportion to the trading volume, e.g. wrapping materials, commission payments.

(c) **Semi-fixed costs**. These contain a fixed element and do not change proportionately to the volume of business, e.g. head office salaries.

13. Expense control

Expenses are inevitably more controllable because of their internal context than other business variables such as sales and gross profit. They can also be used more positively as task-setters for management. The achievement of control depends on these prerequisites:

(a) **Adequate degree of analysis of the actual and budgeted expenses**. For this to be possible the expenses must be:

    (*i*) categorized under homogeneous cost heads, e.g. advertising, so as to make proper comparisons

    (*ii*) not over-detailed so that the reasons for variances are hidden.

(b) **Divergences**. There should be a frequent drawing out of the cost centres and expense sources so that divergences between budget and actual expenses can be quickly spotted. Most retail companies raise detailed expense accounts at least monthly.

(c) **Explanation of the variations between actual and budgeted**. These must be rapid, lucid and accurate so that speedy corrective action can be taken by management (for example, some form of exception reporting can be used to aid the scrutiny).

(d) **Cost heads**. The main cost heads met with in retailing are, roughly in order of magnitude:

    (*i*)   cost of goods sold

    (*ii*) wages and salaries

    (*iii*) accommodation costs (rents, rates, lighting, heating, etc.)

    (*iv*) general expenses (e.g. transport).

14. The operating budget

This pulls together the sales, merchandise and expense budgets and is usually split into either 13 four-weekly periods or, more commonly, into quarters, each three-monthly period containing five, four and four weeks respectively. Comparison is made with the previous year's actual sales with expenses and profits shown as percentages (*see* Table 22.1).

Table 22.1 Operating budget

Four-weekly periods →

	Actual 2003 £	%	Period 1 £	%	Period 2 £	%	Period 12 £	%	Period 13 £	%	Budget 2004 £	%
Sales	3,554,207	100.0	388,000	100.0	402,000	100.0					4,851,700	100.0
Gross profit	1,137,104	32.0	128,400	33.1	135,500	33.7					1,666,000	34.3
Expenses:												
Advertising	84,319	2.4	1,000	0.3	2,000	0.5					127,110	2.6
Branch salaries	178,835	5.0	17,600	4.5	18,390	4.6					285,000	5.9
Head office salaries	102,223	2.9	11,900	3.1	11,900	3.0					188,700	3.9
Establishment costs	250,207	7.0	30,770	7.9	30,930	7.6					400,600	8.3
Overheads:												
Financial	9,885	0.3	1,180	0.3	1,180	0.3					15,330	0.3
Legal	8,489	0.2	960	0.2	960	0.2					12,570	0.3
Distribution	35,066	1.0	3,550	0.9	5,400	1.3					54,500	1.1
Others	48,771	1.4	5,780	1.6	5,840	1.6					79,400	1.6
Total expenses	717,795	20.2	72,740	18.8	76,600	19.1					1,163,210	24.0
Net profit before tax	419,309	11.8	55,660	14.3	58,900	14.6					502,790	10.3

15. The cash budget

This is a forecast intended to ensure the maintenance of a satisfactory balance between anticipated income and expenditure. At its simplest level this can be called the 'cash flow' of the business. The regulation of income and expenditure is particularly important where a company is engaged in forms of hire-purchase or credit transactions (e.g. mail order companies), or when it exhibits a highly seasonal sales pattern where there may be low turnover months when losses are unavoidable. The important ratios to be borne in mind here are the cash level (i.e. cash in hand or at bank or other liquid resources), cash and debtors in relation to current liabilities, and cash, debtors and stock in relation to current liabilities (i.e. working capital).

Both the income and expenditure of the business depend on various factors and these are as follows:

(a) **The income of the business**. This is dependent upon:

(i) cash sales (consider the pattern to date and the balance of sales that are made on credit)
(ii) interest received (easily predictable)
(iii) debtors (these are only likely to be important for the retailer if, like department stores or mail-order houses, they extend a great deal of credit; it is important in these cases to consider the proportion who are likely to pay promptly on arrival of the statement and how many will pay last month's or earlier debts).

Other types of income include interest on investments, proceeds from sale of assets, foreign exchange transactions, etc.

(b) **The expenditure of the business**. This is dependent upon:

(i)   purchases as specified in the merchandise budget
(ii) creditors (their terms and periods of credit permitted)
(iii) wages and salaries
(iv) other overheads
(v)   taxation as and when due for payment
(vi) dividends due to shareholders
(vii) interest due on debentures or other loans
(viii) planned capital expenditure.

16. Cash flow

There are three time-scales that are important when projecting the financing of company activities. These are:

(a) **Short-term cash forecast**. This involves the day-to-day control of the cash position, detailing each financial movement in stock, expenses, capital expenditure and so on (the time-scale is usually up to four to six weeks). The short-term forecast also schedules forward commitments and, if necessary, can allow their rearrangement so that temporary shortage of funds can be overcome.

The short-term forecast is particularly useful for companies trading to the limit of their overdrafts at any time and also companies with surplus funds where management has been charged with making the best use of these funds, e.g. by placing them on 'overnight call' on the London money market.

(b) The annual cash budget. This highlights periods of strain on liquidity so that budgets can be adjusted accordingly. This type of budgeting is carried out by most retailers but is of particular use to those with marked seasonal changes in volume.

(c) Long-term budget. Here the time-scale is up to five years. It is important because:

(*i*)   it will affect the products the company will sell so as to achieve its profitability targets
(*ii*) it will have a bearing on the markets the firm will sell into
(*iii*) it must also help to determine the market share planned by the company
(*iv*) it will affect the size and range of outlets opened by the company.

In other words, the long-term cash budget shows the range of expansion that is possible and will help to answer questions like: Can the company finance the rate of expansion on its existing overdraft arrangements? Should some other form of finance be sought to cushion the company against possible poor trading conditions?

17. The capital budget

Capital expenditure is necessary in the longer-term interests of the firm, e.g. the replacement of or addition to existing assets, such as equipment or buildings. The problems of capital expenditure in retailing revolve around four factors:

(a) Investment is often based on property (the location decision for which few alternatives exist).

(b) The time-scale is longer in retailing than in manufacturing due partly to the fact that leases tend to be for 20 years and also because many retail companies do not receive an acceptable rate of return for one to three years after the investment has been completed.

(c) As far as multiple retailing is concerned, the company's own corporate strategy may determine the capital cost of the project in terms of branch size, cost of fittings and so on.

(d) The income that the retail unit makes may ultimately be significantly larger than that made on an industrial capital project of the same value.

18. Responsibility for budgeting

The gathering and co-ordination of budgetary information is normally the responsibility of the management and cost accountants, whereas the financial accountants are more involved with the historical, end-of-period figures and the construction of the published accounts. In larger companies a budget committee may carry out the co-ordination and represent the buying, selling, property development and other functions. Budgeting should always be carried out backed by the expertise of the operational personnel, who will obviously be interested in seeing that target setting is fair.

19. Reporting

In order that a budgetary control system is made effective key results must be reported upon at regular intervals. The regularity of reports and detail required will vary according to the type of retail operation. With EPOS systems, detailed daily reports can be produced comparing actual sales versus budget and previous years' performance. As well as these, a monthly reporting system for senior management is common.

The components of the monthly report should be the profit-determining variables:

(a) **Sales**. By outlet, four-weekly and cumulatively, giving actual, budget and variances.

(b) **Gross profit**. This should at least cover the sales at selling prices and the purchases at cost of all the major merchandise groups, and the monthly stock movements of each group.

(c) **Expenses**. These should cover the major cost heads, e.g. wages, occupation costs.

The tables should be easily digestible, showing variances and action to be taken. They should include the minimum of verbal data. The main report should be for top management, with subsidiary reports for departmental heads, e.g. sales and buying. Table 22.2 shows an example of a monthly trading and profit and loss summary.

Financial statements

20. The main accounts

Public limited companies are legally obliged to produce final accounts at the end of each trading period. These financial statements should show a 'true and fair' view of the affairs of the company. The most common forms of financial statement are the profit and loss account and the balance sheet. The profit and loss account shows the amount of profit obtained from the use of the assets over a period of time, whereas the balance sheet shows the assets of the enterprise and the sources of capital used to finance these assets. (Tables 22.3 and 22.4 show examples of a profit and loss account and balance sheet respectively.)

Table 22.2 Monthly trading and profit and loss summary

	Period 6				Cumulative						Year-end position					
	Actual		Budget		Actual		Budget		Previous year		Latest forecast		Budget		Previous year	
	£	%	£	%	£	%	£	%	£	%	£	%	£	%	£	%
Sales	382,669	100.0	395,200	100.0	2,622,816	100.0	2,599,700	100.0	1,893,884	100.0	4,930,000	100.0	4,851,700	100.0	3,554,207	100.0
Gross profit	129,775	33.9	130,400	33.0	884,990	33.7	894,500	34.4	616,212	32.5	1,679,000	34.0	1,666,000	34.3	1,137,104	32.0
Expenses:																
Advertising	5,811	1.5	7,800	2.0	95,328	3.6	91,800	3.5	56,506	2.9	130,000	2.6	127,100	2.6	84,319	2.4
Branch salaries	19,693	5.2	20,000	5.1	163,477	6.3	156,600	6.0	85,763	4.5	300,000	6.1	285,000	5.9	178,835	5.0
Head office salaries	15,467	4.0	16,000	4.0	91,175	3.5	88,600	3.4	66,807	3.5	210,000	4.3	188,700	3.9	102,223	2.9
Establishment costs	37,335	9.8	35,000	8.8	178,550	6.8	182,500	7.1	105,540	5.6	385,000	7.8	400,600	8.3	250,207	7.0
Overheads:																
Financial	1,307	0.3	1,250	0.3	7,243	0.3	7,460	0.3	5,442	0.3	15,000	0.3	15,330	0.3	9,885	0.3
Legal	985	0.3	1,000	0.3	5,899	0.2	6,950	0.3	3,907	0.2	11,000	0.2	12,570	0.3	8,489	0.2
Distribution	3,825	1.0	3,600	0.9	31,341	1.2	30,630	1.2	16,638	0.9	56,000	1.1	54,500	1.1	35,066	1.0
Others	5,476	1.4	6,000	1.5	38,777	1.5	40,110	1.5	22,105	1.2	75,000	1.6	79,400	1.6	48,771	1.4
Total expenses	89,899	23.5	90,650	22.9	611,790	23.4	604,650	23.3	362,708	19.1	1,182,000	24.0	1,163,200	24.0	717,795	20.2
Trading profit	39,876	10.4	39,750	10.1	273,200	10.3	289,850	11.1	253,504	13.4	497,000	10.0	502,800	10.3	419,309	11.8
HP finance result: Profit/loss on HP charges	2,786	0.7	3,600	0.9	32,604	1.2	35,000	1.3	22,743	1.2	70,000	1.5	72,300	1.5	49,673	1.4
Provision for unrealized profit	(882)	0.2	(1,000)	0.3	(18,212)	0.6	(19,400)	0.7	(15,255)	0.8	(38,000)	0.8	(39,900)	0.8	(27,474)	0.8
Net profit before tax	41,780	10.9	42,350	10.7	287,592	10.9	305,450	11.7	260,992	13.8	529,000	10.7	535,200	11.0	441,508	12.4

Table 22.3 Profit and loss account for the
52 weeks to 31 January 2004

	£
Sales	600,000
Cost of sales	350,000
Gross profit	250,000
Expenses	190,000
Operating profit	60,000
Interest charges	15,000
Profit before tax	45,000
Taxation	–
Profit after tax	45,000
Dividends	–
Profit retained	45,000

Table 22.4 Balance sheet as at 31 January 2004

		£
Fixed assets		170,000
Current assets	100,000	
Creditors (amount falling due within one year)	45,000	
Net current assets		55,000
Total assets less current liabilities		225,000
Creditors (amount falling due after more than one year)		100,000
		125,000
Capital and reserves		
Called up share capital		100,000
Unappropriated profits		25,000
		125,000

Notes: (*a*) Creditors (amount falling due within one year) = current liabilities.
(*b*) Creditors (amount falling due after more than one year) = debentures and other possible items,
e.g. tax, HP, etc.

Ratio analysis

21. Importance of ratio

Although it should be remembered that factual accounting is historical in character, a business can gain much information from a study of the relationships between various values in financial statements. The regular review of significant ratios enables unhealthy trends to be detected and corrective action to be taken.

22. Return on capital employed (ROCE)

This important relationship establishes how substantial is the return or yield on the money currently invested in the company as measured by the pre-tax profit performance excluding any exceptional profit items, e.g. profit on foreign exchange transactions. The best measure of capital employed is to compute the shareholders' equity at par value (the issued shareholding of the company) plus any reserves (either capital or revenue). All medium and short-term borrowings like debenture issue or bank overdrafts are excluded from this computation. Assuming that shareholders' funds, including reserves, amount to £11.5 million and the pre-tax net profit for the current year is £2.75 million, the return on capital employed is:

$$\frac{£2.75 \text{ million}}{£11.5 \text{ million}} \times 100 = 23.91 \text{ per cent}$$

23. Liquidity ratios

Liquidity determines whether the retailer can meet payment obligations as they arise – there are two commonly used measures:

(a) **Current ratio:** $\dfrac{\text{Current assets}}{\text{Current liabilities}}$

This indicates the retailer's ability to meet current debts with current assets.

(b) **Quick ratio or acid test ratio:** $\dfrac{\text{Current assets} - \text{Stock}}{\text{Current liabilities}}$

This is a more severe measure of the retailer's liquidity position and measures the ability to meet current debts with assets that can immediately be converted to cash.

24. Cost percentages

Most retail companies express their costs by percentage of turnover both at branch level and overall. This allows comparisons to be made and trends to be monitored. For instance, if a branch's turnover was £400,000 per annum, salaries were £32,000 and rent and rates together were £24,000, the respective cost percentages would be 8 and 6 per cent. (The use of salary percentages, for instance, can help decide branch establishments.) If the achieved gross margin (net sales minus net cost of goods sold) was 24 per cent and the planned net contribution was 5 per cent, all the other costs in running the branch could not be more than 19 per cent (these costs might include head office costs, other accommodation costs like lighting and heating and so on).

25. Efficiency of fixed capital utilization

The efficiency of fixed capital utilization can be measured by relating fixed assets to sales, thus giving the speed of fixed capital turnover. Capital development at new and existing outlets unmatched by a corresponding growth in sales volume will be detected by a slowing down in this rate.

Other retail performance measures

26. Sales per square foot

This is one of the basic measures of retail performance and is expressed as follows (taking random figures):

$$\frac{£ \text{ sales per period}}{\text{Sales floor area}} \quad \text{e.g.} \quad \frac{£1,350,000}{3000 \text{ sq ft}} = £450 \text{ per sq ft}$$

The resulting figure is sometimes called the sales conversion factor. This performance monitor is very useful for comparing returns in different branch locations. Due to the extra information often now supplied in retail company accounts and statements it is possible to work out sales per square foot for a number of large companies (and thus to compare performance).

A sophistication on this measurement is net profit per square foot, which shows the actual contribution in profit terms that each branch makes.

27. Sales per linear foot

Many stores also measure their sales and profits in relation to the length of wall runs in their stores. This gives a much better indication of the success of in-store display and merchandising in particular sections and brings out the existence of 'hot-spots' (areas of high volume) and 'dead areas'. For example, a 30-foot wall run with sales of £60,000 per annum gives a sale of £2000 per linear foot.

28. Sales per assistant

This is a key measurement in financial analysis of all kinds and forms a useful comparison between the labour productivity of different branches. It may also assist in working out branch establishments, e.g. sales of £3,000,000 and the number of staff being 25 gives sales per assistant of £120,000.

29. Sales per checkout

By dividing the period's sales in a supermarket by the number of checkouts the operator can find out whether it is 'under' or 'over-tilled' and make adjustments.

30. Rate of stockturn

This is of crucial importance in the retail context and there is a strong correlation between it and the size of net margins and thus return on capital. In food stores, stockturn rates, which are calculated by dividing average stock into sales, may be as high as 60 times (six days' average stock). In non-foods, turns of six to eight times would be considered reasonable.

Progress test 22

1. What is meant by profit planning? Why is it important?

2. What is budgetary control? Describe the advantages and disadvantages of budgeting.

3. Describe the three main types of budget produced by retailers.

4. Why is reporting of results important?

5. What are the two main types of financial statement produced by retailers?

6. What are liquidity ratios? What do they show?

7. Describe four other important measures of retail performance.

23 Human resources

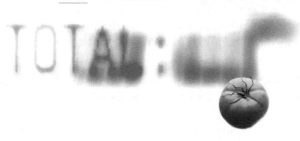

Introduction

The organizing, selecting and training of personnel must be part of the retail planning process. This chapter considers different ways of organizing a multiple retail enterprise, the personnel department and training.

1. Human assets

Human assets are of the utmost importance to retail success, but often plans are made with little regard for the people who will carry them out.

Organization

2. Definition of organization

A comprehensive definition of organization is:

(a) Determining and providing whatever capital, materials, equipment and personnel may be required in an enterprise in order to achieve its objectives.

(b) Defining the duties and responsibilities of the personnel employed and determining the manner in which their activities are to be interrelated.

3. Types of organization (internal structure)

It will be seen from Chapter 2 that each type of retail company tends to operate its own particular kind of organization to meet its objectives. It is very difficult to identify types of organization in a clear-cut fashion, but they are usually labelled for the sake of convenience as:

(a) **Line (or direct) organization**. Here the lines of authority and responsibility come direct from the managing director to the junior. This simple system is only workable in practice in smaller stores because it ignores the growth of the business and the need to rely on specialist functions like personnel, merchandising, etc.

(b) Functional organization. This exists where those in charge of specialist activities or functions are responsible for them throughout every unit of the business, e.g. the chief accountant being responsible for the accuracy of every bill in every branch. The removal of functional responsibility from branch managers, however, vastly reduces their job content, undermines team effort and so on. A wholly functional organization is therefore unknown in retailing, although some multiples through their highly centralized control systems come near it.

(c) Line-and-staff organization. This is simply an extension or development of the line organization in which one or more of the ancillary services have been functionalized. This structure is that most usually adopted by retail firms and combines the line (usually selling), with support functions (like property negotiation) broadening the line organization.

Line management has been described as the relationship in which one person gives an instruction or prescription to another from a different line of command, and staff management as the relationship in which the service offered can be accepted or rejected by others.

4. Centralization

Centralization means the retention of responsibilities in sections attached to head office. Many multiple chains display a substantial amount of centralization in their organization structure. The characteristics of such an organization are:

(a) Considerable consistency throughout the branch network and a rigid control by head office.

(b) Considerable economies from standardized procedures, e.g. the system of stock control.

(c) Competent handling by specialists in such matters as security services, in-store merchandising, payment of staff salaries and so on.

A problem with highly centralized organizations is that managers with initiative or independence of spirit may well leave after a spell of frustration when the power to use their own judgement has been taken away from them.

5. Decentralization

This means that responsibility and authority to make decisions for certain activities have been delegated to subordinate units that are then given discretionary powers. We find in such an organization the following:

(a) A more dynamic business in which the managers of units are encouraged to show initiative and enterprise, and to think for themselves.

(b) The nurturing of creative management talent for higher posts.

(c) A need for area or branch managers of a particularly high calibre, which may be costly if not impossible in a multiple chain running many small branches.

(d) A greater need for checks and controls, whether they are used statistically or appraised by inspection and supervision.

(e) Likelihood of higher morale and greater team effort in branches because of closeness to the 'boss'.

(f) A need for greater specification of duties and responsibilities for field managers because of their proportionately more important roles.

(g) Higher management freed from some routines, allowing more time for determining strategy.

The problem with decentralized control is that many potential economies are lost, because of much duplication of effort.

6. The preferred situation

The principle usually followed is that policies and procedures have an essentially centralized character, but that most day-to-day decisions are, of necessity, decentralized. For example, the complaints procedure in a multiple may be as follows: a centralized control may be expedient to ensure consistency of dealing with justified complaints; the branch manager may be left, however, to decide which are or are not justified, as they arise.

7. The principles of good organization

Some general principles applicable to organization are as follows:

(a) **Objectives**. The goals of the company should be clearly defined, along with the means of achieving them so that the organizers can determine what type of organization is required.

(b) **Flexibility**. When planning an organization structure, provision should be made for adjustments caused by changing circumstances or policies.

(c) **Responsibility**

(i) The responsibility attaching to any post should be clearly defined (e.g. by a job specification).
(ii) Responsibility invested must be balanced by sufficient authority to carry out the functions of the post.
(iii) A person to whom work has been delegated should be responsible to one senior person only (unless the subordinate carries out more than one function).
(iv) If several responsibilities are attached to a particular post they should have some common characteristic.
(v) There should be no duplication of activity by executives.
(vi) Management must ensure that no 'gaps' occur in the organization and that responsibility for each activity or section can be identified with an individual.
(vii) The span of control should be limited to a number that is reasonable in the circumstances.

8. Organization charts

An organization chart should present a diagrammatic representation of the structure of a firm or group of firms. Figures 23.1 and 23.2 show examples of typical organization charts for a large retail multiple company and an individual superstore. The functions of an organization chart are:

(a) Relationships, i.e. line, functional and staff, can be clearly illustrated and may assist in defining the levels and status of individuals.

(b) Responsibility is clearly defined and should show each responsible member of the staff to whom an individual is answerable and who are the individual's immediate subordinates.

(c) A complete picture of the organization is provided in a graphic way and may help to:

    (*i*)   pinpoint any bottlenecks or overloading of executives (e.g. span of control)

    (*ii*) indicate the character of the organization and the degree to which it is centralized or decentralized

    (*iii*) indicate the correct channels of communication for directives, reports and correspondence

    (*iv*) indicate anomalies in the relationship between departments

    (*v*)   secure the introduction of new departments in the right place

    (*vi*) help secure the company structure to new staff and delineate promotion ladders.

(d) Grades and levels within the various functions may also be incorporated in the organization chart. Used in this way the chart can provide a basis for the control of staff and ensure the maintenance of an acceptable balance within the various grades.

The personnel department

9. Responsibilities

The personnel department is responsible for maintaining and supporting the human relationships between management and staff. The detailed functions and responsibilities of the personnel department are as follows:

(a) **Employment**

    (*i*)   Interviewing or arranging interviews of applicants and dealing with any transfers or dismissals.

    (*ii*) Recruitment, including liaison with the Job Centres and any other appropriate source of labour.

    (*iii*) The description of jobs and devising methods of payment and promotion from grade to grade.

    (*iv*) Formulating terms and conditions of service and drawing up of redundancy schemes where appropriate.

    (*v*)   Preparing and maintaining personnel records and statistics.

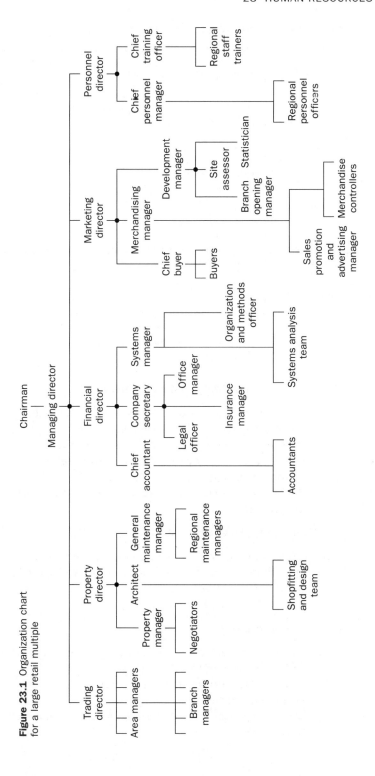

Figure 23.1 Organization chart for a large retail multiple

Figure 23.2 Organization chart for a typical UK superstore

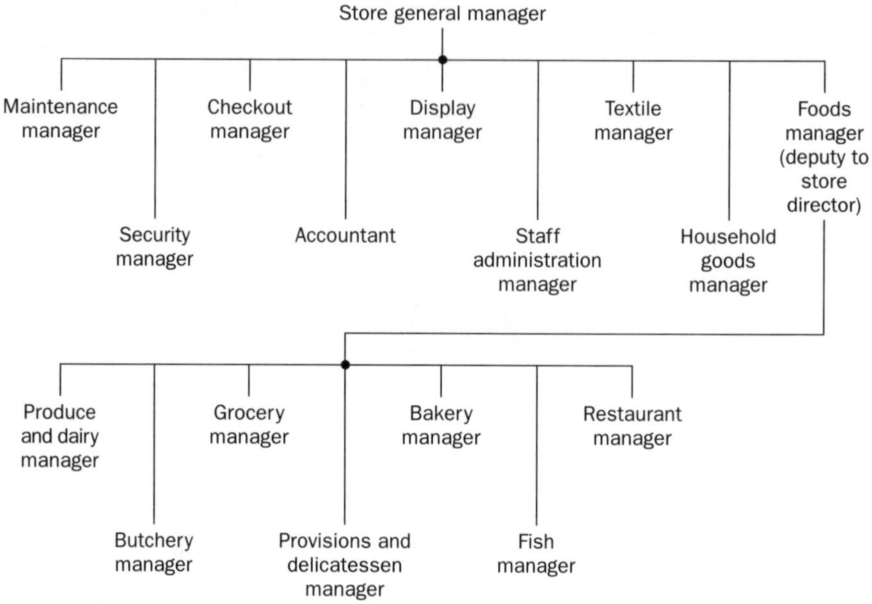

Store general manager

Maintenance manager

Checkout manager

Display manager

Textile manager

Foods manager (deputy to store director)

Security manager

Accountant

Staff administration manager

Household goods manager

Produce and dairy manager

Grocery manager

Bakery manager

Restaurant manager

Butchery manager

Provisions and delicatessen manager

Fish manager

(b) Education, training and development

(*i*) Organizing non-company and external training courses at induction, specialist, supervisor and management levels.

(*ii*) Liaison with appropriate training establishments.

(*iii*) Encouraging further education of all kinds (especially by the provision of financial support).

(*iv*) Dealing with library facilities, the house journal, suggestion schemes, etc., as appropriate.

(c) Wages and salary administration

(*i*) Maintaining the company's accepted wage structure, salary grading, etc., and authorizing rate changes, deductions and special payments.

(*ii*) Consulting management consultants and other specialists concerning proposed incentive schemes.

(d) Health and safety

(*i*) Ensuring compliance with the Offices, Shops and Railway Premises Act and the Health and Safety at Work Act, etc.

(*ii*) Maintaining working medical services.

(*iii*) Keeping health records.

(*iv*) Supervising arrangements for the prevention of accidents and for investigating them.

(e) Welfare

(*i*) Ensuring compliance with the Shop Acts.
(*ii*) Providing social and sports facilities as appropriate.
(*iii*) Advising employees on their individual personal problems.
(*iv*) Administering pensions and superannuation schemes.
(*v*) Supervising staff canteens as appropriate.

(f) Industrial relations

(*i*) Serving as negotiating officers with trade unions and other outside bodies.
(*ii*) Keeping a watchful eye on joint consultative procedures.
(*iii*) Ensuring that company policy towards joint consultation is known, both in theory and in practice.

10. Organization of the personnel function

(a) **The multiple**. Normally a chief personnel officer heads a team that contains a number of travelling branch personnel supervisors. For practical reasons, junior and subordinate staff will be engaged locally by the manager or the staff manager of the branch. Head office will lay down all conditions of service, rates of pay and procedures with regard to sickness and dismissal and may keep a record sheet for all employees that gives a history of their employment. Head office personnel staff should act as final arbiters if field managers are unable to resolve a staff problem themselves.

To sum up, the multiple tends to centralize its personnel function, particularly from a policy point of view, because it allows branch management more time to carry out their main function, which is selling.

(b) **The co-operative**. In co-operative societies, which are self-contained, there is likely to be a personnel officer and, because the co-operative Movement has not yet fully centralized personnel matters, policy is determined by the local management committee.

(c) **Department stores**. Again a chief personnel manager and assistants are likely to make engagements, with departmental managers sitting in. Personnel policy may or may not be made by the personnel manager with the agreement of the board. As in industry generally, personnel management is less likely to be given the accolade of board status, although one director is likely to have responsibility for staff matters.

11. Importance of the personnel function

The importance of the personnel manager has grown in retailing over the past 20 years for the following reasons:

(a) **The size of retail business**. By organic growth and acquisition, some retail companies have tens of thousands of staff, but this has led to greater centralization and a widening gap between management and workers.

(b) **Functionalization**. The personnel manager is now very much a functional (specialist) member of the management.

(c) **Staff problems**. The large number of married and part-time staff employed in retailing creates domestic and other problems and these require careful handling.

(d) **Education and training**. Recent reports by the CBI (Confederation of British Industry) and others have focused on the need for more and better training provision if the UK is to maintain a competitive position.

Training

12. Introduction

Training is concerned with helping staff to make the best possible use of their talents so as to ensure a high level of business efficiency. Good training is particularly important in retailing because of:

(a) High labour turnover and mobility.

(b) Poor recruitment due to:

- (*i*) comparatively low wages
- (*ii*) long hours (seven-day week trading is now common among bigger companies)
- (*iii*) relatively poor working conditions (there are, however, many examples of good conditions, e.g. Marks & Spencer).

The basic requirements of a training system are:

(a) A written company training plan.

(b) Assessment of training needs.

(c) Appointment of a senior executive to be responsible for training.

(d) Appointment of a training officer.

13. Training needs

The training and educational needs of staff in a retail business obviously vary widely. The broad classes of training may be described as for:

(a) New entrants.

(b) Established staff.

(c) Selected staff, e.g. for promotion.

(d) Management.

14. Training new staff

It is vital that training for newcomers to a retail firm is based on a clearly defined, generally understood policy, which is adopted by all members of the company. Success in training new entrants may be reflected in staff turnover figures. Apart from anything else, confidence should be nurtured in the new recruits as soon as they enter the company. The type of information and training required at this level is as follows:

(a) **Induction**. The company must be prepared for the arrival of new entrants and start them on a forward plan of training. This plan can be outlined on the first day, much of which will be taken up with looking around and meeting people, one of whom should describe the company and its organization and relate the recruits' jobs to it as a whole.

(b) **Information**. This may be subdivided into:

   (i) *Essential information*. For example people and places connected with the newcomers' welfare and work, the company's rules and regulations.
   (ii) *General information*. For example contracts of employment, amenities, safety, accident prevention, personal appearance, security (additionally, details of progress and ability assessment, and specialized training opportunities may be given).
   (iii) *Trading information*. Newcomers, particularly, require the knowledge to help provide the public with a consistent trading identity; everyone, however, needs up-to-date information on the company's basic trading policies.

(c) **Customer relations**. Because customers do not distinguish between new and established staff, it may be essential that recruits are quickly advised on situations that are outside their knowledge and experience. Avoidance of these 'on-the-job' situations may, however, be thought more beneficial in the interim stages. Customer service training may include:

   (i) approach to customers, e.g. information offering
   (ii) customers' queries
   (iii) handling difficult customers
   (iv) telephone service, e.g. use of the telephone
   (v) correspondence, e.g. style and content.

(d) **Merchandise knowledge**. This may involve:

   (i) stock identification
   (ii) price and price ranges
   (iii) colour and size availability
   (iv) staple and seasonal lines
   (v) product selling features
   (vi) uses
   (vii) advice on care and after-sales service.

(e) **Salesmanship**. Certain simple sales techniques should be taught in theory and practice and their use supervised until a satisfactory standard is achieved.

(f) **Systems and skills**. A systems syllabus for selling assistants might include:

(*i*) price labels, e.g. location on the merchandise or shelf edge and their use as a sales record
(*ii*) cash sale recording, e.g. running up on the till and writing sales dockets
(*iii*) cash handling
(*iv*) packing goods and delivery
(*v*) alternative methods of payment and sanctioning, e.g. credit, account, hire-purchase, cash on delivery.

(g) **Safety**. The recruits should be acquainted with the health and safety hazards within the working environment, e.g. machines and appliances.

(h) **Security**. Proper systems of checking and surveillance can help prevent dishonesty.

15. Training established staff

Established staff need refresher courses and introduction to new techniques.

(a) **Assessing training needs**. The methods by which the need is established for particular training for existing staff are:

(*i*) *Systems standards*. Checks on skill and accuracy in using the internal systems.
(*ii*) *Sales ability*. Comparisons of numbers of transactions, average sales, selling staff costs.
(*iii*) *Service standards*. Records and detailed analyses of customer complaints.
(*iv*) *Staff turnover figures*. By expressing the number of staff leaving within say a year as a percentage of the average labour force, the staff turnover ratio can be worked out and used either as a trendspotter or as a comparison between branches or departments.

(b) **Topics covered**. Areas of knowledge that may need to be restated are:

(*i*) systems
(*ii*) merchandise, i.e. information and assessing customer needs
(*iii*) expenses control, e.g. telephone, lighting
(*iv*) customer relations.

16. Additional training for selected staff

As a company develops it must help its people to develop along with it.

(a) **Assessing training needs**. In large firms, line and staff managers must advise the personnel and training department as to the job specifications and the qualifications needed to do various types of work so that the recruitment and training of staff produce the right people who are appropriately trained. Training can then continue in individual departments, sections or branches and the personnel department appraised of the results. By co-ordinating these results centrally, training needs can be better identified.

(b) Methods

(i) *Job rotation.* Working for specified periods of time in different departments or branches.

(ii) *Planned experience training.* Undertaking specific projects or responsibilities in departments while working under supervision and reporting on the results.

(iii) *Group training.* This is used when some training needs are common to all group members, but it may have to be supplemented by individual training. Group training lends itself more to classroom-type instruction.

Both the methods in (i) and (ii) can be used for staff who have been specially recruited for their academic achievements or for above-average achievements generally.

17. Management training

(a) **Usefulness.** A systematic training scheme for management will:

(i) enable the business to be run more efficiently and an optimum profit to be obtained from the investment in premises, equipment, staff and stock

(ii) enable individual managers to develop their abilities to full capacity within the firm so that they may be helped to achieve their individual goals and to make a maximum contribution towards the company's goals

(iii) ensure a supply of knowledgeable and competent managers to fill future vacancies.

(b) **Application to existing managers.** Management training is often applied to existing managers in situations of change. Examples of these are:

(i) on promotion or preparation for promotion

(ii) on the expansion or diversification of the business or other changes affecting the duties and responsibilities of managers

(iii) on the introduction of new or different training techniques or policies

(iv) on the introduction of new merchandise

(v) on the introduction of different management employment policies

(vi) on the employment of specialists that require adjustments in working relationships and communications, e.g. computer systems people or personnel officers

(vii) on the availability of new developments in the managers' own and related fields of work.

(c) **Management trainees.** Reliance on outside sources to fill management vacancies can be expensive and often unsatisfactory and therefore planned career training for new recruits and promotables is vital to fill future vacancies. The main points to note in connection with these schemes are:

(i) certain preparatory work should be undertaken before training schemes are started
(ii) the company must have a climate that encourages learning and the progress of individuals
(iii) there must be enough suitable line managers and supervisors to help train the trainees
(iv) individual career training needs careful planning and communication
(v) the number of trainees at any time should be related to known or anticipated vacancies so that expectations held out to trainees on appointment may be realistic.

(d) Management activities and training needs. Management activity in retailing revolves round four sets of resources and these are:

(i) *Finance.* The financial aspects of the business may require training in project appraisal, budgetary control and costing.
(ii) *Merchandise.* The merchandise aspect may suggest training in, for example, sales forecasting, stock control, buying and consumer market research.
(iii) *People.* The personnel aspect may involve training in interviewing, human resources planning, assessment of training needs and salary administration.
(iv) *Premises.* The premises aspect may require training in shop and warehouse site evaluation, planned maintenance or fire practice.

(e) Basis of a sound training scheme

(i) *Assignment of responsibility for training.* Companies with 400 or more employees may find it justifiable to recruit a training officer, while in smaller firms one of the directors may take the function over. In any case the scheme must have full support from top management.
(ii) *Analysis of managerial functions.* This involves the setting up of job descriptions (i.e. lists of management tasks that are being or should be carried out by the company) and their co-ordination and the production of a control chart that will show the training required to match the management requisite of the company.
(iii) *Appraisal of performance.* This is necessary to determine training needs.
(iv) *Assessing future management needs.* By the use of detailed availability/suitability charts, an audit of existing management can be produced and matched against future requirements, taking into account retirements, known leavings and general expansion.
(v) *Design and administration of training.* Training can be either in-company ('on-the-job' and 'off-the-job') or external. It is vital to prepare and maintain personnel records with particular regard to training courses taken, achievement, subsequent promotion and so on.

Progress test 23

1. Define 'organization' and give examples of the various types of internal structure.

2. Discuss the advantages and disadvantages of centralization in retail organizations.

3. What are the functions of organization charts?

4. What are the responsibilities of the personnel department?

5. What are the basic requirements of a training system?

6. Outline the main requirements for training new staff.

7. What methods of training are available to give additional skills to existing staff?

8. What are the advantages of operating a management training scheme?

24 Property and location development

Introduction

This chapter considers the importance and complexity of the property function, how shopfitting operates, the significance of freehold costs and rents, and how retail development occurs.

The property function

1. Importance of the property function

The store premises and other properties owned by a retail company, both freehold and leasehold, may well be its largest asset in value terms. The property department of large multiple retailers serves the trading activity and the company as a whole in a number of important ways, outlined below.

2. Acquisition

Negotiation for the purchase of new property, whether it be new sites or extensions to existing sites, is the lifeblood of an expanding retail company, provided that the acquisitions fall within the limits of an agreed plan of development and that the new-found premises are capable of profitable use. As part of its development plan, the required locations, sites, dimensions and other details will have been sent by the company to estate agents and property developers.

3. Disposals

As a firm rationalizes itself (like many of the multiple food groups have been doing) it will divest itself of the smaller, less profitable branches through estate agents or advertisements in the property press.

4. Surveys

The property department should set up valuation surveys of properties to be acquired to estimate the value to the purchaser as opposed to the rent or price asked. Structural surveys will show defects in the property that would entail expense in reinstatement. It is essential for proper surveys of both types to be carried out before signing a lease or buying a freehold.

5. Scrutiny of conveyancing documents

Although a solicitor is normally retained by a firm when buying or selling properties, leases and title deeds should be examined professionally by the company's property staff. Clauses in short leases are in some cases becoming much more restrictive, for instance in user clauses (restrictions on the use to which a landlord will allow the premises to be put), assignment and subletting rights, right to change the use and right to make alterations, additions and improvements. In addition, length of lease, review clauses, repairing and insurance obligations, service charge, the rent-free period and so on should also be screened on behalf of the company.

6. Planning applications

The property department should make all the necessary approaches to the relevant local authority on planning matters when a new branch or an extension is being developed. This requires the submission of all plans for acceptance by the authority, including shopfronts and fascias, external signs, car parking and so on. The department is also responsible for checking the local plans and the Register of Planning Applications for anything, e.g. road widening, that might affect the site in the future.

7. The Town and Country Planning Act 1990

This Act is the most important successor of the original Town and Country Planning Acts of 1947 and 1971 and it has imposed on each planning authority the duty of preparing a unitary plan.

8. The unitary plan

This is a plan submitted for ministerial approval and is primarily a written statement of policy, accompanied by a diagrammatic structure map for counties and major towns only, designed to expose clearly the broad basic patterns of development and the transport system. Such structure plans form the main link between the policies on a national and regional level and local planning and indicate action areas, i.e. areas where comprehensive development, redevelopment and/or improvement is envisaged in the ten years after submission. The plan, as far as retailing is concerned, will be able to:

(a) Set out the policy and general proposals relating to:

    (*i*)   the hierarchy of centres
    (*ii*) the growth of town centres
    (*iii*) the creation of new centres
    (*iv*) the development of district centres
    (*v*)   the relief of congestion in town centres.

(b) Deal with the quantity of floor space at significant stages and its distribution.

(c) Lay out the broad criteria and policies for:

(*i*)   the location of new development
(*ii*) subsequent local plans
(*iii*) development control
(*iv*) existing development in relation to conservation and conversion.

(d) Deal with priorities and phasing, particularly in relation to action areas, and to deal with implementation, such as the assembly of sites by local authorities and the scope for private development.

9. Project planning and control

When the property department is satisfied that the conditions of a contract are acceptable and that the survey has been competently carried out and is also acceptable, then the actual exchange of contracts takes place (usually through solicitors) and the property is either owned or leased by the retail company. The department then becomes involved in all or some of the following phases:

(a) Rough costing is worked out for project appraisal purposes, probably broken down into shopfitting, shopfront, special equipment (e.g. in-store ovens for a supermarket) and any building costs.

(b) A layout plan is produced by the development department for the shopfitter's use.

(c) Tenders are asked for from two or three shopfitters (although many larger companies have their own shopfitting department). Any building costs may be tendered for separately, along with electrical wiring, air conditioning and so on. Some shopfitting design firms are large enough to take on all aspects of the work but may do some subcontracting themselves. Control of subcontractors is very important for obvious reasons such as work quality and cost overruns.

(d) A shopfitter is selected and a price is agreed.

(e) A programme of work can then be produced by the department based on the progress charts and other documentary estimates provided by contractors (*see* Figure 24.1). The shopfitter will have produced its own detailed drawing of the site. Although the department will wish to oversee the work in progress it may often ask the main contractor (usually the shopfitter) to oversee the project on its behalf. But the department is still responsible for keeping to dates and should be able to hand over the unit to the trader at the agreed time. Some retail firms employ regional property surveyors to look after company projects in their parts of the country.

(f) All through the project the property department should be checking that work is being kept not only up to date but as per plan in terms of layout, materials used, prices and so on by means of site meetings attended by company

Figure 24.1 A programme of shopfitting work (Gantt chart)

Trade	Week comm. 26 April	Week comm. 3 May	Week comm. 10 May	Week comm. 17 May	Week comm. 24 May	Week comm. 31 May	Week comm. 7 June
Builder and plasterer	Floor screed	Walls, ceiling, back area and ceiling retail partitions		Frieze and ceiling (back area)			
Shopfitter		All back shop partitions ceilings and frieze groundings		Light trough, shopfront, fascia, back area doors and facings, etc., unit fitting			
Electrician			Wiring installations back shop area		Retail installation ceiling light fittings etc.		
Heating engineer			Trunking installation		Heating unit installation		
Arcade terrazzo					Terrazzo forecourt doorways, windows and fascia		
Glazier				Glazing shopfront			
Ceiling fitter					Retail ceiling area		
Painter				Frieze and ceiling retail	All back shop areas and finishings retail		
Polisher						French polisher	
Industrial cleaners						Cleaning	

Note: Site programme will commence 26 April and finish 11 June (i.e. extra week in hand) development staff and reporting back to the management. At completion the department should inspect the finished product and accept or reject it on behalf on the company. (Incidentally, it is more probable that operating and development management have caused modifications to be made to the original plan during the fit; this may, of course, increase the final price.)

(g) Each product, whether it is an acquisition or a refit, should be phased into the total development programme for the year (and in line with the agreed budget) so that the department is not faced with an overload situation at certain periods. It is vital, too, that the number of projects in a budget be kept within the ability of the department to plan and control effectively.

10. Costing, budgeting and accounting

The department should be able to cost out in approximate terms the price of a project so that tender prices, if they are requested, can be compared. This will mean that a schedule of standard costs per unit of fitting or per square metre of sales areas must be worked out. A capital budget can then be formulated and this will be incorporated in the master budget for the company. The department will also be responsible for seeing that all invoices sent in by contractors are correct against estimates or tenders and will authorize payment. The department will also negotiate with contractors if there are any changes in invoice details due to alteration in the design of the project.

11. Design

Many of the very large multiple chains have their own architects department. Whether the drawing up of plans is in-house (where the design team would be part of the property function and responsible to the property manager) or whether outside architects are commissioned, adequate drawings must be dated, described and produced for a building project for the guidance of the company shop-planning section, property management, shopfitters, builders and the local planning authority.

These drawings should be to the accepted scale (e.g. 1 centimetre = 1 metre) and should show all or most of the following:

(i)   dimensions, external and internal
(ii)   position and types of all fittings
(iii) lighting
(iv)   heating
(v)   floor covering
(vi)   wall and ceiling finishes
(vii) colour schemes
(viii) materials
(ix)   shopfront and fascia
(x)   stockroom and staffroom facilities
(xi)   stair positions
(xii) any later modifications with dates.

As far as fixtures and fittings are concerned, these may be incorporated later on drawings for internal and shopfitting use (they can, for example, be of help in designing the layout of the branch). The department should produce a catalogue of these fittings, each item being coded and priced. Examples of standard flexible fitments include:

(a) Free-standing wall units.

(b) Gondolas.

(c) Lightweight merchandisers (a light gondola).

(d) Dress racking.

(e) 'Poles' arranged singly or in pairs for bracketing and shelving.

Most proprietary shopfitting systems are today of a modular type. These are standard metric units, which can be run together in sections, that give extra-ordinary flexibility to shop design possibilities in most trades. Much of the design today is, of course, aimed at the open-plan self-selection type store.

12. Maintenance

The property department should make regular inspections of all properties, pre-ferably on a planned basis, and carry out a programme of planned maintenance, which is budgeted for. A maintenance programme will be agreed at head office and initiated both by the latter and by the department.

13. Other statutory duties

(a) Under the Health and Safety at Work Act 1974 the retailer's duty to provide proper fire access, sanitation and staffroom accommodation is normally imple-mented by the department.

(b) If the local authority wishes to purchase a retail property for redevelopment or some other purpose a compulsory purchase order (CPO) is often raised. The department must act on it, particularly in the interests of the retailer so that adequate compensation is possible.

14. Property asset management

One of the most important functions of the department is the control and management of the company's land and buildings. This can mean some or all of the following:

(a) The maintenance of the asset to a level where no loss of value due to dilapidation is incurred.

(b) The collection of subtenants' rent.

(c) The manipulation of the property asset to produce the best return for the company, e.g. whether to lease or to buy, whether to sell freehold and arrange to lease it back as a tenant in order to raise further funds for the business or whether to adopt a policy of redevelopment of owned freeholds in order to enhance their values, and so on.

15. Control of stocks

Although the department may not itself physically control stocks of fittings, it often must organize a system whereby stocks are held at convenient points so that they can be quickly transported to project sites. It may be that shopfitters could hold these stocks on the company's behalf.

16. Other functions

(a) **Keeping of plans**. These documents, which should be kept in special plan chests, will comprise drawings of company properties and key plans (detailed street plans drawn to scale) of shopping centres.

(b) **Liaison**. The department creates a link between estate agents, shopfitters, contractors and builders and the company as a whole.

The cost of sites

Before settling on a particular site the retailer must know something about the cost of shop sites.

17. Definitions

(a) **Value**. The price that a willing seller will accept and a willing buyer will pay. It depends on supply and demand.

(b) **Rental value**. The value as between landlord and tenant.

(c) **Ground rent**. The rent of the site only.

(d) **Rack rent**. The rent of the site improved with buildings. (It is the maximum rent for the value of the property.)

18. Factors relevant to assessment of rack rent

These consist of factual and legal considerations and are as follows:

(a) **Factual considerations**

   (i) *The population of the town*. Generally, the greater the population, the greater the rental value in the principal shopping area.
   (ii) *The classification and type of centre*. Compare a central shopping area in a city such as Glasgow with a main shopping area in a smaller town such as Sevenoaks, Halesowen, Ripon or Penzance.
   (iii) *Position of the shop in the centre*. The rental value in the part of the area favoured by certain multiples is much greater than at the tail end of the area.

(iv) *Side of street.* One side always commands higher rents than the other due to custom, position of shopping magnets, position of the sun, and so on.

(v) *Proximity to key traders.* The arrival of a key trader in an indifferent pitch can transform values overnight.

(vi) *Pedestrian traffic flows.* Pedestrian crossings, bus stops, and crush barriers all affect the flow of foot traffic. Too wide a pavement is a disadvantage because pedestrians are not forced against shop fronts and could miss them entirely.

(vii) *Vehicular traffic flows.* One-way streets are generally unpopular.

(viii) *Parking facilities.* The rental value of shopping positions is enhanced by the provision of nearby parking.

(ix) *Frontage and depth.* Certain multiple retailers are prepared to pay high prices to secure the precise frontage and depth most suited to their trading needs.

(x) *Area.* A rectangular area is worth more than the same area of irregular shape.

(xi) *Other accommodation.* Some trades require almost as much storage as retail selling area. Living accommodation above the shop may be essential.

(b) Legal considerations

(i) *Premium.* A capital payment in lieu of whole or part of the rent.

(ii) *Length of lease.* A retailer proposing to carry out costly capital improvements requires a long lease to write off the investment.

(iii) *Repairing obligations under the lease.* An onerous obligation in respect of a property in bad repair may make the site worthless.

(iv) *Rent review clauses.* The effect of such a clause in a lease is to uplift the rent after a stated number of years, to the rental value at that time. The absence of rent review clauses reduces the value of the lease to the landlord.

(v) *Insurance provisions in the lease.* These determine who pays for the premiums and thus affect the rent to a small extent.

(vi) *Rights set out in the lease.* Rights as to assignment, subletting, to change the use and to make alterations and additions.

(vii) *Service charge specified in the lease.* This is the annual amount to be charged by the landlord for providing services, if any, such as lighting, cleaning of yards, porterage, etc.

19. The relationship between rental and capital values

This is measured by a multiplier, called the years' purchase (YP), which is applied to the net rent to give capital value. It is the converse of the percentage applied to a capital sum to indicate an income. It is worked out by dividing 100 by the percentage. Therefore 6 per cent = 16.667 YP.

20. Valuers' methods of assessing values

There are various methods, the most usual being:

(a) **Comparative.** The direct comparison between the price per square metre and per metre frontage of the shop being considered and other similar shops.

(b) **Residual**. The balance remaining after deducting all the costs of a development from the estimated receipts gives the residual value. If the valuer estimates that a shop and upper part can be sold on completion of a new development for £500,000 and it is going to cost the developer £250,000 to build, including the cost of fees and finance, the developer can afford to pay up to £250,000 as the value of the site.

One method will be used as a check against the other.

21. The points of view of both landlord and tenant in assessing rental values

The rental value is determined by the supply of suitable property and the demand for it.

(a) **The minimum rent required by the landlord**. The landlord requires the highest profitable return. Consider a new development by a landlord (developer) of a single store. Statutory factors affecting the development are planning as set out under the most recent Town and Country Planning Acts and structure plans provided by local planning authorities, building regulations and road improvement lines. The developer must then estimate the following:

(i) *The cost of the site.* If the developer has recently purchased the site it will have had to pay the value of the most profitable development.
(ii) *Cost of building works.*
(iii) *Cost of fees.* This will include the architect's, quantity surveyor's, solicitor's and letting agent's fees.
(iv) *An amount for contingencies.* This is to allow for unforeseen expenses and rising costs.
(v) *Cost of providing finance.* This is necessary to purchase the site and to meet all the above costs. The cost of finance will depend upon the rate at which it is available at the time at current market rates.

The developer will then know the total estimated costs. To ascertain the minimum rent to charge, the developer then applies the percentage return to this total estimated cost. If total estimated costs are £2 million, and 10 per cent is regarded as the correct return on a development of this nature, the minimum rent the developer (landlord) can afford to charge before undertaking the development, will be £200,000 per annum. The resultant rent must not be greater than the rent a tenant can be expected to pay. If the resultant rent is lower than the rent a tenant is likely to pay, the difference represents annual profit.

(b) **The maximum rent the tenant can afford to pay**. The tenant requires to pay the lowest possible rent. An assessment of what is affordable can be made by estimating net profit after deduction of all outgoings.

Stages in estimating net profit are as follows:

(i) *Estimate gross profit.* This is opening stock plus purchases, less sales and closing stock.
(ii) *Estimate net profit.* This is gross profit less outgoings. The outgoings must include the cost of capital invested in the business.

(*iii*) *Estimate outgoings*. Outgoings will include head office expenses, wages, salaries, national insurance, heating, lighting, insurance, stationery, publicity, telephones, postage, vehicle running expenses, repairs, rates, annual depreciation on costs of shop front, fixtures, fittings and vehicles.

For example, estimates result in a gross profit of £700,000 per annum from which are deducted outgoings of £350,000 per annum leaving a net profit of £350,000 per annum. No deduction has been made for rent. The £350,000 per annum is therefore net profit including rent. The tenant must then estimate what can be afforded out of this figure by way of rent and leave sufficient as a reward for running the business. The resultant estimated rent must not be smaller than the minimum rent required by the landlord. If the resultant estimated rent is more than the rental value of the store then the difference represents additional annual profit.

22. Rents based on percentage of profits

Where there is no comparable guide to the property or where the trade is a monopoly, the landlord and tenant may agree on a rent based on a percentage of actual turnover or profits. This type of rent is well known in the USA and is used in several situations in the UK, e.g. motorway retail site rents are based on a sliding percentage of turnover. Some shopping centre sites are also let on this basis.

23. Factors affecting choice on whether to lease or to buy

Owing to substantial rises in property value many retailers prefer to buy freeholds. The return on capital employed in the business should, however, exceed the return on the capital invested in bricks and mortar.

The factors affecting the decision as to whether to buy the freehold or take a lease are:

(a) The availability of capital and the cost of borrowing it.

(b) The availability of either a freehold interest or a lease – whichever is desired in a suitable property. (If a leasehold is required, it is possible to buy a freehold, then to sell the freehold with the benefit of the trader's covenant and the trader takes a lease back at full market rent).

(c) The interest that capital employed in purchase of a property would earn if invested in the business.

(d) The possibility of showing a capital increase in the value of the property.

(e) Taxation:

    (*i*)   capital gains tax and corporation tax
    (*ii*) rent as a charge against profits
    (*iii*) interest charges on capital borrowed being a charge on profits.

24. Valuation of property assets

Because of rises in property values it is necessary to have periodic independent professional valuations to assess the correct return on capital employed and the true profit. As a result of the valuation, the real profit arising from the business may be substantially less than supposed. A book value is only of historic interest to a valuer. It has no relation to market value, i.e. what a property will fetch in the market.

25. Some further points

(a) **Reinstatement values for fire insurance.** In the same way that properties must be valued periodically to ascertain true worth, it is essential that properties should also be valued periodically, say every three years, to ascertain cost of replacement in case of fire. The cost of replacing a property asset destroyed by fire bears no relation to the value of the property for sale. For example, the sale value of a freehold store in a prime position will be higher than the fire replacement value. The value of a tenant's short leasehold interest may well be less than the cost of rebuilding the premises after a fire, for which the tenant may be liable under the lease.

(b) **Rent review clauses.** The object is to secure to the landlord maintenance of the value of the pound (£) and the enhancement values in the area. The rent is assessed periodically by reference to rental values in the locality at the time, but no account should be taken of the value of improvements made by the tenant. The effect of rent reviews is to remove from the tenant a large part of any appreciation in the value of the property that has taken place.

(c) **Clauses in leases requiring special attention.** The following points should be settled and expressly agreed during negotiations for the lease of a property. It is essential that the solicitors to both sides are advised in detail on what has been agreed in order that they may ensure that the terms of lease truly reflect what has been agreed. The points concerned are:

(i) *Assignment rights.* Unless there are special reasons against it, the tenant should have the right to assign to a responsible assignee. It would be reasonable for this right not to be given to the tenant where the tenancy is a short one, because it is agreed by both parties at the time of letting that the landlord is to redevelop at the end of the tenancy.

(ii) *Subletting rights.* The tenant of a large store capable of being split into several units should have the right to sublet to responsible tenants.

(iii) *Right to change the use.* The tenant should have the right to change the use, with consent, which coupled with the right to assign would permit assignment to a tenant of a different trade.

(iv) *Right to make alterations, additions and improvements.* The tenant should have these rights to ensure it is possible to trade effectively. The tenant should be made to apply to the landlord for express consent but the landlord should not be able to refuse unless the carrying out of the work concerned is likely to depreciate the value of the landlord's interest in reversion.

Location development

26. Development management

The development manager, who should be responsible to the marketing or trading director, is in turn responsible for bringing together data so that a plan for the extension and development of a chain is possible. This plan will incorporate some pointers as to the size and type of branches and the general image to be projected.

The main areas of responsibility of the development manager are:

(a) Creating, reviewing, updating the development plan.

(b) Finding new sites in conjunction with the property department.

(c) Producing viability studies on new projects, meeting viability timetables and ensuring these are adhered to.

(d) Recommending properties to the board.

(e) Organizing regular site visits, in conjunction with the property department and monitoring the progress of work on site.

(f) Advising on layouts, lighting, signage, display, systems, colours, etc. of new branches.

(g) Co-ordinating and controlling development teams, which may comprise representatives from merchandising, architects, surveyors, administration, operations, security, finance, personnel and training.

(h) Monitoring the performance of new, resited, extended and modernized branches once opened.

In carrying out these functions the development manager and their team will use much of the methods and information contained in Chapter 11.

27. Planning retail development

The broad methods by which this part of the company's strategic plan can be framed are as follows:

(a) **Possible areas**. Determine the geographical areas for possible and profitable retail expansion. This will depend on the minimum acceptable support population to show the desired return on investment and other factors detailed below.

(b) **Branch potential**. Determine the sales and profit levels and market share that each potential (and existing) outlet can reasonably take as its objective by examining its strengths and weakness and matching these up with a standard

store performance profile for the grade of branch being examined. This will produce pointers to extension and modernization needs.

(c) **Diversification.** Examine the possibilities of diversifying into other market
areas by the acquisition of existing businesses. This may also involve diversifying into other product groups or even abroad.

28. Constraints on development

Before producing a development plan as part of the corporate plan, the constraints on extending market coverage must be discussed:

(a) **Physical distance.** This does not affect the large multiple as much as it
might the smaller chain run possibly by one person, the proprietor, who must
be readily able to control the shops, travelling between them by car. The bigger
retail chain normally controls branches on a territory basis, each area being in
the charge of an area or regional manager.

(b) **Lines of communication.** Branches, no matter whether they obtain supplies
direct from the manufacturer or from a company warehouse, must be reasonably
accessible by road or rail. This is particularly true of stores selling daily lines, e.g.
bread and newspapers.

(c) **Type of trade.** Except in the very largest cities, variety chain stores and
other large space users will operate only one branch. The exceptions are some
food and convenience stores which, because of the lower support populations
required, are able to open more than one branch in many towns, very often in
the suburbs.

(d) **Existence of market potential.** Certain areas offer no scope for development
for the following reasons:

    (*i*)   low catchment populations
    (*ii*) over-heavy competition
    (*iii*) small, underdeveloped or otherwise unsuitable shopping centres
    (*iv*) competition from another branch of the same company
    (*v*) company image does not fit the socio-economic profile of the area.

(e) **Finance.** Capital must be available to support an expansion plan. The number of outlets planned, although not necessarily the geographical extent of the
development area, may be stultified by high interest rates, lack of self-financing
facility or government intervention in capital projects.

(f) **Availability of sites.** Some shopping centres are highly constricted and the
number of sites appearing either in a private sale situation or on the open market
may be severely limited. Once on the market the sites must be of a suitable
size and shape; variety chains particularly have encountered problems in land
assembly in some town centres. High rents are unlikely to deter most big chains
these days from seeking and finding representation in prime sites.

(g) **Legal restraints**. Until fairly recently, supermarket chains had difficulty in securing licences from local courts to incorporate the sale of wines and spirits in their branches. They are still not allowed under the Food and Drugs Act 1963 to dispense ethical drugs except from a separate in-store pharmacy run by a qualified pharmacist.

(h) **Lack of management**. Two limitations could exist here:

  (*i*) training and successions plans in the company may not be advanced enough to provide new branch management quickly
  (*ii*) an expansion plan can be stultified by a lack of professional skills at head office.

(i) **Lack of other resources**. A big proportional jump in the number of branches operated, perhaps from acquisition, could strain internal departments such as buying, accounting or personnel.

29. Branch profiles

Before a development plan can be implemented a retail chain must have a concrete idea of what sort of units it wishes to operate. Tesco, for example, aims for its stores to be what it calls 'conforming stores'. As part of the pinpointing of the company's strengths and weaknesses for corporate planning purposes, it is essential for the existing stock of branches to be completely appraised. This appraisal is meant to help planners to decide how to improve the current resources and build up for the future. The aspects of the 'profile' examined are as follows:

(a) **Layout**. This is invaluable in deciding how best to lay out an existing store, how it can be improved in the future (e.g. by extension) and what a standard unit should look like in terms of frontage, depth, etc.

(b) **Shopfront and fittings**. Again the store layout revolves round fittings, as does the shopfront to some extent (e.g. if the front is arcaded or angled). A chain will aim eventually to standardize in this as in many other areas. Standardization helps reduce the price of fittings and is also instrumental in creating a consistent store image.

(c) **Ranging**. A retail chain should have some means of finding out in some detail the product mix in each of its branches. This will have implications for gross margin, buying, layout and display, staffing, deliveries, and so on. The idea is to achieve as much standardization in ranging as possible, taking into account local market differences.

(d) **Operating costs**. As standardization in branch size and staffing continues, standard operating costs can be more easily budgeted for new branches.

(e) **Sales**. Many multiple retailers categorize branches in particular sales or profit bands.

30. Development lists

At the core of the development plan are the lists of towns and shopping centres within which representation is desired. On the basis of the standard branch profile (or profiles if more than one class or size of branch is envisaged within specific market sizes) and the estimated branch sales, a clear idea of net contribution and therefore return on investment can be gained. If the (apparent) return on investment is acceptable in a particular market, then it will be incorporated in the development plan.

31. Investment and rationalization

After appraising its stock of stores a retail chain will concentrate its development efforts on:

(a) **Modernization**. Branches are normally refitted every three to five years depending on the trade (fashion stores need a facelift more often). Sometimes strong local competition may speed the process. However, only branches that are likely to benefit should be so treated; they would be expected, as the minimum requirement, not only to be capable, from the extra sales that should flow from the investment, of paying the annual depreciation charge on the new fittings but at least of servicing the capital investment.

(b) **Resites**. It sometimes occurs that a branch has to relocate within a shopping centre because of changes in the environment, e.g. the movement of a key multiple or a new traffic management scheme. Leases fall due, compulsory purchase orders are tendered, or it is felt that the branch has outgrown its size for the business it is doing and cannot be extended. Resites should be considered very carefully because they occasionally produce a less than satisfactory return if the old branch benefited from cheap rents and other low charges while the new branch opens with expensive fittings and at a much higher rent and rates charge. Turnover may consequently have to be much higher.

(c) **Extensions**. It is often possible to extend branches that have become too small for their sales level. Sometimes it is possible to take over stockrooms or other ancillary accommodation for sales area extension, but it may often mean the purchase of flanking shops. When Dixons took over Currys, the former was able to expand its branches in this way in several locations.

(d) **Acquisition of existing businesses**. By buying existing shops owned by competing or even non-competing traders a chain can sometimes not only extend its development area but also allow rationalization of its existing spread of shops by closing nearby, less effective units. A list of businesses to be taken over in the future can be framed as part of the acquisition strategy.

(e) **Overseas expansion**. Many UK retailers have expanded abroad with varying results.

Progress test 24

1. Why is the property function so important in retailing and what are its main functions?

2. What are the factors relevant to the assessment of rack rent?

3. Describe the points of view of (*a*) the landlord and (*b*) the tenant, in assessing retail values.

4. What factors are important when deciding whether to lease or buy?

5. Explain what factors a retailer would consider before embarking on a retail development plan.

25 Store management

Introduction

The task of putting into operation the policies of the organization on a day-to-day basis falls substantially on the store managers. In this chapter we consider the duties of the store manager, measures of store productivity and other aspects of retail operations management.

The store manager

1. Unit management

In an independent retail outlet the store manager may well be the proprietor but in multiples a branch manager will be employed. Although much of this chapter will be relevant to the independent trader, it is primarily focused on management of a unit within a multiple retail chain.

2. Duties of store management

Broadly, the store manager must put into full and effective operation in the branch at all times the company's policies and procedures. The day-to-day operations of the branch must be organized and directed to its full trading potential within the constraints of position, size of unit, etc. Detailed duties will encompass some or all of the following, in the style of a job specification:

(a) **Sales.** To achieve budgeted sales for the period.

(b) **Costs.** To maintain controllable costs within a budget, e.g. lighting, telephones.

(c) **Profit.** To achieve planned levels of profit, both gross and net for the period.

(d) **Stock**

    (*i*)   To maintain a level of stock within the current budget.

    (*ii*) To keep stock shortages to a minimum.

    (*iii*) To count and record stock in the branch from time to time as required by company policy.

(e) **Buying**. To ensure that if local buying is permitted, purchases are made only in line with company policy, taking into account the total budgeted stockholding.

(f) **Presentation**. To maintain standards of display and presentation that encourage and retain trade and contribute to the identity the company wishes to project. This particularly entails that:

- (*i*) sales areas, windows and shopfronts are maintained in a clean and tidy condition (this applies also to stock areas, rest rooms, toilets, etc.)
- (*ii*) all merchandise is displayed in line with company standards, including the open display of all lines appropriate to the grade of branch, the correct price marking and ticketing of products, etc.

(g) **Sales promotions**. To carry out the company sales promotion policy and to initiate and execute local sales promotions in agreement with the area manager.

(h) **Staff**

- (*i*) To ensure by interview and selection (agreed with the area manager) that the branch is properly staffed to its budgeted establishment with competent section management and assistance.
- (*ii*) To train staff in the basic functions of branch operation.
- (*iii*) To terminate their employment within the scope of company policy and with regard to legislation such as the Employment Protection (Consolidation) Act.

(i) **Premises**. To protect and maintain the building, machinery, equipment, fixtures, fittings and vehicles of the branch and to report any action needed to maintain trade assets in good working order and at acceptable safety standards.

(j) **Administration**

- (*i*) To carry out company procedures as published from time to time for the reception and disposition and safe custody of cash, stock and other assets.
- (*ii*) To prepare, maintain and submit such records and reports as may from time to time be required by the company.
- (*iii*) To observe the large amount of legislation that surrounds retailing today.

(k) **Communication**

- (*i*) To establish and maintain adequate means of communication within the branch of the company's objectives as they affect branch personnel, including in-store meetings.
- (*ii*) To keep area management aware as far as possible of local news and developments likely to affect the company's present or future interests.
- (*iii*) To play an active part as far as it is feasible in the civic and cultural activities of the locality in which the branch is sited in order to foster confidence and goodwill towards the company.

3. The branch manual

This document lays down the standing orders of the business as far as branch operation is concerned. There should be arrangements in its make-up for additions, amendments and deletions, each of which should be serially numbered and dated for identification and insertion. The manual or bulletin should be signed for, each copy numbered and located (one for each branch) and handed over formally as one manager takes over from another. The wording requires careful consideration as there should be no ambiguity or misinterpretation between different sections of the business. One criticism of the manual is that, if possible contingencies are legislated for, a deadening effect resulting in some loss of initiative may occur. The quasi-permanent manual may in some businesses be supplemented by such ancillary instructions as the shrinkage manual, the sales promotion plan or the training manual. Many firms send out sales or display memoranda to branches which may then be incorporated in a manual.

4. Responsibility of managers

It will be seen that a number of the unit managers' duties are quantifiable and therefore controllable through budgets. These budgets should, in well-run companies, be agreed with the managers by their immediate superior (usually an area manager). Once standards of performance and competence have been published, monitoring can be carried out through exception reports on sales and profit performance and by physical inspections. Breaches of the standards laid down by the company may not, of course, always be the responsibility of the branch manager. For example, an accident occurring to a customer because of the faulty maintenance of fittings would not necessarily rebound on the manager.

Measuring a manager's performance

5. Skills

The manager of a retail operation requires two primary skills: trading skills and management skills.

(a) **Trading skills**. These are based on the ability to spot opportunities within a business environment in order to maximize store profit.

(b) **Management skills**. These are concerned with maximizing the resources within their control – the major resource over which the retail manager has substantial control is the human resource (*see* Chapter 23).

6. Store productivity

Productivity involves producing better results with the same mixtures of resources or producing the same results with fewer resources. This means that stocks have to be sufficient to meet (uneven) demand but not excessive and so leading to the tying up of capital. Similarly, employing too many staff with insufficient work to do is wasteful, while employing insufficient staff at peak times causes queues and customer dissatisfaction.

The task of operating management is to balance the load of customers against the capacity (resources) available to it. This means that store management has to generate the best possible performance and results at the least cost from:

(a) Customers

(b) Merchandise

(c) Store human resources

(d) Store physical resources – including space.

7. Measuring store productivity

The most effective way of measuring productivity is to calculate ratios of resource to results, e.g. profit per square metre of selling space, and comparing these ratios with pre-set standards, e.g. budgets. Productivity ratios can also be compared against industry norms, competitor results or even against other company stores or sections within a store.

The following is a list of some important measures of store productivity:

(a) Sales per employee

(b) Sales per labour hour

(c) Staff costs as a percentage of sales

(d) Labour costs per activity

(e) Average wage costs per hour

(f) Sales per square metre of selling space

(g) Sales per linear metre of fixture

(h) Sales per customer (by value, number of items or departments)

(i) Customers per time period (e.g. hour)

(j) Items per time period

(k) Sales per checkout

(l) Sales: total assets

(m) Sales: stock

(n) Gross margin return on investment

(o) Gross profit per square metre

(p) Net profit per square metre

(q) Gross and net profit on sales

(r) Shrinkage as a percentage of sales

(s) Wastage as a percentage of sales

(t) Mark-downs as a percentage of sales

(u) Other costs as a percentage of sales.

There are also other qualitative measures such as service to customers and merchandise availability. Unfortunately, these cannot be easily measured but the level of customer complaint may be an indicator. Stock-age rating is also important to identify slow-moving stock which unnecessarily ties up capital or requires markdown, thus reducing profitability.

As an example, a typical grocery multiple will have a gross profit on sales of approximately 17 per cent. Staff costs will typically run at 5 to 6 per cent and other operating costs at 2 to 3 per cent of sales. With overhead and allocated costs of 4 to 5 per cent it can be demonstrated that net profits are in the order of 4 to 5 per cent of sales. It is therefore clear that savings in staff or operating costs (i.e. controllable by the operating manager) can have a dramatic effect on the net profit (the 'bottom line').

Other aspects of store management

8. Health and safety

The store manager is responsible for the health and safety of both staff and customers in the store. The two main aspects are the prevention of ill health arising from working conditions and circumstances, and safety – the prevention of accidents.

Branch mangers have to comply with the Health and Safety at Work Act 1974 which lays down minimum standards on such aspects as lighting, cleanliness and accidents.

9. Heating

Many larger modern stores are fitted with sophisticated ducted heating systems that are often expensive to install and to run. Smaller stores may use convector heaters and in these and larger stores the use of warm-air curtains at entrances keeps in much of the internal heat. Heat conservation of this kind is particularly important with open-fronted units in covered air-conditioned shopping centres.

Some points to note on the subject are:

(a) Capital cost and the use of fuel should be economic, particularly in view of today's energy costs (e.g. thermostatic control).

(b) Planned maintenance is needed.

(c) Safety is important, particularly from the point of view of fires.

(d) Equitable distribution of heat is necessary, according to the position and size of the selling or ancillary area.

10. Ventilation

Many larger stores are now fitted with air-conditioning equipment for summer use. Again the capital cost and fuel consumption of air cooling and changing systems can be high. Smaller units are more likely to rely on simpler means of ventilation such as louvres or air extractors. The following points should be considered:

(a) The alternative benefits of natural and mechanical ventilation.

(b) Elimination of draughts is essential.

(c) Spread of clean air is also to be desired.

(d) Unsightly ducting, motors and so on should be eliminated.

11. Lighting

Although expensive, effective lighting is essential to attract customers and enhance the surroundings. The cheapest and most efficient store illumination is still a variation on fluorescent lighting. For example, mercury halide gives as much light as conventional fluorescent lighting but uses 30 per cent less electricity. Spot lights are extensively used in clothing and some durable stores to add atmosphere or to highlight products. Spots, however, can be expensive to run. In larger stores, an emergency lighting system is often installed, powered by a diesel generator. The following points should be noted:

(a) Natural lighting should be used as far as possible.

(b) It is necessary that light diffusors are kept clean.

(c) Spare tubes and spot bulbs should be kept in the branch.

(d) Time switches on window lights can save expense.

(e) In summer, some 'starters' should be removed from tubes to reduce the ambient heat.

(f) Different colour tubes can be used for special effects, e.g. meat counter illumination is usually 'pink'.

12. Cleanliness

The multiple organization often leaves it to the branch manager to organize cleaning on a local basis. Most large shopping centres have several professional window cleaners who 'tout' for work as soon as a shop starts fitting-out ready for the opening. Some multiples, however, use national contract cleaning that can bring considerable savings in a large chain. Again, large multiple branches may carry their own heavy-duty vacuum cleaners and polishers that may be operated by the staff or by part-time cleaners.

13. Accidents

Points to note in this connection are:

(a) All accidents to customers and staff should be recorded in an accident book and a report sent to the legal department.

(b) First-aid facilities should be provided in the staffroom.

(c) Staff should be helpful but non-committal in customer accident cases.

(d) Arrangements should be made with the local hospital for treatment in cases of emergency.

Security

14. Pilferage

Pilferage is the theft of cash or stock and contributes much of the 'unknown shrinkage' in retail organizations, of which there are basically two types: shop-lifting (*see* **15**) and staff pilferage (*see* **18**). Depending on the firm and its security management, shrinkage of this kind amounts to between 0.5 and 4 per cent of total turnover. However, about 10 per cent of shrinkage is not deliberate, e.g. inadvertent undercharging or the giving of too much change. In 1995, the UK retail trade was estimated to lose over £2 billion per year in shrinkage, representing approximately 1.5 per cent of turnover.

15. Shoplifting

This is the work of members of the public and is estimated to make up 30 per cent of unknown shrinkage. The methods used to combat shoplifting include the following:

(a) **Store detectives**. These are either recruited by the retail group or hired from a security organization. Although they tend to be expensive, their success rate is reckoned to be good.

(b) **Electronic systems**. There are a number of proprietary brands of systems used in the UK, all with tags that are removed at the point of sale. Most potential shoplifters notice the sensitized tags that set off alarm bells at the entrance to the store if taken through a photo-electric curtain and are therefore deterred from stealing. These systems, although expensive, are said to be beneficial, even reducing staff thefts of stock. The tags can also be used for stock control.

(c) **Closed-circuit television**. Cameras, which are mounted in the store, transmit to monitor screens either in the sales area or the manager's office.

(d) **Security mirrors**. These convex mirrors, which are available in various diameters, are relatively cheap and therefore more within the range of the smaller retailers. Positioned in blind spots, they act as a deterrent to shoplifting. One-way mirrors are also useful for manager's offices overlooking the shop.

(e) **Chains and loop alarms**. These are popular in electrical goods stores for smaller audio, kitchen and personal-care items. The simple chain is locked round a number of items, while allowing them to be examined individually. Loop alarms are similarly locked and, if broken, send out a high-pitched buzz.

(f) **Fitting-room tags**. The fitting room is a favourite place for shoplifters to operate and some store groups allow customers to take in only a maximum number of items, with hanger tags that have to be returned with the goods.

16. General security

An open display of merchandise undoubtedly increases the risk of shoplifting so other precautions that may be taken could include:

(a) Encouragement of staff alertness.

(b) Well lit, properly laid-out sales floor.

(c) 'Closed' display of small items such as pocket calculators and electric shavers.

17. Apprehension

A person can be arrested without warrant if he or she is seen stealing or if a theft has occurred and there are 'reasonable grounds' for suspicion of that person. It is usual to give suspected customers the opportunity to pay by asking them if there is anything they wish to pay for. If they decline it is obligatory to wait until they have stepped out of the store before requesting their return to the manager's office for a check of their purchases. A witness to the incident should be present and the local police should be called. All should be done as quickly as possible. Most retail groups now make it a policy to prosecute shoplifters, but it is vital that the staff involved work to a prearranged system of apprehension.

18. Staff pilferage

An estimated 60 per cent of shrinkage is caused by direct staff thefts of stock or cash and collusion with delivery people, salespersons and customers. Supermarkets seem to have the worst record here and shrinkage rates of 2–3 per cent have been described as workable by supermarket management. Again, supermarkets are estimated to have 25 per cent of their losses in the cash system through direct theft from tills and dishonesty with floats, cashing up and banking. One of the 'black spots' for staff pilferage is the goods reception and stockroom areas where security is often lax. For internal security the following precautions should be taken:

(a) Security staff should check employees for suspected stolen merchandise.

(b) Tills should be spot-checked from the till roll sporadically.

(c) All credit notes and refunds should be signed by the manager.

(d) Employees' handbags, coats and effects should be left in separate cloakrooms or hung well away from stores or in a position where managers can see them.

(e) Reserve stock should be kept either caged in or out of the way of staff, with valuable stock like cigarettes and watches locked up.

(f) Staff should be instructed on the correct acceptance of deliveries.

(g) Stock should be kept in sealed outer packing. This minimizes pilferage and helps stocktaking.

(h) There should be a clause in the letter of appointment allowing spot searches of clothing and hand-luggage.

(i) Staff purchases should be isolated from the customer sales system.

It is important that any staff security measures be put out as a precaution for the general good of the majority who are honest.

19. Shopbreaking

This occurs when a retail unit is forcibly entered. Shopbreaking is rarer than customer/staff pilferage but each particular loss is likely to be much greater. The type of theft is of course 'known' and amounts stolen can be checked after the event. Points to observe in this context are:

(a) A strict locking-up procedure should be followed each night and in reverse in the morning.

(b) There should be secure locks on doors and windows at the front, side, rear and on the roof.

(c) Grille and other types of alarm should be set at a low 'sensitivity' because they are liable to be disturbed by heavy traffic – over 90 per cent of alarm calls are false in the UK, due to incorrect setting.

(d) Duplicate keys should be held by the branch manager, security officer and/or the local police station.

(e) A security light should be left on in the branch.

(f) A full audit of stock should be made as soon as possible in the event of a break-in. Many large multiples send out an audit team, including one of the group accountants, to check stock units and values.

Progress test 25

1. Outline the duties of the store manager.

2. What are the two primary skills required of the store manager?

3. What is meant by store productivity?

4. List ten measures of store productivity.

5. Why is the measurement of store productivity important?

6. Describe the main aspects of health and safety for which the retail manager is responsible.

7. Define the terms (a) pilferage, (b) shoplifting, and (c) shopbreaking.

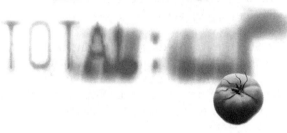

26 Technology in retailing

Introduction

Information technology (IT) and information and communication technology (ICT), which is the marriage of computers and telecommunications, is enabling the conversion of retailers from their traditional role as product-led merchants to consumer-driven marketers, allowing them to compete in the increasingly mature markets of the West. In this chapter we consider technology used in retailing, technology applications and database marketing.

1. IT in retailing

The applications of IT to retailing are numerous and continually expanding. The functions of retailing (*see* Chapter 1) are being revolutionized through investment in IT systems. The whole supply chain is in a process of integration through electronic data interchange. Lower stock investment is possible at store level because IT monitors sales on a continuous basis and calls up appropriate replenishments. IT enables stores to stock more appropriate merchandise and to target specific customers with relevant promotions. An important substitute for conventional shopping is e-commerce – the use of the internet.

Uses of technology

2. Electronic point-of-sale systems

A variety of EPOS systems have been developed, all of which utilize micro-processors: either 'stand alone' or connected to an in-store computer. The EPOS systems generally offer three functions:

(a) A price look-up (PLU) facility.

(b) The ability to record and store information on the sale of individual items.

(c) The capacity to print a till receipt that shows an abbreviated product description and a price.

The most commonly found EPOS system is the 'stand-alone' till. This offers a PLU facility, whereby the machine is able to store the price of fast-selling items and, through the application of an appropriate code, checking out is considerably speeded up.

The most sophisticated EPOS systems enable the automatic input of a code to the system. This is effected by the application of a machine-readable code to the product, which is then passed over a suitable light scanner enabling the code to be transmitted to the EPOS computer. These systems are now well established in most retail sectors using a code consisting of bars that enables the speediest checkout by a laser scanner.

The central computer is able to communicate with the in-store computer overnight to gauge total stock levels and to produce individual store order requirements for next-day delivery.

The introduction of EPOS systems offers scope for a degree of automatic re-ordering, when stock falls below certain pre-set levels. This enables overall stock levels to be kept at a minimum, while maintaining a maximum service level.

3. Bar coding

The bar code consists of a series of bars that can be read by the laser scanner, in addition to a human-readable number. This coding system, known as the European article number (EAN), has been developed on an international basis, enabling compatibility for imported and exported goods.

The human-readable code normally consists of 13 digits known as EAN–13; a shorter code, EAN–8, does exist for smaller products. The codes are shown in Figure 26.1.

The first two digits or 'flag characters' identify the nationality of the numbering authority registering the product. The UK number bank is controlled by the Article Number Association (ANA) and the UK flag characters are 50.

The next five digits are allocated by the ANA to the distributor (retailers have a code for own-label products). The second set of five digits is used by the distributor to identify the product (by price, size, colour, flavour and pack size). The final digit acts as a check to ensure the product code is correctly composed.

Figure 26.1
Bar-coding system

9 780712 112888

| Country code | Manufacturer reference | Product code | Check digit |

EAN–8

The EAN system also allows for a 'variable weight' code to be used for goods that are weighed in-store (e.g. produce, meat).

4. Advantages of EPOS systems

The hard benefits are:

(a) Higher checkout productivity – up to 15 per cent increase.

(b) Labour savings – items do not need to be individually priced.

(c) Reduction in 'mis-rings' at the checkout.

(d) Price changing is easier since only the computer price-file and shelf-edge label need be changed.

The soft benefits are:

(a) More management information on:

    (*i*)   customer flows on an hourly basis
    (*ii*) product sales, by line and over time
    (*iii*) checkout operators' productivity
    (*iv*) the effects of advertising and new product introduction.

(b) Better stock control management.

(c) Automatic ordering facility.

(d) Closer identification of shrinkage (i.e. theft, breakages, fraud, etc.) points.

(e) Better in-store labour scheduling.

The growth of EPOS systems has enabled the instantaneous collation of sales information in a more refined manner. The scanning systems provide detailed sales performance by product and outlet over days and hours. Very detailed market research can thus be quickly produced, which is of invaluable use to the retailers and their suppliers. All the leading grocery operators have now installed scanning systems and have integrated these EPOS systems into existing information networks.

An extension of EPOS is EDI (electronic data interchange) where the scanning of an item at the retailer's checkout provides information not only to the retailer but also is sent directly to the supplier to trigger a replenishment decision in the supplier's warehouse. The overall effect is that inventories decrease and stock-outs become less common.

The only significant disadvantage to these systems is the cost, but with this coming down gradually most retailers will find that the need to install systems increases.

5. Portable data capture units

The portable data capture unit (PDCU) is a miniature version of the EPOS scanning system and is now widely used in many sectors of the retail trade, largely for stock-control purposes. The PDCU consists of a small hand-held computer and an attached fixed light 'pen' or 'wand' for scanning bar codes. The PDCU is used to collect information on stock quantities, which can be entered either manually or by scanning a stock control bar code. Having collected stock information, the PDCU then interfaces with other computerized systems (e.g. buying office, warehouse ordering).

6. Viewdata

With a suitably adapted television set and a computer key pad, it is possible to transmit and receive information via the telephone lines. Such a system has opened the way for communication between the private and commercial sectors.

The UK's main public viewdata network is Prestel, operated by British Telecom, which enables the user to link cheaply into other users' computers. The BBC's Ceefax and ITV's Oracle Teletext services are of a similar nature, but with little scope for communication between users. The QVC shopping channel allows real 'teleshopping' with some interactivity. These systems, plus several privately operated viewdata services, offer significant scope for the transmission of information, with tremendous implications for retailing. The technology is an ideal medium for linking consumers directly to suppliers or retailers, enabling the concept of 'armchair' or teleshopping. There are, however, few examples of significant teleshopping schemes in operation. This is largely due to relatively few consumers possessing viewdata technology and the limited range of products that are presently supplied.

7. Electronic funds transfer

Electronic funds transfer has operated for some time, and enables the direct transfer of funds from one bank account to another electronically, particularly in the area of personal banking, where auto-teller machines (ATMs) allow the withdrawal of cash, statements and cheque books to be ordered and accounts to be settled at some high street banks and building societies; ATMs are increasingly appearing in stores also.

The wider use of electronic funds transfer at the point of sale (EFTPOS) in retail outlets has required new technology to be installed at the checkout, into which a customer debit card, e.g. Switch is fed. By the use of this card customers are then able to transfer money to the retailer from their bank account.

8. Other applications

As well as the accounting and financial systems that have historically been the reason for installing computers, the following areas are increasingly using new technology:

(a) **Space allocation.** Knowledge of specific product sales enables the retailer to make the best use of shelf space. Techniques such as direct-product profitability (DPP) identify precise profit contributions for specific products, which naturally affects space allocation.

(b) **Energy management**. Energy costs for retailers are significant and many are now using computers to monitor and minimize their energy costs (heat, light, refrigeration).

(c) **Security**. Over £2 billion worth of goods are lost by retailers annually as a result of shrinkage, stock loss, theft or fraud. By tracking individual stock items through the EPOS system such losses can be reduced. Sophisticated electronic surveillance devices are also being used.

9. Electronic data interchange

EDI systems send the data captured at store level direct to the supplier (initially it was to the company's warehouse). This is an important addition to the value chain and EDI transaction volumes have been growing at 20–25 per cent a year since international standards for documents such as orders and invoices became established in the 1980s.

EDI has become a standard way of trading for the majority of big companies. It enables just-in-time (JIT) ordering, speeding up stock turnarounds and creating close partnerships between retailers and suppliers as companies share trading data for mutual benefit. Cost of sales, which represent about 75 per cent of sales for food retailers, can be managed down. The EDI system has also enabled the development of efficient consumer response (ECR).

10. Efficient consumer response

At the centre of ECR is the sharing of sales information with suppliers, something that EDI has begun. But ECR is much more than this. It involves just-in-time deliveries and partnership sourcing. Instead of sending orders to suppliers as stocks get low, retailers have the task of generating orders to the manufacturers. Both parties jointly agree forecasting techniques and the supplier takes over responsibility for replenishment using up-to-date sales information from the retailer. It also involves the retailer informing the supplier about sales promotions that will affect the volumes sold and thus those ordered.

These systems that are based on trust and confidentiality may not work in all circumstances. Both supplier and retailer must gain from the systems and it may be that critical mass needs to be reached for benefits to be shared around.

11. Virtual shopping

Virtual means 'almost' or 'nearly' in the sense that the processes required can be activated without any tangible aspects. We read of 'virtual corporations' (a telephone that can be used to order from outsourcing agencies) and virtual reality (VR) is a now commonly used term. Most human activities can be virtualized, given the technology and the belief of the subject. Shopping is no exception. Imagine a supermarket with no checkout queues, no need to push an unruly trolley and no cars in the car park. Here you can 'fly' around the stores at speed, even pass around shelves and walls and buy products by pressing a button on a handset. Such a system can exist in a computer if appropriate software is developed. Users of the system wear headsets and hold handsets to 'take' products from the shelves as they move through the store. The products reappear in a shopping basket at the virtual checkout.

Such systems are now being developed by companies such as Sainsbury. In the motor distribution sector Ford has offered virtual test drives for the launch of its Galaxy multipurpose vehicle (such systems have been common in simulation for training pilots). The big advantage of such an approach is that buyers do not need to be physically present at the point of distribution and can, therefore, save time and money. There are clear advantages for distribution in dispensing with expensive outlets. The logistics of delivering the goods is the biggest problem and needs addressing by the industry. E-commerce, too, will generate more volume of goods moving by road to fulfil customer orders. It can be argued that consumer vehicle traffic to conventional retail outlets will reduce but that large warehouses, to serve the London region, for instance, will need to be built around the M25. An increase in the use of larger delivery vehicles may be the result.

12. Electronic commerce

The development of the internet and the World Wide Web has potentially major consequences for retailing in the long term. It is possible to envisage Western countries without many retail shops as more customers buy through electronic commerce (e-commerce) means. Objections to this future range from the increase in logistical problems (actually delivering the products) to the fact that many consumers will still want to shop in conventional environments because currently many websites are 'boring'. On the other hand the Web enables prospective buyers to roam the system to identify best prices.

It is clear that many current online retailers need to increase their investment in technology and learn to use marketing skills if they are to turn the millions of internet users into customers. One of the most successful companies using the internet is Amazon, the US bookseller. It provides the widest possible selection (over a million books), discounts of up to 40 per cent and an easy way to find titles and order them. In addition, if customers order a book, they are shown a list of other titles that previous buyers of the book have also purchased. One problem online retailers face is drawing internet users to their website. Amazon is so firmly established that it uses reminder advertising in, for example, *The Sunday Times*. A favourite method is to ensure that a website establishes links on busy or related sites; this, of course, can be expensive. Website design is also important in terms of initial attractiveness, navigation aids around the site, and so on. Loyalty programmes modelled on airlines' frequent-flier offers are also beginning to appear on the Web. Database marketing can also be used to develop relationships with customers. This is the key to Amazon's success.

One of the biggest problems facing e-commerce relates to the concerns that customers have about credit card security. To alleviate these fears stores have adopted security measures such as encrypting transactions (use of codes such as PIN numbers) and using 'firewalls' (blocks) to protect customer data stored on their computers. These measures obviously add to costs.

In mid-2003 there were estimated to be 600 million web users worldwide with over 30 million in the UK. However, growth in e-commerce has slowed down substantially, reinforced by the events of 11 September 2001. Some of this downturn was triggered by the dot-com 'bust' in early 2000, which launched the bear market in equities.

When examining e-tailing (B2C) futures most commentators argue that the future is hybrid and that the 'clicks-and-mortar' retailer will constitute at least the mid-term future. A good example of such a twin-path approach is Tesco. Having established itself as the UK's most successful supermarket chain the company has built up a very competitive online shopping service. But instead of building highly automated new warehouses dedicated to fulfilling orders from the internet – the strategy of rivals such as Sainsbury – Tesco is exploiting its network of 650 stores nationwide. Orders are sent from the Tesco Direct website to the store nearest the customer and picking is done from the store shelves. Tesco says that this is profitable on the average shopper's baskets of £100, but in the longer-term future this homespun approach may have to be transformed into a dedicated warehouse-based fulfilment system in order to preserve the integrity of the store merchandising.

13. Multi-channel retailing

Alongside the growth of the internet, the phenomenon known as multi-channel shopping has aroused much interest among retailers. Customers are starting to think of shopping not just as visiting shops but as browsing the Web, buying through the TV, selecting goods from catalogues and using the telephone and direct mail channels for contacts. The advent of 3G mobile telephones, which can intercept promotional text and video messages, may be a further development.

Many retailers from Argos to Ann Summers (which also sells through party-plan) are realizing the potential of this type of cross-selling, marketing and relationship building. For example, according to Zygon, a software specialist, Tesco added 146,000 entertainment products to its online offer for Christmas 2002, Argos's click-and-collect service operates from all its showrooms and online tailoring is now offered by Lands' End.

Database marketing

14. Background to database marketing

Database marketing is yet another application of information technology to retailing. It involves the linking of the normal EPOS systems in a retail store with loyalty or preferred customer cards.

These plastic cards are sometimes given to any customer who applies for one, although many schemes have 'spending thresholds' that customers must meet. The application form includes the name and address of the customer and other segmentation data (much of which could be non-obligatory). The EPOS system captures the details of the products purchased on each visit to the store and the loyalty card is 'swiped' at the same time, enabling the retailer to record purchases per household.

The cardholder may be given discounts on a variety of goods and the cumulative savings can be used by the shopper to buy more in future. This is the so-called 'loyalty' aspect, where shoppers are supposed to develop a preference for shopping in a certain store. More important, retailers can use their databases to identify particularly large or frequent purchasers at their stores. This is the basis of relationship marketing: these preferred customers are offered further discounts and these offers may be delivered by direct mail to home addresses.

15. Applications of database marketing

Whereas the basic use of loyalty cards has been to sell more to existing customers rather than attracting new ones, the potential from data mining of customer records is only just being realized.

An early US experience was at Smitty's, a Phoenix, Arizona store chain. By examining database details a number of shoppers who avoided the delicatessen counter were identified. They were targeted with special offers on deli lines and 60 per cent of these were redeemed. Subsequently, it was found that 35 per cent of these shoppers had made further visits, without the pull of incentives.

In another US example, Camelot Music, a 500-outlet operation based in Ohio, faced cut-pricing on CDs from the big discounters such as Wal-Mart. Its normal loyalty programme was not helping so it decided to focus on its best shoppers using ICL's Corema software to segment them into musical genre categories. For example, offers to jazz enthusiasts increased spending by 21 per cent in that category.

16. Benefits of database marketing

The advantages of database marketing are somewhat similar to those for direct marketing and sales promotion (to which it is closely linked).

(a) **Targeting**. It is relatively easy to use micromarketing techniques and to identify individual households. Depending on the amount of information on the database about each household, there are possibilities of segmenting each not only on the basis of geographic and demographic data but on income, lifestyle and other aspects.

(b) **Measurement**. Having a specific target household to monitor means that it is relatively easy to see whether or not a promotion has worked and to reinforce it with further incentives.

(c) **Immediacy**. Such activities have a marked impact on short-term sales. A longer-term goal of retailers today, however, is to try to lock customers in by substituting transactional marketing for relationship marketing (i.e. the difference between treating each sale as a stand-alone event and attempting to build a platform from the continuing links between customer and retailer).

Asda, the supermarket chain, published four areas of potential from the use of data mining:

(a) Helping to reduce customer defections to rival chains.

(b) Sharper focusing on product lines.

(c) Developing secondary shoppers into primary customers.

(d) Targeting and recruiting new shoppers.

17. Problems of database marketing

There are numerous disadvantages to the use of database marketing.

(a) **Costs**. Although database marketing is cheaper than an earlier promotional tool, trading stamps, costing 2 per cent of turnover as opposed to 4 per cent for stamps, it is still expensive. The Boots Advantage scheme cost £25 million in its first year, including setting up the database. Tesco has said that it needs an annual 1.5 per cent increase in sales to cover Clubcard running costs, i.e. around £50 million each year.

(b) **Consumer apathy**. As each retailer launches its own version of a loyalty card there is the possibility of a 'zero sum game'. Loyalty will reside less with the cards than with the overall image that the retailer prefers. Tesco and Sainsbury's have issued more than 20 million cards between them. Many households have three or more of these cards. Taking into account the costs of database marketing, some retailers talk of putting resources into the traditional ways of appealing to customers through convenience, choice and value.

(c) **Data protection**. Some customers may be wary of the amount of information that retailers and others are able to gather on them and how the data could be used. In the UK, the Data Protection Acts 1984 and 1998 (*see* Chapter 27) offer some relief.

18. Direct marketing

A database can be used to target any customer who is within a particular segment. A mail shot can then be sent to them. More sophisticatedly, customers can be targeted through the internet. The point here is that prospective customers can be identified by using many methods of data collection, e.g. filled-in coupons, loan applications and so forth. Computer technology enables companies to record more data about specific populations than ever before: Who? Where? What do they buy? When? How?

To use this information effectively a relational database is essential. Here, files are indexed against one another and they are linked in a way that expresses the logical connections between different types of data: one-to-one or one-to-many. This reflects the fact that a company may offer many products but that each product is desired by different target audiences. Figure 26.2 shows a typical consumer database.

Figure 26.2 A typical
consumer database

Note should be made of the growing use of call centres in direct response situations. Call centres are crucial to the success of telemarketing, which again relies on databasing. Another application is the use of facsimile machines. Many households possess such hardware: the growth of 'junk fax' has become a grumble for many, particularly because it uses the owner's paper.

Supply chain management

19. Supply chain management

Until fairly recently the prime operational activities of retailing were seen to be the purchasing of products, their storage and ultimately sale to the consumer. However, particularly for the large-scale multiple retailers this is a very narrow view. Increasingly retail management is expanding its activities to incorporate principles of supply chain management.

Supply chain management can be defined as the organization of all the business processes that enable the profitable transformation of raw materials or products into finished goods and their timely distribution to meet customer demand. There are two components of the retail supply chain: the external supply chain and the internal supply chain.

(a) **The external supply chain.** Includes such aspects as sourcing, supplier–distributor relationships, merchandising and strategic and operational partnerships. For example sourcing should consider not just the cost of the product itself but also all the costs of delivery of the product to the retailer's central warehouse, store and also beyond to the customer. A number of large retailers for whom promotional activities are particularly important have also developed alliances and partnership relationships within the supply chain to ensure the efficient delivery of manufacturers' display and promotional materials to the retailer's stores.

(b) **The internal supply chain.** Consists of activities related to the relationship between the retailer's central warehouses and the individual stores. Thus the main activities involve facilities and material handling, transportation, stock management, capacity utilization and information management.

20. IT in supply chain management

There is little doubt that this whole area has been transformed by the introduction of IT. This started with the introduction of EPOS and subsequent development of EDI and developed into the more recent acceptance and development of specialized software for the efficient management of the supply chain across the internet.

Sainsbury's is an example of a British company at the forefront of developments in this area. At the heart of its newly introduced supply chain management system is a web engine that allows complex business transactions to be built and presented to a browser so everyone sees the same up-to-date view of the data. Some 700 suppliers, 50 hauliers and 40 Sainsbury's supply chain and finance users can access the system 24 hours a day from the Sainsbury's Information Direct (SID) website. Suppliers and hauliers are responsible for entering their own data on product movements. It is claimed that the system is benefiting everyone across the supply chain. Sainsbury's customers benefit from improved in-store availability, suppliers and hauliers benefit from improved data, which reduces administration and speeds invoice-processing, and Sainsbury's benefit from increased loyalty of their customers because product is on the shelf when they want it and in the right quantity.

21. The supply chain management system

For the large retailer, supply chain management systems can become very complex. It may be helpful therefore to imagine the whole system working in concert to minimize costs while maximizing customer service but, in fact, as being made up of a number of more digestible sub-systems:

(a) **Demand management**. Co-ordinating sales forecasts from all the players at the point of sale through production to raw material suppliers, so that everyone is working to the same plan, rather than creating unnecessary safety stocks.

(b) **Distribution resources planning (DRP)**. Keeping track of the status of production and procurement of materials for each order: where the goods are located, what transport and warehousing is in use, what stock to keep and when to reorder. Also, if it all goes wrong, what resources are available to mitigate problems and costs.

(c) **Transport management systems (TMS)**. Determining what methods of transport at what cost are available to the shipper; what costs and timings are associated with each route; the order in which to load transport; optimization of multi-segment deliveries; compliance with documentation required for customs and shippers.

(d) **Warehouse management system (WMS)**. Systems to optimize the storage and picking of goods in a warehouse, including compliance with carrier and customer documentation standards.

(e) **Supplier relationship management (SRM).** Information about suppliers of direct and indirect materials, such as agreed terms of trade such as delivery and price associated with them, records of status, records of contacts between the enterprise and the various points of contact in suppliers.

Implications of the new technology

22. Management training

Unless management fully understands and is able to operate the new systems, many benefits will be lost. It is therefore important that managers are trained in the capability of the system and how to use it; a broader appreciation of the application of computers is also vital. This might be achieved by short courses on the capabilities of computer systems, keyboard operation, how to read and use print-outs, etc.

As procedures change to meet the requirements of new technology, reporting structures also may well change. Management should be aware of these changes and how they will affect the staff. Technology is a management tool and it is vital that managers are aware of the role played by new equipment; they need to understand fully the basic principles and draw on the specific training offered by the equipment suppliers.

Progress test 26

1. What are the advantages of EPOS systems?

2. What is a PDCU?

3. What are the implications of the new technology for the manager?

4. With reference to particular examples, examine the contribution, if any, of IT investment to the ability of retailers to survive the growing competition in the retail sector.

5. Discuss the development of multi-channel shopping.

6. What are the main components (subsystems) of a supply chain management system?

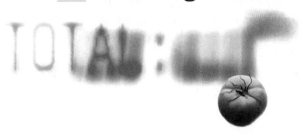

27 Retailing and the law

Introduction

This chapter considers how legislation affects retailing in general, how consumers are protected and how retail staff are protected.

1. Development of the law regarding retailing

There have been two main threads in the development of the law affecting retailers. One concerns the sale of goods, regulations for which date back certainly to 1226, while the other concerns the status of employees within the industry. In the latter case, specific legislation was not passed until 1912. Legislation of both kinds has been increasing in volume and complexity during the past ten years and this chapter discusses some of the more important Acts. Note that the information here is intended for guidance only. The reader is advised to refer to specific texts for more detailed, authoritative and up-to-date information.

2. Some general points

(a) The retailer is legally entitled to demand the exact purchase price for its goods, in cash.

(b) Strictly speaking, cheques are not legal tender – payment by cheque is a concession offered to the customer by the retailer.

(c) A deposit paid by a customer in relation to merchandise ordered to the customer's particular specification is not normally returnable to the customer (unless the seller is unwilling or unable to deliver the goods or to pass good title).

(d) There is no obligation for a customer to produce a receipt, and the law allows customers to prove their purchase verbally.

(e) In the absence of any fixed delivery date the retailer must have the goods available for delivery within a reasonable time. The place of delivery depends on what has been agreed.

(f) A retailer commits a criminal offence and may be prosecuted if it displays a notice saying 'No money refunded' or 'Sale goods not exchanged or money refunded'.

(g) If a retailer gives the consumer extra rights, e.g. 'Your money will be courteously and promptly refunded if you are not satisfied', then it must make it clear that these rights are in addition to the usual statutory rights, e.g. by stating, 'This does not affect your statutory rights'.

Consumer protection

3. Sale of Goods Act 1979

This Act replaced the Sale of Goods Act 1893 and the Supply of Goods (Implied Terms) Act 1973. It relates to all transactions in which ownership of goods passes in exchange for money – it does not apply to services. But similar provisions apply where goods are transferred under a contract for services, e.g. servicing a car (see the Supply of Goods and Services Act 1982).

The three most important aspects of the Act are:

(a) **Goods must be of merchantable quality**. They must be fit for sale, but customers have no right to reject goods in respect of defects brought to their attention before the sale (but they must have been specifically pointed out to the customers), or if the customers examine their goods, they have no right to reject goods because of defects that their examination ought to have revealed.

(b) **Goods must be fit for the purpose**. This means fit for the purpose for which the customer is buying them. However, if the goods are required for a special purpose, the customer must make this known to the retailer, who, if it then supplies a particular item, would be liable if it was unfit for this purpose. The retailer would not be liable, however, if the buyer does not rely on the seller's judgement, or if it is unreasonable for the customer to so rely.

(c) **Goods must correspond with their description**. For example, machine-made items should not be described as hand-made.

The retailer must rectify the situation relating to faulty goods by offering a refund. Alternatively, the customer may accept a credit note, repair of goods or a replacement.

It should be noted that the retailer may be liable for consequential loss caused by defective goods, e.g. if a faulty gas oven explodes and ruins the customer's kitchen. The customer has a right to bring a claim against the retailer at any time up to six years from the date of purchase of the product. In the event of a dispute the courts will decide how long a particular component or product ought to last.

4. The Supply of Goods and Services Act 1982

The provision of a service by the retailer to customers is outside the protection of the Sale of Goods Act 1979, but is covered by similar provisions in the Supply of Goods and Services Act 1982. This Act requires goods supplied under the contract to be of merchantable quality, fit for their purpose and to comply with any description. In addition, services performed under the contract must be completed with reasonable skill and care.

Further protection is available under the Trade Descriptions Act 1968, which makes it a criminal offence for a retailer knowingly or recklessly to make false or misleading statements relating to services.

The law of contract applies, and the customer is entitled to sue the retailer for breach of contract if something goes wrong. Unless a fixed price has already been agreed between the parties, the customer is entitled to expect that the price for the service will be a reasonable price.

5. Sale and Supply of Goods Act 1994

This Act, which came into force in 1995, amends the Sale of Goods Act 1979 and changes the words 'merchantable quality' to 'satisfactory quality' (a more modern phrase) which may include fitness for purpose, appearance and finish, freedom from minor defects, and safety and durability. The customer's rights as outlined in the 1979 Act remain unaltered.

6. Food Act 1984 and Food Safety Act 1990

The purpose of these Acts is to protect the consumer from the sale of inferior food products and the Acts consolidate previous legislation on food, drugs, markets and cold stores. The provisions of the Food Act 1984 have largely been repealed, and are replaced by new provisions in the Food Safety Act 1990 concerning food safety and consumer protection. The 1990 Act makes it an offence to render food injurious to health (e.g. by adding things to it or subjecting it to a process or treatment). It is also an offence to sell food that has been rendered injurious to health, or is unfit for human consumption, or is so contaminated that it cannot reasonably be used for human consumption. It is also an offence to sell food that is not of the nature, substance or quality that is demanded by the purchaser. It is also an offence to describe or present food falsely, e.g. by means of labels or advertisements, or to mislead as to the nature, substance or quality of the food. It is also an offence to sell or offer for sale food, the presentation of which is likely to mislead as to its nature, substance or quality.

Food that is suspected of not complying with safety requirements can be seized and condemned, and the use of processes or treatments used in the preparation of food can be prohibited.

Ingredients must be listed in order of weight on jars and packages, and the name or address of the packer or labeller added.

If a food retailer is accused of contravening the Food Safety Act it can plead 'due diligence' in defence. This protects traders who can show that they have observed all reasonable precautions to safeguard products and customers.

7. Food Hygiene (General) Regulations 1970 and Food Hygiene (Amendment) Regulations 1990

The 1970 regulations were originally made under the Food Act 1984, which has been substantially replaced by the Food Safety Act 1990, but the 1970 regulations continue in force as if made under the Food Safety Act 1990. The regulations place certain responsibilities on employees or persons handling food:

(a) Foods must be protected from the risk of contamination.

(b) People handling food must keep the parts of their body that are likely to come into contact with food as clean as is reasonably practicable. Cuts and abrasions must be completely covered with waterproof dressings. The prohibition of smoking and spitting is also included in this regulation. All clothing must be kept clean.

(c) Those handling open food are to use clean (washable) overalls.

(d) Persons suffering from certain infectious diseases (e.g. typhoid fever, salmonella infection or dysentery) must inform the person in charge, who in turn must inform the local authority medical officer.

(e) Premises should be clean and in good condition so that food cannot be contaminated directly or indirectly.

(f) Equipment that comes into contact with food must be kept clean to prevent the risk of food contamination.

(g) Certain foods are to be stored at temperatures laid down in the regulations; the foods covered include cheese, cooked products containing meat, fish, eggs, cereals, pulses, smoked fish, prepared salads, sandwiches, pies, etc.

Further regulations exist under the Food Safety (General Food Hygiene) Regulations 1995.

8. Food Standards Act 1999

The Food Standards Agency was established by this Act in response to public concerns about 'mad cow disease' and other suspect contamination in the food chain. The Agency's main objective is to help protect public health from risks which may arise in connection with the production and consumption of food.

9. Resale Prices Act 1976

This repeals and consolidates the provisions of earlier legislation, e.g. the Resale Prices Act 1964. It is unlawful for individuals as well as collective suppliers to fix minimum prices. A manufacturer can still recommend selling prices for its goods but sellers do not have to observe them, although in some cases they may be bound not to exceed them.

10. Trading Stamps Act 1964

This Act places restrictions on persons carrying on business as promoters of trading stamp schemes. The cash value of the individual stamp must be clearly marked on its face and the Act also makes it possible for retail customers to obtain this cash value rather than 'gifts'. The Act also makes it obligatory for shops operating these schemes to display notices stating the cash value of the stamps and to keep for public inspection a copy of the promoter's current gift catalogue, which must contain the promoter's name and registered office.

11. Trade Descriptions Act 1968

This Act is based on the recommendations of the Molony Committee, which reported in 1962. The Act imposes commercial penalties on any person who:

(a) Applies a false trade description (as defined by the Act) to goods.

(b) Sells goods to which a false trade description has been applied.

It should be noted that a description can be verbal as well as written. The Act gives powers to the Department of Trade and Industry to require information to be marked on goods or to be included in advertisements.

12. Unsolicited Goods and Services Acts 1971 and 1975

These Acts seek to protect people to whom goods are sent or delivered, without being asked for. Section 1 of the 1971 Act provides that in certain circumstances receivers of unsolicited goods may use, deal with or dispose of them as if they were an unconditional gift to them, thus extinguishing the sender's rights. It is a criminal offence for senders to demand payment where they have no reasonable cause to believe there is a right to payment. It is also a criminal offence in such cases to threaten to take legal action, to have the receiver's name put on a list of debtors/defaulters, or to initiate collection procedures.

13. Fair Trading Act 1973

Further strengthening of consumer protection legislation occurred when this Act enabled the setting up of the Office of Fair Trading (OFT) run by the Director-General of Fair Trading and supported by a Consumer Protection Advisory Committee. The Director-General had powers to investigate both general consumer trade practices and the activities of individual traders and, if there was sufficient evidence, to obtain their discontinuance or modification by a court order or a statutory instrument, which is a type of delegated legislation. Under the Enterprise Act (see below) the post of Director General has been abolished and the OFT now operates as a board with at least four members and a chairman.

14. Competition Acts 1980 and 1998

The 1980 Act authorized the Director-General of Fair Trading to carry out a preliminary investigation to determine whether a course of conduct being pursued amounts to an anti-competitive practice.

If the existence of an anti-competitive practice was identified, the Director-General was empowered to refer the matter to the Competition Commission (formerly the Monopolies and Mergers Commission) for further investigation, and for their report as to whether the practice was against the public interest. If it was against the public interest, the Director-General could ask the parties to undertake to refrain from the practice or take action in order to remedy the defect. The Act's purpose was to encourage competition and prevent anti-competitive practices such as monopoly situations.

The Act defined the existence of a monopoly situation as being when at least one-quarter of the supply of goods or services supplied in the UK is supplied by one person, or one company, or group of interconnected companies, or where two or more unconnected persons do so, and so conduct their affairs in any way to prevent, restrict or distort competition.

The 1998 Act gave the OFT sweeping new powers to fine companies up to 30 per cent of turnover for price fixing. The Act also renamed the Monopolies and Mergers Commission (see above) as the Competition Commission which has the same role.

15. Enterprise Act 2003

A much tougher, U.S.-inspired approach has been introduced by this legislation which can impose criminal penalties on those who engage in cartels, grants new detection powers to the OFT and replaces the mergers code in the Fair Trading Act. Ministerial involvement is ended and competition, not public interest, is the new test applied in investigation. There is also a new independent Competition Appeals Tribunal.

16. Consumer Credit Act 1974

This very important piece of consumer protection legislation is based on the report of the Crowther Committee, which looked into the whole question of credit trading, particularly how it affects the consumer. The Committee suggested important reforms such as the concept of 'truth in lending' so that borrowers can know the exact rate of interest they have to pay. Much of the previous legislation on the subject, such as the Hire-Purchase Acts of 1964 and 1965 and money-lending legislation, has been swept away. Nearly every credit trader is affected, from the shop offering 'easy terms' to the department store operating budget accounts and, indeed, to many firms that offer support services or advice to credit users.

Supervision and control of the Act is carried out by the Director-General of Fair Trading. The main provisions of the Act are as follows:

(a) **Licensing**. The Act requires anyone carrying on a credit or hire business (e.g. TV rental) to obtain a licence from the Director-General. Before granting the licence the Director-General will want to know:

(*i*)   the type of activity to be carried out
(*ii*) the type of agreements the trader will want to enter into
(*iii*) whether the person obtaining the licence is 'a fit person to engage in the activities covered by the licence'. (The fitness to hold a licence may depend on past behaviour as reflected in court records or engagement in business practices that the Director-General feels to be unfair.)

The licence may be either 'a standard licence' issued to the person named, or a 'group licence' covering a group of persons or a group of activities, e.g. a limited company.

(b) Advertising and canvassing. False or misleading advertisements are automatically illegal under the Act and an offence is committed not only by the advertiser but by anybody who publishes the advertisement or even draws it up. The Act seeks to control 'high-pressure' doorstep selling by providing that customers have a right to cancel the agreement where oral representations have been made to them in their presence, and the agreement was signed anywhere other than the creditor's business premises. This cuts out the risk that consumers will enter into agreements 'on the doorstep'.

(c) Entering into agreements. Important and complicated provisions are set out in the Act regarding the actual form of credit or hiring agreements, particularly for a 'cooling-off period' of five days in order for the prospective debtor to reconsider the matter and, if necessary, get out of the agreement. Specific information must also be supplied before customers sign, regarding their rights (e.g. to cancel the agreement) and duties, the amount and rate of the total charge for the credit, and the protection and remedies available to them under the Act.

(d) Default and termination. If the vendor wishes to terminate the agreement for reasons such as non-payment, notice must be given to the debtor with full reasons for termination. With hire-purchase and conditional sale agreements many of the basic provisions of previous legislation are carried on. For instance, a vendor is still prevented from repossessing goods under these types of agreement, other than by means of a court order, once one-third of the total price has been paid. Customers must also have the right to terminate the agreement at any time and their maximum liability in such an event is to make the payments up to one-half of the total price (and possibly pay for any damages for failing to keep the goods in proper condition).

(e) Extortionate credit bargains. Where there is an extortionate credit bargain (an agreement requiring grossly exorbitant interest payments, or that is otherwise grossly unfair), the court has power to reopen the credit agreement, and can totally rewrite its terms, having regard to the circumstances of the debtor and creditor (the court could, for example, reduce the rate of interest).

17. Consumer Credit (Advertisements) Regulations 1989

These regulations provide rules on how the retailer must conduct its credit advertising.

At the heart of the legislation is the requirement to define two standard measures of credit cost, namely:

(a) The total charge for credit.

(b) The annual percentage rate of charge (APR). The APR must be stated more prominently than any other rate, e.g. annual flat rate or monthly period rate, and at least as prominently as any other piece of credit information.

The regulations also set out the minimum amount of information required in credit advertisements. Also, some expressions may only be used in credit advertisements in restricted circumstances, e.g. words such as 'overdraft', 'interest-free' and 'no deposit' carry special meanings and therefore must not be used loosely.

Where the creditor requires security in the form of a mortgage or charge on the debtor's house, a statement must be made in the advertisement in the form: 'Your home is at risk if you do not keep up repayments on a mortgage or other loan secured on it'.

If the advertisement is for a mortgage or other loan secured on property and repayments are made in a currency other than sterling, a statement is necessary in the form: 'The sterling equivalent of your liability under a foreign currency mortgage may be increased by exchange rate movements'.

18. Unfair Contract Terms Act 1977

This Act reduces the degree to which the liability can be limited or excluded in contracts. It is not possible to exclude liability for death or personal injury caused by negligence.

Exclusion of liability for breach of contract is also controlled. Where the buyer acts as a consumer the seller cannot exclude or limit the requirements of the Sale of Goods Act (*see* 3). In other cases exclusion of liability for breach of contract may be allowed if the exclusion clause is reasonable. Ultimately it is up to the courts to define what is or is not reasonable, and this depends on the circumstances in each case, for example:

(a) The relative bargaining positions of the parties.

(b) Whether there was any inducement for the consumer to enter the contract, e.g. 'low price' (this would make the exclusion more likely to be reasonable).

(c) Whether the consumer had knowledge of the clause (if so, more likely to be reasonable).

(d) Whether the consumer could have gone elsewhere and entered into similar contracts without the clause (more likely to be unreasonable as, if other traders do without the clause, then this one should be able to also).

(e) Any other circumstances.

19. Theft Act 1968

This Act allows a store's security officer or other person to arrest a suspected thief. A person is guilty of theft if he or she dishonestly appropriates property belonging to another with the intention of permanently depriving the other of it.

The use of force is allowed in making an arrest, but only such as is reasonable in the circumstances in the prevention of crime. Where an arrest is made, the person making the arrest must take the arrested person to a magistrate or to a police station as soon as is reasonably possible, i.e. within a reasonable time.

20. Consumer Protection Act 1987

This Act introduced the concept of 'product liability', namely that:

(a) A person who puts an 'own brand' mark on goods may be liable to any person who is injured by those goods if they prove defective.

(b) A retailer may be liable to any person injured by defective goods supplied by it, unless it can identify its own supplier.

The Act also empowers the Secretary of State to make regulations in respect of certain types of goods, e.g. oil heaters and fireguards, flame-resistant nightwear for children, electrical appliance wiring, colour codes and children's toys. Local authorities are responsible for protecting shoppers. Trading Standards or Consumer Protection Departments see that laws concerning trading are met and investigate complaints.

The Consumer Protection Act repeals Section 11 of the Trade Descriptions Act 1968 (which concerned giving misleading information, e.g. as to the price of goods). Section 20 of the Consumer Protection Act 1987 creates a new offence of giving misleading price indications, and detailed guidance on this new offence is given in the Code of Practice for Traders on Price Indications (*see* 20).

21. Disability Discrimination Act 1995

This act introduces laws aimed at ending the discrimination that many people face. The Act gives disabled people new rights in the areas of access to goods, facilities and services. For example, a newsagent may say that people with learning disabilities from a nearby training centre cannot use its shop to buy snacks at lunchtime because the attention they need delays service to other customers. The newsagent is discriminating against them because of their disability. This is unlawful. (*See also* 32.)

22. Consumer Protection (Code of Practice for Traders on Price Indications) Approval Order 1988

This order is made under the Consumer Protection Act 1987. It gives guidance as to what constitutes the offence of giving misleading price indications, and aims to promote desirable practices among traders when they are giving price indications. The Code of Practice for Traders on Price Indications is set out as a Schedule to the Order; it states that in general if a trader is making a price comparison it should do so in terms that are clear, and if it is not intending a price comparison, it should not use words that suggest that one is being made.

Price comparisons should always state the higher price as well as the price that is intended to be charged. Statements like 'sale price £5.00' or 'reduced to £39.00' should not be used without quoting the higher price to which they refer.

If expressions like 'usual price', 'normal price' or 'regular price' are used they should make clear whose regular, usual or normal price it is.

If a trader is making a comparison between the present selling price and another price at which it has offered the product in the past, it should state the previous as well as the lower price.

In any comparison with the trader's own previous price:

(a) The previous price should be the last price at which the product was available during the last six months.

(b) The product should have been available to consumers at that price for at least 28 consecutive days in the previous six months.

(c) The previous price should have been applied at the same shop where the reduced price is now offered.

If any of this is departed from, this is not necessarily a breach of Section 20 of the Consumer Protection Act 1987, so long as the comparison is fair and meaningful, and a clear and positive explanation of the period in which the higher price applied is given.

The Code also deals with 'introductory' and 'promotional' offers, 'when perfect' comparisons, comparisons with other traders' prices and comparisons with recommended retail prices. Again the comparison must be fair and meaningful; for example, an introductory offer should state for how long it applies and should not carry on for so long that it seems to be the permanent price (this could mislead the customer into thinking they are getting a bargain if they buy the item now, whereas the price is not in fact going up for a while yet).

The Code deals with the actual price to the consumer, and this covers things like indicating two different prices, e.g. a lower price shown in the window while a higher price is charged at the point of sale (this would be an offence under Section 20 Consumer Protection Act 1987). Also covered is incomplete information given as to price and non-optional extras, postage, packing and delivery charges, VAT and professional fees.

The Code also deals with price indications that become misleading after they have been given (e.g. newspaper and magazine offers), which would happen if:

(a) Consumers could reasonably be expected still to be relying on them.

(b) The trader does not take reasonable steps to prevent consumers so relying.

If the magazine does not state otherwise, the price should apply for a reasonable period, i.e. at least seven days, or until the next issue. If the advertisement has become misleading due to, for example, changes in VAT, the correct price should be indicated to customers who place orders, before they commit themselves to buying the product.

The Code also applies to the sale of 'new homes' and this expression carries a restricted meaning and should not be used loosely.

The Consumer Protection Act 1987 does not require traders to observe the Code – they can still give price indications that do not accord with the Code, provided they are not 'misleading' as defined by Section 21 of the Consumer Protection Act 1987; the definition covers indications about any conditions attached to a price, about what is expected to happen to a price in the future, and what is said about price comparisons, as well as indications about the actual price the consumer will have to pay. It also applies in the same way to any indications given about the way in which a price will be calculated.

23. Weights and Measures Act 1985

This Act makes it an offence to give short weight, or inadequate quantity, or a wrong indication of amount.

Certain listed foods are required by the Weights and Measures (Miscellaneous Foods) Order 1988, when pre-packed, to be sold in prescribed quantities. These items include foodstuffs such as salt, sugar, flour, chocolate bars, milk, butter, coffee, pasta and potatoes.

Pre-packed food stuffs, whether in packets, bottles or tins, must be marked with the weight or quantity, otherwise an offence is committed.

The Weights and Measures Act 1963 (Cheese, Fish, Fresh Fruits and Vegetables, Meat and Poultry) Order 1984 requires that meat, fish, poultry, cheese and fresh fruit and vegetables must have either the weight marked on the packet, or the weight must be made known before purchase, otherwise an offence is committed.

24. Data Protection Acts 1984 and 1998

Retailers and others who hold personal information on computers are responsible for obtaining, storing and disclosing it in accordance with stated principles. One of the most important of these is that the information must have been obtained fairly. Consumers who have given information need to know how it will be used, otherwise they have the right to withhold it. The 1998 Data Protection Act came into effect in 2000. This deals with data gained indirectly (e.g. from the electoral register) with further consumer protection regarding this data.

Employee legislation

25. Shops Act 1950

This is aimed very largely at protecting staff from exploitation and long hours. The Act lays down fairly tight controls over three main areas:

(a) **General closing hours** (i.e. the ordinary week-day closing times). Serving of customers generally must not be later than 8 pm, and 9 pm on a late closing day. To accommodate the special position of confectioners, tobacconists and newsagents (CTN), special differing provisions apply.

(b) **Early closing days.** There is a statutory requirement for every shop to close at 1 pm for one half-day each week. The local authority can, however, make shops in a particular area exempt from this provision, if that is the wish of the majority of shopkeepers in the area. Such exemptions are common. The early closing day requirement does not apply to shops at certain airports.

(c) **Staff employment conditions.** The Shops Act also contains many conditions of employment for staff. For example, no more than six hours can be worked by an adult shop assistant without a 20-minute break. Where the hours of employment include the hours 11.30 am to 2.30 pm, at least 45 minutes must be allowed for lunch (one hour if lunch is not taken in the shop) and if an assistant works between the hours of 4 pm and 7 pm, a minimum of 30 minutes should be allowed for tea.

These provisions do not apply to a shop if the only persons employed as shop assistants are members of the occupier's family, maintained by the occupied and dwelling in the occupier's house. Persons under the age of 18 may not be employed for more than five hours without an interval of at least 20 minutes.

26. Shops (Early Closing Days) Act 1965

This Act allows the occupier of the shop to select the premises' early closing day. This revokes local authority powers in this respect as laid down under the Shops Act 1950. Occupiers are obliged to display a notice specifying the early closing day and this notice should be readable from the shop entrance.

27. Offices, Shops and Railway Premises Act 1963

Under this Act, shopkeepers must register with the local authority on a form known as OSR1. The Act lays down certain minimum standards concerning health and safety.

(a) Standards of comfort

(*i*) *Cleanliness.* All premises, fixtures and fittings must be kept clean, including staff-rooms, stairways, exits, halls and lifts.

(*ii*) *Overcrowding.* Office staff must have at least 400 cubic feet (11 cubic metres) of area each in which to work, but this stipulation does not extend to the public areas of shops or showrooms (although there is still a general responsibility here to avoid overcrowding likely to cause risk of injury to health).

(*iii*) *Temperature.* Staff are entitled to a reasonable room temperature, laid down in the Act as a minimum of 16 degrees Centigrade after the first hour.

(*iv*) *Overall comfort.* Adequate ventilation, lighting and drinking water must be provided, along with seating and outdoor clothes storage.

(b) Standards of safety. Staff must be able to move around the building in safety. This means that all areas must be soundly constructed, properly maintained and free from obstruction and slippery substances.

(*i*) *First aid.* A proper first-aid box or cupboard must be provided for each 150 people employed.

(*ii*) *Dangerous machinery.* Great care must be taken to see that staff are not injured by machinery, such as preparation machines in the butchery section of superstores. All dangerous parts of machinery must be properly fenced in either by a fixed guard, or, if this is not possible, by an automatic safety device. Certain machinery that is prescribed by the Minister as dangerous must be operated by trained staff, who must be supervised.

(c) **Hygiene**. Adequate washing facilities for staff are required under the Act, along with a minimum of one lavatory per 15 members of staff of each sex.

(d) **Fire precautions**. The Fire Precautions Act 1971 and the Fire Precautions (Factories, Offices, Shops and Railway Premises) Order 1989 apply, and the following requirements are laid down:

(i) *Fire-fighting equipment*. This must be suitable and properly maintained, and must be kept ready for immediate use on the premises.

(ii) *Proper means of escape*. In case of fire, a proper means of escape, which is signposted for shoppers as well as for staff, should be available. The fire exits should be kept uncluttered and the fire doors themselves should have panic bars.

(iii) *Inspection for fire certification*. The local authority has a duty to inspect the premises before issuing the certificate. However, the Fire Precautions (Factories, Offices, Shops and Railway Premises) Order 1989 states that a fire certificate is not required where not more than 20 people work at any one time, or where fewer than 10 people work at any one time in upstairs rooms in the building.

(iv) *Fire alarms*. These will also be required to have a certificate. The most important point here is that the noise must be heard clearly in all parts of the building.

(v) *Fire drill*. This is required if the retailer's shop is large enough for fire certification. A set routine in event of fire should be known to all staff and random practices carried out for test purposes.

This Act is now largely regulated under the workplace (Health, Safety and Welfare) Regulations 1992.

28. Health and Safety at Work Act 1974

This Act provides a comprehensive and integrated system of law dealing with the safety, health and welfare of people at work and even the health and safety of the public. Employers must tell their employees what the policy of the firm is towards health and safety. Guidance notes are available from the Health and Safety Executive. Local authorities through their inspectorates are responsible for the general enforcement of the Act's provisions, which include the serving of two notices, detailed below.

(a) **Improvement notices**. These state how the Act has been contravened and calls upon the shopkeeper, for example, to put it right within a particular time.

(b) **Prohibition notices**. If inspectors feel that some activities involve a risk of serious personal injury, they may serve a prohibition notice that has an immediate effect and may involve the full or part closure of the store.

The employer's duties under this Act are to:

(a) Draw up and publish a safety policy statement.

(b) Ensure that safety procedures are implemented.

(c) Keep and publish safety records.

(d) Advise staff and others of their responsibilities.

Employees are also liable under this Act if they fail to follow safe methods of working.

29. Equal Pay Act 1970

This Act came into force in 1975 with the purpose of eliminating discrimination between men and women in regard to pay and other terms of employment contracts, i.e. basic rates of pay, overtime, bonus and piece-work payments, holiday and sick pay entitlement. Under the Act, an individual woman has the right to equal treatment with a man when she is employed on like work, or on a job that has been given equal status under job evaluation, or on work of equal value. Minimum wage legislation was also introduced by the Government in 1999, based initially on a minimum of £3.60 per hour and increased in later years.

30. Employment Protection (Consolidation) Act 1978

This Act replaces the Contracts of Employment Act 1972 and the Employment Protection Act 1975. It is a complicated piece of legislation and is subject to periodic modification, e.g. the Employment Acts 1980 and 1982. The following are some important provisions of the Act regarding:

(a) **Contracts of employment**

(*i*) A written statement of main terms and conditions of employment must be provided to the employee within 13 weeks of the commencement of employment.

(*ii*) There must be written notification, within one month, of a change in the name or identity of the employer.

(*iii*) Employees working more than 16 hours per week are entitled to an itemized pay statement.

(b) **Maternity rights**. These include maternity leave, etc.

(c) **Dismissal and redundancy**. For example redundancy pay, notice of termination of employment, written reasons for dismissal, compensation for 'unfair' dismissal.

31. Employment Rights Act 1996

This further regulates the Sunday working of shop and betting workers, their time of work and amends laws on wage protection and unfair dismissal.

32. Employment Act 2002

The Act makes provision regarding adoption and paternity leave and pay, maternity leave and pay, flexible working, employment tribunal reform and resolving disputes between employers and employees.

33. Sex Discrimination Acts 1975 and 1986

It is unlawful to discriminate on the grounds of sex in employment, training and education, as well as in the provision of goods and services. Individuals have the right to complain to courts and industrial tribunals. The Equal Opportunities Commission was established to help enforce this legislation promoting sexual equality. The law covers both recruitment and existing employees in matters like appointment and promotion. Firms with fewer than five employees are excluded.

Discrimination on the grounds of sexual orientation is covered by the Employment Equality (Sexual Orientation) Regulations 2003.

34. Race Relations Act 1976

By this Act discrimination on the grounds of race, colour, creed or religion is unlawful in employment, training and related matters. Individuals have access to industrial tribunals and civil courts. The Race Relations Board was replaced by a new Commission for Racial Equality for the elimination of racial discrimination.

Specific regulation on religious discrimination is covered by the Employment Equality (Religion or Belief) Regulations 2003.

35. Social Security and Housing Benefits Act 1982

As a result of this Act employers are responsible for paying Statutory Sick Pay (SSP) to their employees for up to eight weeks of sickness absence in one tax year. The retailer is required by law to keep records of:

(a) Dates of sickness absence (including Saturdays and Sundays) reported by employees.

(b) Any days within such sickness absences for which SSP was not paid, with reasons.

(c) Details of each employee's qualifying days in each period of incapacity for work.

These records should be kept in such a way that DSS inspectors can have access to them on request. The Social Security Benefits and Contributions Act 1992 consolidates much of the previously enacted legislation on social security matters.

36. Disability Discrimination Act 1995

This Act, mentioned earlier in section 19, also applies to employment. Although employers naturally want the best person for the job, it may be unlawful to discriminate against disabled people in certain circumstances. For example, Jo has a learning disability that has prevented her from gaining a certain qualification. Although she is the best candidate she is refused the job on the grounds that she does not possess the qualification: but the qualification is not necessary to do the job. Here the employer has discriminated unlawfully against her.

Every aspect of jobs is covered by the Act including selection, doing the work, career development and redundancy or dismissal.

Note: This chapter on Retailing and the Law is intended for guidance only and is not intended as a comprehensive overview of statutes. The reader is advised to refer to specific texts for more detailed, authoritative and up-to-date information.

Progress test 27

1. Outline the main provisions of the Sale of Goods Act 1979. How was it updated in 1994?

2. Explain how the Food Safety Act 1990 protects consumers. What defence can a food retailer offer to an alleged breach of the Act?

3. Describe the general provisions of the Consumer Credit Act 1974. What is the connection with the Fair Trading Act?

4. How has the Enterprise Act altered the way in which competition is regulated in Britain today?

5. Briefly discuss the several Acts that try to protect employees from discrimination at work. How effective do you think they are?

28 The future of retailing

Introduction

It can be argued that the pace of change in retailing – as in the environment generally – is accelerating. The key drivers are technology, increasing maturation and therefore competition in the retail sector and changes in social and cultural attitudes. This chapter considers how retailing is affected by social and economic variables, the political and legal system and technological and sectoral-specific trends.

1. Change

We have already discussed some of the current alterations in the retail climate. For instance, Chapter 26 focuses on technology in retailing. It is impossible, however, to discuss the future of retailing without reference to the changes going on in the macro-environment.

One of the crucial questions is how retail managements can respond to the massive changes that will affect the retail sector over the next 25 years. This chapter outlines some of the challenges that companies face. Some responses are already being made today. Students of retailing will be asked continuously as success and failure unfold how valid strategies are or have been.

We discuss the major changes that appear to be occurring and then how retail management is responding or could respond to each variable.

Economic changes

2. Globalization

Whatever this term means it is certainly reflected in the cross-border moves made by retailers discussed in Chapter 5. These changes are likely to continue for the next few years until overtaken, perhaps, by a new retail cycle, based on store-less shopping through the internet or its successor.

3. Deflation

Deflation can be defined as a consistent fall in the level of prices – the opposite of inflation which we have suffered for 50 years. Deflation or falling prices has been a common feature of economic conditions at times for many centuries. Japan and Hong Kong have suffered deflation since the late 1990s. It is possible that a new long economic cycle is beginning that will involve falling prices for a period. This will have major lessons for retailers as they juggle with their costs and their output prices to try to maintain profitability.

4. Economic integration

By this is meant the growing tendency for adjoining countries to form trading blocs. As discussed in Chapter 5, this has implications for all industry sectors, including retailing, with regard to cross-border moves and their implementation. These economic and political trends are likely to continue with the extension of the European Union to Eastern Europe. The launch of common currencies is part of this trend, with the shortening of retail life cycles. Even the most innovative new retail ideas are quickly copied, thus losing their pre-eminence, for example various fast-food formats.

Technology

5. Space usage

Whereas space is still a major resource for most retailers, the rise of e-commerce has shown that its long-term place in the planning of even a food chain may be finite. On the other hand, many people will still want to shop conventionally. Hybrid systems are likely to be common for the next quarter century, where well-known brands like Tesco offer both internet and conventional shopping to cater for the existing and new consumer segments.

6. Micromarketing

To address the new explosion in segmentation, retailers will need to focus even more on the micromarkets, using the database techniques described in Chapter 26. Refinements in software and in computer power will make this approach much more cost-effective for retailers.

7. Value chain aspects

The value chain, discussed in Chapter 4, involves the complete flow of goods and services from suppliers, through intermediaries like retailers to the final customers. IT can thoroughly enhance the usefulness of the value chain as manufacturers and retailers swap information on current operations and trends. This more open approach to managing the supply chain will be one of the most important changes in the future.

Social variables

8. Increase in one-stop shopping

Shopping, particularly for food, is regarded by many consumers as time-consuming and boring. Superstores are now 'creaming' and 'scrambling' more to improve shopper footfall and profitability. Creaming involves adopting the most popular lines from a range of other retailers, e.g. newspapers and magazines, over-the-counter medicines, fresh flowers and plants, alcohol and so on. Scrambling means taking risky, high-margin foods and services from other suppliers. These include banking, post office operations, medical and dental services and the like. This could also be described as a growth in intertype competition.

9. Destination and 'hangout' centres

One important social trend is the rise in the number of people living alone, working at home or living in isolated and sprawling suburbs, which has increased the popularity of stores that, regardless of product or service offered, provide a place for people to congregate. These not only include superstores and shopping malls (where 'events' take place) but also the new trend towards coffee bars (last seen as a new trend in the late 1950s).

10. Consumer learning

Marketing is constantly evolving and one assumption is that buyers do not always know what they want; instead they learn what they want, partly through marketers who 'teach' new consumer buying patterns. Examples might be Starbucks in the coffee market and Amazon in internet bookselling.

Regulatory environment

11. Regulatory bodies and policies

In the UK, government bodies such as the Office of Fair Trading and the Competition Commission (formerly the Monopolies and Merger Commission), along with Parliament, will continue to investigate the activities of firms in sectors such as food retailing. The policies of UK governments since 1979 have been to support competitive environments through deregulation and privatization. These trends are likely to continue within democratic systems and across pan-national groupings such as the European Union.

Sectoral trends

These are largely to do with the environment described by Michael Porter in his Five Forces Theory (*see* Chapter 3).

12. New retail forms

One of the key characteristics of change in most industry sectors is that new forms often appear from the most unexpected sources. Conventional insurance brokers in town centres now have to compete against direct (telephone-based) selling of their products. The so-called 'category killer' opens huge retail sheds devoted to just one product like toys while a new firm may be set up to retail merchandise on the internet.

13. Non-store retailing

The growth of direct selling to households, vending and the internet have all replaced possible store-based retailing and these trends are set to continue with changing consumer lifestyles.

14. Changes in sizes of outlets

The growth of giant retailers of the category killer type is knocking out medium-sized operations and tending to polarize size between big and small. This is particularly obvious in food retailing.

15. Polarization in retailing

Both food and clothing stores are polarizing. In food, the polarization is based on large and small stores with few medium-sized outlets. In clothing a polarization between upscale label outlets and discounters like Matalan has occurred, adding to the problems of 'middle-way' chains like Marks & Spencer.

16. Grand strategies

These are discussed in Chapter 4.

17. International expansion

This is discussed in Chapter 5.

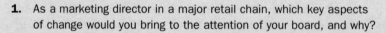

Progress test 28

1. As a marketing director in a major retail chain, which key aspects of change would you bring to the attention of your board, and why?

2. Discuss the possibility that non-store retailing will eventually replace store retailing.

3. What do you think are the implications for logistical planning posed by the growth of non-store retailing?

4. Describe the key opportunities and threats facing retail business today.

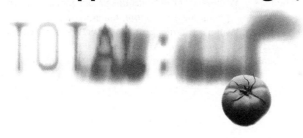

Appendix 1 Bibliography

Alexander, N. (1997), *International Retailing*, Blackwell.

Baron, S., Davies, B. and Swindley, D. (1991), *Macmillan Dictionary of Retailing*, Macmillan.

Bevan, J. (2002), *The Rise and Fall of Marks & Spencer*, Profile Books.

Brown, S. (1992), *Retail Location: a Microscale Perspective*, Avebury.

Christopher, M. (1985), *The Strategy of Distribution Management*, Gower.

Collins, A. (1992), *Competitive Retail Marketing*, McGraw Hill.

Cook, D. and Walters, D. (1991), *Retail Marketing: Theory and Practice*, Prentice Hall.

Corstjens, J. and Corstjens, M. (1995), *Store Wars: the Battle for Mindspace and Shelfspace*, Wiley.

Davies, G. (1993), *Trade Marketing Strategy*, Paul Chapman.

Davies, G.J. and Brooks, J.M. (1989), *Positioning Strategy in Retailing*, Paul Chapman.

Drucker, P. (1954), *The Practice of Management*, Harper & Row.

Fernie, J. (1990), *Retail Distribution Management*, Kogan Page.

Fitch, R. and Knobell, L. (1990), *Fitch on Retail Design*, Phaidon Press.

Freathy, P. (2003), *The Retailing Book*, Pearson Education.

Gardner, C. and Sheppard, J. (1989), *Consuming Passion*, Unwin Hyman.

Gilbert, D. (2003), *Retail Marketing Management*, Pearson Education.

Guy, C. (1994), *The Retail Development Process*, Routledge.

Harris, D. and Walters, D. (1992), *Retail Operations Management*, Prentice Hall.

Hart, C. *et al.* (1997), *Cases in Retailing*, Blackwell.

Herzberg, F. (1966), *Work and the Nature of Man*, World Publishing Co.

Howe, W.S. (1992), *Retailing Management*, Macmillan.

Jones, K. and Simmons, J. (1990), *The Retail Environment*, Routledge.

Johnson, G. (editor) (1987), *Business Strategy and Retailing*, Wiley.

Kay, J. (1993), *Foundations of Corporate Success*, Oxford University Press.

Kay, J. (1996), *The Business of Economics*, Oxford University Press.

Kay, W. (1989), *Battle for the High Street*, Corgi Books.

Kent, A. and Omar, O. (2002), *Retailing*, Palgrave Macmillan.

Knee, D. and Walters, D. (1985), *Strategy in Retailing*, Philip Allan.

Kotler, P. (2002), *Marketing Management* (11th edition), Prentice Hall.

Maslow, A. (1970), *Motivation and Personality*, Harper & Row.

McDonald, M.H.B. and Tideman, C.C.S. (1993), *Retail Marketing Plans*, Butterworth Heinemann.

McGoldrick, P. (1994), *Cases in Retail Management*, Pitman.

McGoldrick, P. (2002), *Retail Marketing*, McGraw Hill.

McGoldrick, P. and Davies, G. (editors) (1995), *International Retailing: Trends and Strategies*, Pitman.

McGregor, D. (1960), *The Human Side of Enterprise*, McGraw-Hill.

Porter, M. (1980), *Competitive Strategy*, The Free Press.

Porter, M. (1985), *Competitive Advantage*, The Free Press.

Seth, A. and Randall, G. (2001), *The Grocers*, Kogan Page.

Sullivan, M. and Adcock, D. (2002), *Retail Marketing*, Thomson.

Varley, R. (2001), *Retail Product Management*, Routledge.

Walters, D. (1988), *Strategic Retailing Management: a case study approach*, Prentice Hall.

Walters, D. (1994), *Retailing Management: Analysis, Planning and Control*, Macmillan.

Walters, D. and White, D. (1987), *Retail Marketing Management*, Macmillan.

Wileman A. and Jary, M. (1997), *Retail Power Plays*, Macmillan.

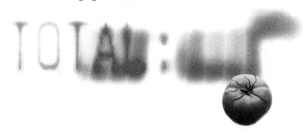

Appendix 2 Retail trade associations

Alliance of Independent Retailers and Businesses
Adam House
Waterworks Road
Worcester
WR1 3EZ
Tel: 01905 612733
www.indretailer.co.uk

Association of Convenience Stores
Federation House
17 Farnborough Street
Farnborough
Hampshire
GU14 8AG
Tel: 01252 515001
www.acs.org.uk

British Council of Shopping Centres
1 Queen Anne's Gate
London
SW1H 9BT
Tel: 020 7222 1122
www.bcsc.org.uk

British Franchise Association
Thames View
Newtown Road
Henley-on-Thames
Oxfordshire
RG9 1HG
Tel: 01491 578050
www.british-franchise.org.uk

British Retail Consortium
2nd Floor
21 Dartmouth Street
London
SW1H 9BP
Tel: 020 7854 8900
www.brc.org.uk

British Shops and Stores Association
Middleton House
2 Main Read
Middleton Cheney
Banbury
Oxfordshire
OX17 2TN
Tel: 01295 712277
www.british-shops.co.uk

Independent Retailers Confederation
21 Baldock Street
Ware
Hertfordshire
SG12 9DH
Tel: 01920 468061

Institute of Grocery Distribution
Grange Lane
Letchmore Heath
Watford
Hertfordshire
WD2 8GD
Tel: 01923 857141
www.igd.com

The Mail Order Traders Association
Drury House
19 Water Street
Liverpool
L2 ORP
Tel: 0151 227 9456
www.emota-aevpc.org

Index